The Unfulfilled

INDIAN
SUMMER
OF 1996

Published by   Russell Schneider Enterprises, Inc.
              P.O.Box 347156
              Cleveland, Ohio 44134
Copyright 1996 by Russell Schneider Enterprises, Inc.
All rights reserved
Published November 1996

Printed by Fine Line Litho, Cleveland, Ohio

ISBN 0-9649813-1-9

The Unfulfilled

INDIAN

SUMMER

OF 1996

Members of the Cleveland Indians, led by Manager Mike Hargrove and Kenny Lofton march toward center field to participate in the raising of the Central Division championship flag at Jacobs Field, September 19, 1996.

By Russell Schneider

About the Author: *Russell Schneider*

In some ways it's easier - in others more difficult - to write objectively about a team a man has lived (and died) with all his life, and even covered for 32 years for the largest newspaper in Ohio, *The Plain Dealer* in Cleveland.

Which is the problem Russell Schneider had in writing this book, as well as others about the Indians: *Frank Robinson, the Making of a Manager*, in 1975; *Lou Boudreau, Covering all the Bases*, in 1993; *The Glorious Indian Summer of 1995*; and *The Cleveland Indians Encyclopedia*, also in 1995.

The fact is, this book - *The Unfulfilled Indian Summer of 1996* - perhaps most accurately depicts professional baseball in Cleveland now and in the past (hopefully not the future) as it is a story of the ups and downs of a major league team on a roller coaster ride.

A team, the Indians, that was expected - even *pre-ordained* - to win, not merely another pennant, but the World Series.

As we all know now, they did not.

But it was a helluva ride while it lasted, until Roberto Alomar, the (in)famous spitter and his Baltimore cohorts got in the way.

Nevertheless, 1996 was a good season for the Indians, one in which record crowds saw them play, which was suspenseful from beginning to end, and which provided plenty to anticipate in 1997.

Schneider, after a two year stint in the U.S. Marine Corps (1946-48), played minor league baseball in the Indians farm system (a good field, light hitting catcher), and was recalled to active duty with the Marines during the Korean War. Later he played and managed semi-pro baseball teams in an around the Cleveland area.

Schneider covered the Indians for 14 years, from 1964-77, and also covered the Cleveland Browns of the National Football League for six years, before concentrating on investigative reporting, special assignments and writing a sports column, *Schneider Around,* for the Plain Dealer.

Schneider and his wife Catherine have three children, Russell Jr., who played a major role in the writing, editing and production of this book, Bryan and Eileen, who is married to former Indians pitcher Eric Raich.

Foreword: *By Bob August*

Sports Columnist, *Lake County News-Herald, Lorain Morning Journal*

For 14 years, starting in 1964, Russ Schneider covered the Indians for The Plain Dealer. It must have seemed longer. Those who were there, like the soldiers who later recalled Napoleon's winter retreat from Moscow, did not remember many high points.

Then, in 1995, after having gone on to other things, Schneider returned to chronicle the day-by-day unfolding of a different Indians season than he'd ever experienced, a time when all the days seemed bathed in sunshine, the nights balmy and, until well into October, only good things happened to the ball team. Some called it "a magical season." The only deficiency in the narrative was the ending, the World Series loss to the Atlanta Braves.

Now Schneider is back with a book about another Indians season, one starting with the hope, often rising to an expectation, that the 1996 Indians would deal with the one imperfection in the 1995 scenario. He was there for the start in March in Winter Haven, Florida when the Indians' gaze already was directed far off to October.

It is a more complex story line he traces this time, a season of paradoxes. The Indians, for a second year, had the best regular season record in the major leagues, their third best in 42 years, and didn't get past the first playoff. They not only wound up frustrated but were often troubled. This was no longer the best of all possible baseball worlds. Reality came crashing though the clubhouse door.

Albert Belle had another outstanding season but was engulfed by controversy. Carlos Baerga, one of the most popular Indians, went into inexplicable decline and was traded. Jim Thome had a breakthrough season but Julian Tavarez was a flop, and the years caught up with Dennis Martinez. Jose Mesa no longer was the invincible closer. There were injuries and occasional anger, with some players reacting to the trades of Baerga and Eddie Murray.

Even from the perspective of a few months, the 1996 Indians season is intriguing, the success somehow baffling in relation to all that went wrong. It's a record worth examining and this book makes it accessible for every Indians fan.

Dedication, Credits and Acknowledgments

To my wife, Kay, for her encouragement, patience, support and editing; and to my son, Rusty, for his invaluable help in the writing, editing, and production of this book; and to Joe Simenic, a dear friend, a valued colleague, a remarkable researcher, and one of the best baseball fans anywhere; and to Bob DiBiasio, Bart Swain, Joel Gunderson, and Susie Gharrity of the Indians Public Relations Department; and to Indians beat reporters Jim Ingraham of the Lake County News-Herald, Paul Hoynes of the Plain Dealer, and Sheldon Ocker of the Akron Beacon-Journal; and to Joe Corrado, Angelo Murracco, and John Krepop, press box attendants at Jacobs Field, for their friendship and help; and to Mike Hargrove, who was, is and will be my Manager of the Year for many years; and to his coaches, Jeff Newman, Charlie Manuel, Dave Nelson, Mark Wiley, Toby Harrah, and Luis Isaac; and last but not least, to the players on the team that almost brought another pennant to Cleveland and made 1996 another wonderful Indian Summer, though our cheers turned to tears at the end.

The Batting Order

Foreword by Bob August

Prologue

PROLOGUE

More than 50,000 fans rallied at Public Square that chilly day, October 30, 1995, to celebrate what had been a glorious Indian Summer, the renaissance of baseball in Cleveland.

The Indians had won the American League pennant after 41 years of disappointment and frustration, and came within one game of beating Atlanta in the World Series.

After congratulatory speeches by Governor George V. Voinovich and Mayor Michael R. White, Indians owner Richard E. Jacobs told the cheering fans, "We are not selling hope and patience anymore. We have a proven winner."

Indeed the Indians did.

Then Jacobs promised that the players would have a "single mission" in the coming season: It would be to win the World Series in 1996.

Jacobs' pledge was well received - and believed by the fans and media.

It also triggered the start of efforts by General Manager John Hart, Dan O'Dowd, director of baseball operations, and Manager Mike Hargrove to boost the Indians to the next level.

To shore up the weaknesses that had prevented the Tribe from going all the way in 1995.

First, Hart courted Paul Molitor, the 39-year old Hall of Fame-bound first baseman-designated hitter.

After several days of negotiations, however, Molitor decided to return to his roots, St. Paul, Minnesota, and to play for the Twins.

Undaunted, Hart turned his attention to two other veterans, in no particular order of preference, Julio Franco and Mark Grace, who could do the job that Eddie Murray did in 1995 - serve as a DH and/or first baseman.

Each had pluses: Franco was a right handed hitter, which Hart felt the team needed, had played shortstop and second base for the Indians from 1983-88, and had won the 1991 American League batting championship with Texas.

Grace, at 31, was three years younger than Franco, and was an accomplished first baseman who was coming off a .326 season with the Chicago Cubs, his best year at the plate.

It was never made clear if Grace spurned the Indians to re-sign with the Cubs and remain in the National League, or whether Hart chose Franco.

Whatever, Franco came highly recommended by Bobby Valentine, who had managed him in 1995 with the Chiba Lotte Marines in Japan, and he was signed to a two year contract on December 7.

With that, Hart went back to Murray, offering him a one year contract at a salary of $2 million, which was $1 million less than he was paid in 1995.

Hart justified the cut in pay because, with Franco the first baseman (backed up by Herbert Perry, if necessary) Murray, who would turn 40 before the season started, would not be called upon to see much, if any service at first base.

It was perceived by Murray as an affront, something that bothered Murray (and would become a major factor later), but he re-signed with the Tribe, also on December 7.

Then Hart went after Jack McDowell - a "bulldog" the likes of Orel Hershiser - to replace Ken Hill, the "rent-a-pitcher" the Indians acquired from St. Louis in July 1995, but declined to re-sign when he became a free agent.

McDowell, also given a two year contract, signed on December 14.

But that didn't end Hart's efforts to ensure that the Indians would repeat in 1996, even climb one level higher - and that the key players would still be on the team beyond the coming season.

Manny Ramirez was signed to a new, four year contract with a club option for the 2000 season, Hershiser's contract was extended through 1997, Charles Nagy was signed for two more years with a club option for 1998, and Omar Vizquel was signed to a six year contract through 2001 with a club option for 2002.

All told, Hart committed more than $55 million of Jacobs' money and, it appeared, all the pieces were in place, not only for greater things in 1996, but for several years beyond.

Obviously, the fans thought so, too.

On December 2, 1995, four months before the Indians would play their first game, on April 1 against New York, it was announced that Jacobs Field was completely sold out for all 81 games in the 1996 season.

It was unprecedented in major league baseball - and to think that, prior to Jacobs' purchase of the franchise in 1986, and before there had been an agreement to construct a new ball park for the Indians, the American League considered moving the team out of Cleveland.

And, lest there be any doubt that the players themselves were impressed with Hart's acquisitions of McDowell and Franco, and the granting of extended contracts to the players, Albert Belle went on record with a startling prediction.

Arguably the best hitter in baseball, Belle said he thought the 1996 team would break the American League record for most victories, 111, set by the Indians in 1954.

Unfortunately, it didn't turn out quite that way.

Oh, the Indians won more games than any other major league team, but fell short of their avowed goal.

They lost to Baltimore in the Division Series, and the New York Yankees played Atlanta in the World Series.

And there was no rally on Public Square in October.

The cheers that had reverberated through Jacobs Field all summer, turned into tears, as there was nothing to celebrate, only to mourn what might have been - what many thought *should* have been.

1

IN THE BEGINNING IT LOOKED SO EASY

Spring Training, February 15-April 1

It was expected to be another cake walk for the Indians in 1996 - even to the next level, winning the World Series - when they reported to Winter Haven, Florida for spring training on February 15.

And, why not?

Not only were the key members of the American League championship Tribe returning for an encore - Albert Belle, Kenny Lofton, Jim Thome, Omar Vizquel, Carlos Baerga, Eddie Murray, Sandy Alomar Jr., Orel Hershiser, Charles Nagy, Dennis Martinez and Jose Mesa - two proven stars were added to the cast.

Signed as free agents during the winter were Jack McDowell, the A.L.'s winningest pitcher in the 1990s, and Julio Franco, who won the A.L. batting championship with a .341 average in 1991 and was returning after one season in Japan where he hit .306 in 127 games for the Chiba Lotte Lions.

McDowell, the A.L. Cy Young Award winner in 1993 who won 98 games for the Chicago White Sox and New York Yankees from 1990-95, would be the fourth established starter in the pitching rotation.

Franco, who'd played shortstop and second base for the Indians from 1983-88, would be the first baseman, the position he played in Japan.

The master plan - really, the *expectation* - of General Manager John Hart and Manager Mike Hargrove was that McDowell would pick up the slack created by the departure of Ken Hill, and Franco would be more productive than Paul Sorrento.

Hill was the "rent-a-pitcher" who went 4-1 in 12 games in 1995 after being acquired from the St. Louis Cardinals on July 27 for three minor leaguers.

Sorrento, who represented one of Hart's best deals when he was obtained in a 1992 trade with the Minnesota Twins for two minor leaguers, hit 25 homers and drove in 79 runs, but his .235 batting average was the lowest among Tribe regulars in 1995.

Both were deemed expendable and weren't offered 1996 contracts, and both went on to sign as free agents - and to perform well - with other clubs; Hill with the Texas Rangers and Sorrento with the Seattle Mariners.

Just as it was taken for granted that Franco would be the Indians' regular first baseman, allowing Murray to serve strictly as the team's full time designated hitter, so it was figured that the fifth spot in the pitching rotation would be filled by either Mark Clark, Chad Ogea, Albie Lopez or Brian Anderson, whomever stepped forward to win the job in spring training.

Anderson, who was born and raised in Geneva, Ohio, about 40 miles east of Cleveland, and grew up rooting for the Indians, had been acquired on February 15 from California after the Angels had made what could have been a costly contractual mistake.

During the off-season they had tried to cut his salary by more than the allowable 20 percent, an oversight that was caught by Anderson's agent, Ron Shapiro, which could have resulted in the pitcher being declared a free agent.

LONG A TRIBE FAVORITE

However, Shapiro - whose son, Mark, is the director of minor league operations for the Indians - proposed that the Angels either re-negotiate Anderson's contract, or trade him.

The Indians, who had coveted Anderson in 1993 when he was the Angels' first pick (third overall) in the amateur draft, and also tried to trade for him in December of 1995, moved swiftly.

They offered pitchers Jason Grimsley and minor leaguer Pep Harris for Anderson, a deal the Angels - this time - readily accepted rather than risk losing the left-handed pitcher.

Ironically, when the Indians had tried to trade for Anderson two months earlier, the Angels wanted Lopez and Ogea in exchange, a deal that Hart summarily rejected.

So it was that, because of the Angels' mistake caught by Ron Shapiro, Anderson's price tag was drastically reduced.

Upon signing a two year, guaranteed contract worth a reported $1.35 million, Anderson joined Ogea and Lopez - the two pitchers California originally had wanted - in the competition, along with Clark, for the fifth spot in the pitching rotation.

Thus, it was virtually taken for granted that the major question concerning the Indians was not *if* they'd repeat in 1996, but *how much better* they'd be than in 1995 when they clinched the AL Central Division title on September 8, and finished 30 games ahead of second place Kansas City.

And, of course, if they'd fulfill the promise made three and a half months earlier in the wake of the Glorious Indian Summer of 1995 when 41 years of futility and apathy were discarded like yesterday's newspaper.

A 'SINGLE MISSION' IN 1996

Then, as the organization took a curtain call attended by more than 50,000 adoring fans on Public Square on October 30, owner Richard Jacobs pledged that the players would have a "single mission ... to prepare ourselves so the 1996 World Series will be won by the Cleveland Indians."

But it wasn't long before some unexpected questions arose, and it soon became evident there'd be more to spring training than simply preparing to win again.

It began on a nearly tragic note as McDowell, returning from a visit with his former White Sox teammates in Sarasota, Florida, totaled his rented automobile in an accident on a rain-slickened highway near Winter Haven.

Fortunately, perhaps even *miraculously,* McDowell was uninjured, although the car he was driving skidded off the road and rolled over. It left McDowell, who was wearing his seat belt, hanging upside down, but unhurt.

Was the accident a portent of things to come?

Perhaps so, as McDowell, who'd signed a two year, $9.6 million contract with the Indians on December 14, 1995, almost immediately suffered what he called a "minor" physical problem. Pitching in the Tribe's first exhibition game on March 1, he limped off with a strained flexor muscle in his hip.

McDowell attributed the injury to "trying to throw the ball 110 miles an hour against the Yankees," for whom he'd gone 15-10 in 1995, and with whom his relationship was much less than ideal.

Hargrove agreed at the time that McDowell's injury was "nothing serious," although it idled the pitcher-musician for ten days before he was able to take the mound again.

TOO MANY CALORIES

Another warning sign surfaced when Carlos Baerga and Manny Ramirez reported to camp and their uniforms - the same working clothes they'd worn in 1995 - proved to be a size or two too small.

Sure enough, at least in the case of Ramirez, management's fears were confirmed when he stepped on the scales for the first day of practice.

The dial spun and didn't stop until it reached "224," which was 29 pounds more than Ramirez weighed in 1995 when, in his second season in the major leagues, he batted .308, hammered 31 homers and drove in 107 runs.

Hargrove didn't even try to disguise his displeasure. "It fries me that Manny let four months of the off-season go by (without getting in better shape). He lifted weights, but he didn't push himself away from the table, and that bothers me."

Julio Franco was quick to offer some advice. He said of Ramirez, "He's young, immature and he's going to make mistakes. I told Manny he shouldn't come to spring training 20 pounds overweight. He said he won't again. I said, 'If you do, they'll kill you.'

"I understand (Ramirez). I see a kid with a lot more talent than I had. If I can help him grow up - not the hard way like I did - that's what I'm going to do."

Franco admitted that, when he was with the Indians previously, "I was young and dumb. My biggest mistake was that I didn't listen to anybody. If I hadn't changed, I don't think I'd be alive today."

Hargrove agreed with Franco's self-analysis. A former teammate of Franco's, Hargrove said, "I can tell you right now that the old Julio Franco would not be back with the Indians."

ACCENTUATE THE POSITIVE

Though little was said about Baerga's additional baggage, it was an issue that would be well-aired later.

But in February, when Baerga was heralded by the Indians as the "heart and soul" of the team, nothing negative was said of the popular second baseman.

Baerga, who'd strung together six outstanding seasons after coming in trade from San Diego in December 1989 - including a .314 batting average with 15 homers and 90 RBI in 1995 - reportedly checked in at 220. (It was later learned that Baerga's weight was close to 230 pounds at the onset of spring training.)

It elicited a non-critical comment from Hart, to wit: "That (220) is about 10 or 12 pounds less than what Carlos has come to camp at the last two years."

However, Hart ignored the fact that Baerga's playing weight as listed in the Tribe's 1995 media guide, was 200 pounds, and the general manager's subsequent comment - "Carlos is in good shape" - proved to be something less than 100 percent accurate.

The first indication that Baerga had a way to go before being in good shape came the first day the Indians took the field.

As has become an annual ritual as designed by strength coach Fernando Montes, all the players were required to begin training camp by participating in the hated "Warrior Run."

It's an 880 yard race around Chain O' Lakes Park and provides an unmistakable, albeit non-scientific measurement of a player's general physical condition.

Baerga not only finished last, but was lapped by several of his teammates.

When he staggered to the finish, Baerga, sweating profusely, breathlessly stated, "I'm no track and field man. I'm a baseball player. We just need to hit and field."

'I HAVE MY OWN PROGRAM'

One player who didn't even run the race was Kenny Lofton. He'd won his fourth consecutive A.L. stolen base championship with 54 in 1995 when he suffered an assortment of minor injuries that limited him to 118 games, and batted .310, which was 39 points below his 1994 average.

"I have to try to peak at the right time," said Lofton. "I don't want to try to fit into someone else's program, I want to fit into my own. I let the team (management) know that. They said to 'do what you have to do to get ready,' which I am."

Not present for the opening exercises, and absent with permission for the next 11 days, was Murray who, this spring and into the season, rejected all requests for interviews. It was unlike Murray's previous two years in a Tribe uniform when he was considered a team leader.

Murray, who in 1995 became the 20th player in major league history to make 3,000 hits in his career, was closing in on another significant milestone in 1996 - he needed 21 homers for a total of 500 and become the 18th player to reach that plateau.

By doing so, Murray would join Hall of Famers Willie Mays and Hank Aaron as the only players to achieve both levels of excellence.

In retrospect, Murray's silence during spring training also could have been considered as another sign that all might not be well with the defending A.L. champions.

On one of the few occasions in which he spoke to the media, Murray made very clear his disdain for sportswriters when he was asked about his never having won a Most Valuable Player award despite his outstanding career record.

"I have no faith in the people in that occupation (members of the Baseball Writers Association of America who do the voting)," responded Murray. "Besides, I will not have them dictate how I feel or play. Why let someone who has never put on a major league uniform judge you?"

Hart, who approved Murray's request to observe his 40th birthday, February 24, at home with his family, said he was satisfied that the veteran would be in shape to start the season.

"I was with Eddie for years in Baltimore and I know him," said Hart. "This (coming to camp late) is par for the course for him."

Hart also took the occasion to praise the veteran first baseman-designated hitter. "Ed Murray was one of our first major free agent signings because of his talent and character."

It was speculated, however, that it no longer was a matter of mutual admiration between the two men, never mind Hart's perfunctory praise.

FIRST GRACE AND MOLITOR

Murray reportedly was miffed at Hart because of the way the general manager conducted contract negotiations during the off-season.

Murray had been signed to a one-year pact in 1994 with a club option for 1995, which was exercised, paying him a salary of $3 million.

However, after Murray batted .323 with 21 homers and 82 RBI in 1995, he was allowed to become a free agent as Hart went shopping during the winter.

Among the first basemen-designated hitters courted by Hart to replace Murray were Mark Grace and Paul Molitor. Both eventually said no to the Indians and signed with other teams - Grace returned to the Chicago Cubs and Molitor joined the Minnesota Twins.

Hart then signed Franco to play first base, and offered a contract to Murray at a $1 million reduction in the salary he was paid in 1995.

Murray never came out and said he resented the way Hart dealt with him - but then, Murray said nothing to the media after he eventually, reluctantly agreed to the Indians' $2 million offer.

It was later reported that Murray stipulated that he was rejoining the Tribe only as a designated hitter, that he would not play first base as he did in 21 games (including three in the post season) in 1995.

It was a report that was never confirmed by any of the principals, but neither was it specifically denied.

When Hargrove was asked in spring training if Murray would play any games at first base, the manager replied, "Eddie has never come to me and said, 'I don't want to play first base anymore.' (But) I'd like to keep him as the DH. It's something I'd like to do."

MURRAY'S ATTITUDE NO PROBLEM

If Murray's attitude bothered Hargrove, the manager wouldn't admit it.

"Eddie is not real talkative, even with his teammates," said Hargrove. "But he's a very honest person. He has a lot of integrity. That's something you don't hear a lot about.

"I'm not worried about Eddie's attitude. No. 1, he's not in this only for the money. And, No. 2, Eddie has too much respect for the game and his teammates to let anything happen that might hurt the team."

When Murray finally reported on February 26, he was greeted by his teammates with a gag celebration of his 40th birthday. And, when members of the media requested interviews, he told them he didn't feel like talking. It was a feeling that never changed thereafter, as long as Murray wore a Tribe uniform.

Shortly after his arrival in Winter Haven, Murray came down with what was first described as "a sinus-flu condition." Later it was said to be an "ear infection" that caused him to sit out the Tribe's first 11 exhibition games.

Murray finally made his first appearance in a competitive situation on March 12 when he went 0-for-3, grounding into two double plays in the Indians' 4-1 loss to Pittsburgh.

Through the rest of spring training Murray hit .271 with two homers and eight RBI. He went 8-for-16 in the Tribe's final four games, including a perfect 4-for-4 with one homer in the second last exhibition game, an 8-6 victory over the Pirates in front of 41,280 fans at Jacobs Field on March 30.

Another sometimes unhappy camper was Clark, the pitcher who was competing for the fifth starter's job in the rotation, but didn't think he should be required to do so.

DOWN TO THE WIRE

It was Clark's impression that he'd established himself in 1994 when he went 11-3 with a 3.82 ERA before suffering a broken wrist that ended his season on July 21. After opening the 1995 season at Class AAA Buffalo, Clark was recalled on June 27 and compiled a 9-7 record, but was not placed on the postseason eligibility list.

The Indians re-signed Clark on December 20 to another one year contract that would pay him $900,000 with a club option on his services in 1997, but he was given no assurance of remaining with the Indians.

Through the first couple of weeks of spring training Hargrove was non-committal regarding Clark's chances, as well as those of Ogea, Lopez and Anderson.

"The decision for the fifth spot (in the rotation) will go right down to the wire. There are some front runners, and some are lagging behind, but that's all I want to say," Hargrove said.

With less than two weeks remaining, Hargrove was much more open, calling Clark's performance "outstanding" against the Yankees on March 16. "That's the best I've seen him in a long time. I guess we should threaten him every time he goes out."

The latter was a reference to speculation that the Tribe would try to obtain waivers on Clark for the purpose of sending him back to Buffalo, or that he would be traded.

Rumors persisted that Pittsburgh, Toronto and Seattle were interested in dealing for Clark, though Hart maintained, "We like Mark Clark," and, "We're not shopping any of our guys."

On March 20, Clark had another good outing, allowing six hits and three runs in five innings as the Indians beat Detroit, 20-3, but Hargrove was still unwilling to give him the fifth starter's job.

OGEA LEADS THE PACK

"The media seems to have anointed Clark as the fifth starter, but this thing is not over," said Hargrove, perhaps because Ogea also was pitching very well.

When Ogea pitched six scoreless innings on March 27 against Toronto, facing the minimum 18 batters with two reaching base (both of whom were wiped out in double plays), the Indians were convinced they could afford to trade Clark.

That victory over the Blue Jays gave Ogea a 3-0 record and 3.60 ERA in 15 innings in five Grapefruit League appearances. Hargrove was well pleased - and this time didn't mind saying so. "That was Chad's best outing all spring," he said.

"If you match Ogea's stuff against Lopez's, it pales in comparison. But when it comes to knowing how to pitch. Ogea is right up there with anyone. The only thing Chad has done wherever he's pitched is win. That has to count for something."

Four days later Clark was traded to the New York Mets. It wasn't a major deal, based on the players the Indians received in return, but it solved the problem of what to do with Clark and his $900,000 salary.

The Indians denied speculation that the deal was made to unload Clark's hefty contract. "This was not a money deal," said Dan O'Dowd, director of baseball operations. "The (coaching) staff just liked our young pitchers better than Mark."

In exchange for Clark, the Indians received two minor leaguers, outfielder Ryan Thompson and pitcher Reid Cornelius, both of whom were assigned to Buffalo.

Clark was ambivalent about the trade. "There were times this spring that I felt the Indians didn't want me around, then there were times when I felt they did," he said.

"But if they don't want me to pitch for them, I don't want to pitch for them. I'm glad I'm going some place where I'm wanted."

'CLARK WAS A ROAD BLOCK'

Hart said, "It was a tough trade to make because Mark Clark is a good kid. But (he) was a road block in the way of our young pitchers like Chad (Ogea), Albie (Lopez) and Brian (Anderson). And behind them we have (Paul) Shuey and Bartolo Colon (in the minor leagues).

"We also have acquired two players (Thompson and Cornelius) we like."

Ironically, the deal for Clark came on the exact third anniversary of the date the Indians acquired Clark from the St. Louis Cardinals (along with minor leaguer Juan Andujar) for outfielder Mark Whiten.

Clark's three year statistics with the Indians: a 27-15 won-lost record with a 4.46 ERA in 68 games, 56 as a starter.

Trading Clark left Ogea as the leading candidate for the fifth spot in the pitching rotation, though the issue wasn't completely settled until after the season began.

From the time Clark was sent to the Mets on March 31, through the first month of the season, Ogea got the first opportunity as the Tribe's fifth starter. He was not an immediate hit, however, and Anderson and Lopez subsequently also were used in that role.

The other two roster decisions to be resolved by Hart and Hargrove, while important in the makeup of the 1996 Indians, were much less difficult - choosing two utility infielders and two extra outfielders.

Hargrove made that point clear in his opening remarks to the team. "I told (the squad) that I'd heard a lot of managers say that 'everybody has a chance to make this team.' When they did, I kind of looked at them like they were stupid," he said.

ESPINOZA HAS INSIDE TRACK

It was obvious that Alvaro Espinoza had the inside track to one of the jobs as an extra infielder because of his ability to play all four positions, including first base.

The competition for the other infielder's place on the roster was up for grabs between Scott Leius and Herbert Perry, though Mario Diaz, a 34-year old career minor leaguer also was said to be under consideration.

For Leius, who'd been signed as a free agent after six seasons with Minnesota, his versatility also was a plus. Perry was basically a first baseman, though it was said that he could, if necessary, play third and the outfield in an emergency. Diaz had had brief, but unsuccessful trials with Seattle, the New York Mets, Texas and Florida, and also had been signed as a free agent.

In Perry's favor, though it wasn't something the hierarchy liked to discuss (or even think about) was that Franco's inexperience at first base, combined with the intention of using Murray strictly as the team's designated hitter, might require keeping a backup first baseman.

The preference, however, was for Perry, who batted .315 in 52 games in a couple of stints with the Indians in 1995, to return to Class AAA Buffalo and continue his development as the Tribe's first baseman of the future.

As for the competition for the two vacancies on the roster for extra outfielders, the candidates were Wayne Kirby, Jeromy Burnitz, Brian Giles and Dave Gallagher.

Kirby was the Tribe's regular right fielder in 1993 but lost his job to Manny Ramirez in 1994 and was trying to retain his backup status; Burnitz was acquired in November 1994 from the New York Mets and batted .284 with 19 homers at Buffalo in 1995; Giles, a 17th round selection in the 1989 amateur draft, had progressed steadily through the Tribe's minor league system, hitting .310 with 15 homers at Buffalo in 1995; and Gallagher was a 35-year old veteran who played 15 games for the Indians in 1987, then served with six other major league clubs, including the Chicago White Sox, Baltimore, California, New York Mets, Atlanta and Philadelphia.

KIRBY AND BURNITZ FAVORED

The fact that neither Kirby nor Burnitz could be sent back to the minors without obtaining waivers established them as front runners to make the team, though both - as well as Giles - were left handed hitters.

In his early appraisal of the four outfielders, Hargrove said, "Kirby is the best defensively, Giles is the most consistent hitter, Burnitz has some serious giddy-up in his bat, and Gallagher is a good, all-around player."

Hart also made it clear that he favored Burnitz, saying, "He is an interesting guy. He's got power, he can run and play all three outfield positions, and he has a pedigree. He was the Mets' No. 1 pick in 1990."

Hargrove sloughed off the fact that Kirby, Burnitz and Giles all batted left handed. "Having two left handed hitters on the bench doesn't bother me," he said, "because, no matter who we keep, we'll have two right handed hitters as extra infielders." Espinoza, Leius, Perry and Diaz all batted right handed.

As it turned out, and as expected, Espinoza and Leius survived. Perry was returned to Buffalo where he was to have been the Tribe's first baseman in waiting - until a mid-season knee injury required surgery and put him on the disabled list - and Diaz was released.

Perry was disappointed, but not surprised when informed of his demotion. "It's not often that a rookie hits .315 one year and gets sent down the next," he said.

"But the Indians are going for a championship. They went out and got Julio Franco who's a great hitter, an established hitter. I am a good hitter, but I'm in the wrong place at the wrong time. I want to play for this team, but there are not a lot of jobs (open) on a championship team."

Kirby and Burnitz also made the final 25 as expected, as Giles was optioned to Buffalo, and Gallagher, reading the writing on the wall, quit and went home, retiring from baseball.

"I've played a long time and I know what's going on," Gallagher told reporters before he departed on March 22. "I went to talk to John Hart and Dan O'Dowd with the idea of making it easier on them."

'BEAR DOWN OR ELSE'

Still, it was an over-simplification by those who wrote that Hargrove's "only" major decisions were to choose two utility infielders and two extra outfielders.

He also had to guard against a problem that confronts the managers of most defending championship teams - complacency. Especially, in the Indians' case, considering how easily they prevailed in 1995.

Hargrove insisted, "I won't let it (complacency) happen."

The first to feel his sting was Julian Tavarez when the young relief pitcher failed to properly execute a fielding drill on February 25. Hargrove made Tavarez repeat it several times, until he got it right.

"It was that Julian didn't know where to go in the drill," Hargrove explained. "We told him twice in an hour's time, and he still got it wrong. Then he thought it was funny, but I didn't. There's a time to work, and there's a time to joke around.

"I realize, if you don't allow players to have some fun with the drills, you don't get anything out of it. But you also have to define things, and I think things were redefined with Julian."

Hargrove also came down hard on another of the Tribe's young relievers, Alan Embree, this time during a game against Philadelphia on March 23 when he delivered a "bear-down-or-else" message.

It was during the sixth inning, with Embree struggling, that Hargrove called time, strode to the mound and gave a finger-pointing lecture to the left handed pitcher.

"I told Alan that the way he was going about things wasn't working. I told him to let the ball go," Hargrove said - among other, more forceful things.

A WAKE-UP CALL FOR EMBREE

"Basically, I thought Alan needed to wake up. He's been trying to throw the ball into a tea cup all spring, and he doesn't have to do that. Maybe he will in 10 years, but right now he just has to pick out a location and turn the ball loose. He has to trust his stuff."

Embree's response to Hargrove's scolding: "We had a little pow-wow. What Grover said to me turned out to be the best thing I've heard all spring. Instead of saying, 'Don't worry, it will come,' he said, 'Get it done now. He also told me to 'throw the ball through Sandy (Alomar), not to him.' That made a big difference."

Then, with a week left in spring training, Hargrove further showed his growing intensity. He was ejected by N.L. umpire Angel Hernandez in the first inning of a game against the Braves.

The argument resulted from what Hargrove perceived as Hernandez's "arrogant treatment" of Lofton, who was called out on strikes and dropped his bat at the plate. Hernandez took offense and kicked the bat which, in turn, angered Lofton and Hargrove.

"I've never seen an umpire do anything so unprofessional in my life," said Hargrove. "It was real obvious he was looking to throw somebody out, and I'd rather it be me than one of my players. They need the at-bats."

Lofton said of the incident with Hernandez, "An umpire shouldn't be able to do anything to me bodily, or to my equipment, and not have something done about it. I think the league should do something. If baseball can do something about Albert Belle just for saying something, they can do something about this.

"It's not right for someone to kick somebody else's equipment. If I had kicked a piece of Hernandez's equipment, I would have been thrown out, fined, whatever. But he can kick my stuff and what happens?

"The umpires are considered the bosses of the game. I'm only using this as a comparison, but it's like the police. You can't do anything about the police. They're the law."

SIX GAMES: FOURTEEN ERRORS

There also was concern throughout spring training about the Indians' defense - or lack of same. Through their first six exhibition games they committed 14 errors, including four on March 6 in a 7-4 victory over Houston.

"We're a better defensive team than this," Hargrove said. "I'm not overly worried," he added - with emphasis on "overly."

But obviously, there was concern, especially when the number of errors climbed to 17 in the first nine games, plus several of the mental variety.

It got even worse - much worse - 12 games later. On March 18, in a 10-9 loss to Kansas City, the Indians committed four more errors, two by Baerga, giving the team a total of 31 in 21 games.

Hargrove was very upset. "The errors fry me ... and there's no excuse for Manny Ramirez letting a fly ball fall behind him (for an uncharged error). All he had to do was be a little observant," he said.

At the same time, perhaps because of Baerga's two errors, both Hargrove and Hart spoke more openly regarding their concern about the second baseman's weight.

"It's the same thing every spring," said Hart. "For Carlos to be at the top of his game he has to be at a certain weight."

Initially, Franco's play at first base also proved to be a distinct cause for concern as he was making errors and seemed to be unsure of the fundamentals required of a first baseman.

"We're working with him," said Hargrove. "We are satisfied that Julio, having been a darned good middle infielder in his career, can make whatever adjustments will be necessary. He'll be okay."

Hargrove's comments came in the wake of Franco's debut at first base, in the Tribe's first exhibition game, which was less than scintillating.

'GIVE FRANCO A CHANCE'

Franco was unable to scoop out of the dirt a throw by Jim Thome, and was "picked off" himself on a throw by Anderson with a Yankee runner on first base.

Afterwards, Hargrove was unusually testy in responding to questions about Franco.

"Give the guy a chance before you go out and say he can't play first base," said Hargrove, a major league first baseman himself for 12 years for Texas and San Diego, as well as the Indians.

"That's a new field out there. It's soft and the balls stayed down. Julio will be OK. Just give him a chance," Hargrove said again.

Hart also defended Franco. Of his inability to scoop up Thome's throw, Hart said, "Jimmy threw a hand grenade to first base."

Franco said that Hargrove told him, "First base is the easiest position to play," though the manager subsequently clarified that statement to the media.

"What I said," said Hargrove, "was that, if you're just going to stand there and catch balls hit to you and run to the bag, it's the easiest position. If you play it right, it's much tougher."

But Hargrove also vowed: "We're going to work with Julio on every part of playing first base. We're going to break it down and address every aspect. Julio wants to do this, and he's staying with it."

'KIND OF RIDICULOUS' - LOPEZ

Another who wasn't happy, though for a different reason than the impatience harbored by Hargrove, was Lopez.

It was during the winter that the Indians, in a routine check of their players' status by O'Dowd, discovered they had another option on Lopez. It meant they would be able to send him back to the minors one more time without fear of losing him to another major league club on a waiver claim.

Lopez didn't like it, and was outspoken in his complaint. "I thought it was kind of ridiculous for them to go digging and find a special clause," he grumbled. "They might as well just let me go instead of sitting on me."

Of course, Lopez's lament made no difference in his status, or the Indians' evaluation of his ability, and it wasn't until the end of spring training that he was returned to Buffalo.

'NO PROBLEMO' - JOSE MESA

It was late in spring training that the first sign surfaced of doubt about Jose Mesa's ability to repeat his remarkable 1995 performance when he was the most successful closer in the major leagues. Mesa racked up 46 saves in 48 chances, breaking Doug Jones' 1990 record of 43 in one season.

With a week remaining in spring training Mesa was tagged for three runs in the ninth inning of a game against Baltimore, almost blowing what turned out to be a 4-3 Tribe victory.

"Jose has not shown the kind of velocity he had last year," said Hargrove, admitting his concern even though Mesa had converted five saves in five spring training opportunities. "We're waiting to see it (the velocity he showed in 1995), and though it's getting late, he still has time."

Mesa shrugged off the implied criticism. When asked if he was ready to open the season, he said, "You better believe it."

Was he a flash in the pan in 1995? No, said Mesa. "I think people will be seeing me pitch the way I did last year for a long time. I feel very strong."

Of his 1995 performance, Mesa said, "It's like God was holding a lot of things for me and gave them all up in one year. That's why I don't get cocky. I know I've got to keep working hard to stay in the game."

MARTINEZ IS HURTING

Another key player around whom the Indians' hoped-for success in 1996 would depend was Martinez.

The soon-to-be 41 year old pitcher was beset by injuries - right shoulder, right forearm, left knee - the second half of 1995. He opened the season with nine straight victories (and a 2.35 earned run average), but finished with a 12-5 record and 3.08 ERA.

Initially in spring training "El Presidente," as Martinez was nicknamed, reported that he was free of pain. "I feel like a kid again," he said.

However, nine days later, on Feb. 26, Martinez admitted to having a sore shoulder.

"I'm trying not to think about it," he said. "I can throw better than I did (late) last season, but for some reason there's a little discomfort in there. It's not the same amount of pain as last year, so it did get better. It's like a little pain that won't leave me alone.

"It might have something to do with age. It seems like its saying to me, 'Get out of the game, or something.'"

Hargrove claimed he wasn't worried. "That's Dennis," said the manager. "We saw the stories in the paper where he said his shoulder and elbow were bothering him. When we asked him what the deal was, he said nothing was wrong. I'm satisfied with that (explanation)."

A couple of weeks into spring training it was obvious that Martinez was becoming very sensitive about his tendency to complain about physical problems.

'A 100-TO-1 UNDERDOG' - MARTINEZ

Prior to pitching the third game of the Indians' exhibition season, Martinez candidly discussed his career. "I overcame my drinking problem to go to four All star games, pitch a perfect game and win 100 games in each league," he said.

"And last year, before Game 6 (of the AL Championship Series), I had to be a 100-to-1 underdog against Randy Johnson and Seattle. I bet a lot of people lost a lot of money on that game."

Martinez, with eighth and ninth inning relief help from Tavarez and Mesa, beat the Mariners, 4-0, to keep the Indians alive to win Game 6 and the A.L. pennant, vaulting them into the World Series against Atlanta.

"If we had lost Game Six, I know we would have lost Game 7, and who would have been the scapegoat?

"Me," Martinez answered his own question. "I would have been blamed. I know the press would have said, 'This guy has done all these things, but he can't win a post season game.'

"I've been thinking a lot about my career. I don't want to be suffering at the end. I want to leave the game with my head up and thinking about the good times. I don't want to leave the game feeling down, and with a lot of pain.

"I know I have to be patient. This (the injuries) didn't happen in one day and it's not going to go away in one day.

"And, from now on I'm not going to say anything more about my arm when reporters ask me. I'll just keep throwing the ball until my arm falls off. I came here to fight like a young kid in the game. I know what is here today might be gone tomorrow.

"But I get hot when I read things that ... I have a thousand aches and pains. What more can I do to get credit for what I've done?"

'WHO WILL FEEL THE PRESSURE?'

Then Martinez talked about the Indians, and in doing so, said what others also believed.

"There is a lot of pressure on this ball club," he said. "With the team we had last year we reached the World Series, and now we've added Jack McDowell and Julio Franco. If we don't win it now, the question is, 'What's wrong?'

"I don't know who will feel the pressure and maybe give in to it, but the pressure is here. I hope it doesn't bother anyone because there is always pressure in this game.

"You also have to wonder if this team has enough talent to keep a dynasty going. Orel Hershiser, Tony Pena, Eddie Murray and Paul Assenmacher might not be around too much longer, and you hope the young guys can take over."

Martinez followed his discourse by pitching three solid innings against Florida in his first competitive appearance of the spring. He surrendered a run on three hits in the Indians' 12-10 victory.

Martinez entered the season needing 12 victories to match Juan Marichal as the winningest Latin American pitcher in major league history. Marichal retired in 1975 after winning 243 games (and losing 142). Martinez's record going into the 1996 season was 231-176.

"Ideally," Martinez continued, "we can get back in the World Series and (I can) get the record at the same time. But this year we want to win it all. We want the big prize, the big check - and the ring. We've already finished second (in the World Series)."

THE OPENING DAY ASSIGNMENT

With 2 1/2 weeks remaining in spring training, Hargrove announced that Martinez would be the Tribe's opening day pitcher against the Yankees in Cleveland on April 1.

Hargrove's explanation: "We've got four No. 1 starters. We felt confident with any of the four but we felt Dennis should be the one." Hargrove also announced that Martinez would be followed in the rotation by Jack McDowell, Hershiser, and Nagy.

It would be Martinez's third consecutive opening day assignment for the Indians, and probably the final of his career as his three year contract with Cleveland would expire at the end of the 1996 season.

Martinez said of the assignment: "When Mike got the starters together and told us I'd start on Opening Day, I was shocked ... believe me, I was."

But he also was pleased. "I think (Hargrove) may have done it to make an old man feel good. It's psychology, and I like those kind of tricks.

"Maybe it had something to do with my experience, but I still think the difference was age. But that's good. Sometimes when you get old, people forget about you. This is a good move by the manager. It makes me feel like I'm home again.

"The only problem about pitching on Opening Day is that I won't get to be introduced and run on to the field to get my American League championship ring with the rest of the team. I'll be warming up in the bullpen.

"I'd like to lift (the ring) up and show it to everyone and say, 'See what we won for you.'"

In handing the Opening Day assignment to Martinez, Hargrove also re-established that Alomar - not Tony Pena - would be behind the plate when Martinez pitched.

Through most of the 1995 season Pena had been Martinez's personal catcher. But Hargrove decreed that, "Since Alomar is our No. 1 catcher, he will catch Martinez."

It, of course, pleased Alomar, though neither Martinez nor Pena commented on the decision.

BELLE'S $50,000 FINE

Another issue that commanded the attention of virtually everybody in spring training was anticipation of disciplinary action expected to be taken against Albert Belle. He had directed an obscenity-laced tirade at telecaster Hannah Storm prior to Game 3 of the 1995 World Series.

It was during the first week of camp that Belle, who was at that time talking to the Cleveland media, said of the incident:

"I think it's being blown out of proportion. I treated (Storm) just like any other reporter that day. I just wanted everybody out of my way. I didn't discriminate against her because she's female.

"Over the course of baseball history, reporters and baseball players have had their problems. I think it would be a big injustice for a fine or suspension to take place because of this. It would be the first time a player has been suspended or fined for yelling at a reporter."

Finally, on Feb. 23, acting commissioner Bud Selig notified the Indians and Belle that he was being fined $50,000. It was the largest amount ever assessed a player in the history of baseball.

The Players Association said it would help Belle fight the fine.

Hart said, "We support our ballplayer, but this is not our call."

However, there was no doubt that Hart and the Indians' hierarchy felt the fine was excessive. The amount might have been that high because Belle had said on several earlier occasions that he "would do the same thing over again."

Belle's agent, Arn Tellem, said, "This is akin to Marcia Clark being the judge and jury, as well as the prosecutor in the O.J. Simpson trial."

'THE FINE IS RIDICULOUS' - LOFTON

Lofton was one of the few players willing to comment, and he came on loud and strong.

"The fine is ridiculous," he said. "It doesn't make any sense for someone to get fined $50,000 for saying a curse word. Albert didn't hurt anyone. He just walked through the dugout before the game, said what he said and walked back. There was no more to it than that.

"I think they're just out to get Albert. Maybe it's because he does not talk to the media. I don't know.

"I'm not saying Albert was right. But if he's going to get fined $50,000, I need to keep my mouth closed." Then Lofton exclaimed, "Wow!"

When it was pointed out that Belle intimidated Storm and other reporters, Lofton responded, "What difference does intimidation make? It doesn't matter if it's Pee Wee Herman or Hulk Hogan. (Belle) shouldn't have done what he did, but the fine is not right.

"It's going to be interesting to see what happens to the next player who curses a reporter. We'll see what happens then. Then we'll know if they are just trying to get Albert or not."

At the time, Belle also was sweating out a lawsuit. It was filed against him by the parents of a boy Belle had chased three months earlier. It was alleged that Belle hit the boy with his vehicle after the boy and three others egged Belle's house Halloween night.

HOW MUCH IS BELLE WORTH?

Belle continued to be in the news through most of spring training as negotiations on a new contract got underway March 7 between the Indians and his agent. That initial meeting also was attended by Belle's father, Albert.

After it ended Hart said, "Don't read anything into this (but) there's been no progress, nothing is close. We're just talking. This could be something that takes us all year. No timetables have been set."

Neither Belle nor his agent would comment.

The next day the Indians delivered their offer in a meeting that, this time, also included owner Dick Jacobs, as well as Hart and O'Dowd.

Reportedly, it was a five year contract worth between $37 million and $38 million, but was rejected by Belle, after which Tellem returned to his office in California.

Before leaving Winter Haven, the agent said, "Both sides are working toward the same thing. The Indians want Albert to stay, and he wants to stay. He loves the city."

Despite being unable to reach agreement, Tellem said, "This was a very productive day (and) we'll keep the dialogue going. If something happens, I can come back in another couple of weeks. We don't want this to be a distraction during the regular season. Things would probably slow down, but we'd still keep talking."

Hart said, "There are a lot of things to get done. This is a process. It will take time."

There was speculation - which neither Tellem nor Hart would confirm - that Belle was seeking a contract worth more than the four year, $34 million deal (which broke down to $8.5 million annually) given Ken Griffey Jr. by Seattle, and better than the $18.3 million, three year pact ($6.1 million annually) that Mo Vaughn received from Boston.

TRADING BELLE 'A NON-OPTION'

In view of the fact that Belle would be eligible for free agency at the end of the season, Hart was asked if the Indians would consider trading the recalcitrant outfielder.

"Trading Albert is a non-option," replied Hart. "We've never even thought about it. We built this team and Albert is part of the team."

As for the temporary breaking-off of negotiations, Hart said, "There is no timetable (for signing Belle). If we don't get it done in spring training, maybe we'll get it done during the season. If not, then maybe we'll get it done at the end of the season.

He also said, "We are not going to let this become a distraction. Albert says he wants to stay. We want him to stay. The only problem is money."

Of the coming season, Belle predicted the Indians could break the 1954 team's record of 111 victories "if all our pitchers stay healthy."

He also said, "People expect us to win it all, and we expect to win it all, so we are all on the same page."

During the interview, one of the few he held with the Cleveland media, Belle said he might hold post game conferences in the coming season.

But then he told the assembled reporters, "I'll see you guys in October."

It also was during the first week of spring training exhibition games that Belle agreed to do a televised interview with Roy Firestone of ESPN.

However, after Firestone had flown to Winter Haven and waited two days to meet with the outfielder, the interview never took place because Belle failed to appear.

Belle also was requested for interviews by *Newsweek* and *Sports Illustrated,* but agreed only to talk to the former not the latter. It did not endear him to *Sports Illustrated* - or to Roy Firestone.

PICKING UP WHERE HE LEFT OFF

In his first at-bat in the Indians' exhibition opener on March 1 in the Yankees' new stadium in Tampa - and one day after being assessed the largest fine in baseball history - Belle smashed a two run homer off David Cone in the first inning, accounting for the Tribe's only runs in a 5-2 loss.

Afterwards, Hargrove commented: "Albert has a tremendous ability to focus. When they coined the term 'tunnel vision,' they had Albert in mind. He has a strong ability to shut things out and keep concentrating on his job."

Other than his contract negotiations and the controversy that arose over his being fined $50,000 by Selig, it was a relatively calm spring for Belle.

Until March 21, that is, when he was ejected from a game against the Blue Jays in Dunedin, Florida by plate umpire Matt Malone (an American Association umpire).

It happened in the first inning of what became a 6-5, 10 inning victory for the Indians. Belle was called out on strikes. He argued briefly, then returned to the dugout and shouted at the umpire, at which point Malone ejected Belle.

Hargrove wouldn't fault Belle: "It's getting near the end of spring training and I like to see Albert turn up the intensity a little."

When asked what Belle shouted at Malone, Hargrove said, "I didn't hear Albert say what the umpire said he said (but) I did think the ejection was a little quick."

'WE WANT ALBERT BACK' - HART

In the wake of subsequent bad press on the national level, as well as criticism directed toward the Tribe after the World Series, Hart wondered: "Why are the Indians a bad story?

"People in the national media want me to come down hard on Albert Belle and run him out of town. Guess what? This is not going to happen. I have never said that Albert wasn't wrong (about his tirade against Storm).

"At the same time, Albert is part of our family. He's been here eight years. We want him back next year, and I believe we will have him back when all is said and done.

"It's not like we have not disciplined Albert. We sat him down. We sent him out (to the minor leagues). But he is the centerpiece of what is arguably the best offensive team in baseball.

"He is always in shape. He has put in the work in the outfield. He is the only player who keeps a log on every single pitcher. And he is the most popular athlete in Cleveland.

"We like Albert because he is part of our family. If I had to take a hill, I'd want Albert there when I charged."

VIZQUEL'S SHOULDER IS HURTING

With the Indians getting ready to break camp and head north, the potential for more trouble surfaced on March 27. Omar Vizquel, the A.L.'s Gold Glove shortstop, returned to Cleveland to undergo an examination of his aching shoulder at Lutheran Hospital.

Though nothing had been said of Vizquel's ailment previously, the Indians revealed he had been suffering with it all spring.

"I am not worried but I am concerned," said Hargrove. "Omar has been playing with pain (and) we want to be sure what's causing it. We sent him back for an MRI because it is better to be safe than sorry.

"But don't make too much out of this. Let's wait to see what the tests show. This is strictly a precautionary measure."

Hart said, "Even if the news is bad, I think we have the best backup shortstop in baseball in Espy (Alvaro Espinoza)"

The next day Vizquel returned and it was reported that the injury was not serious. As publicist Bart Swain told the media, "There was no damage to the rotator cuff, but there was some fraying of the labrum, and some tendinitis."

The labrum was described as "a lip-like structure in the cartilage of the glenoid cavity in the shoulder."

Vizquel said, "I'm taking anti-inflammatory pills and I should be able to play with (the injury). I think it would clear up if I rested for a week. But I don't want to do that. That's why it will take a little longer than normal to go away."

Asked how the injury occurred, Vizquel said he didn't know, but speculated, "This was the first year that I haven't played winter ball in my career. Maybe the time I didn't spend on the field affected it."

Hargrove said he would give Vizquel more rest this season. "We might hold him back from taking infield every now and then, and we'll pay more attention to giving him a day off. But that's something we were going to do anyway.

"It comes down to Omar tolerating the pain. We've been assured he can't do further damage to the shoulder.

HARGROVE LIKES WHAT HE SEES

With three days remaining before Opening Day, Hargrove said he was pleased because the Indians were peaking at the right time.

"I like the way the club has built momentum," he said. "We started slowly, especially on defense. In the last two weeks, however, we've really started to focus. Our defense has improved and we've played well. This is how you'd like a camp to work. We're playing the best heading into the season."

The Indians went on to win two of their final three games - 8-6 over Pittsburgh at Jacobs Field on March 30, and 5-3 over Cincinnati for the "Ohio Cup" in Columbus on March 31 - for a final Grapefruit League record of 21-14.

"I think the most pleasant surprise was Paul Shuey coming in and throwing strikes," said Hargrove - though Shuey's spring training performances weren't enough to keep him on the roster.

With Mesa the closer; Assenmacher, Poole, and Plunk the set-up men; and Tavarez and Ogea working in middle and long relief, there was no room on the roster for Shuey, the second player selected in the 1992 amateur draft.

"I don't see where Paul fits in right now, but the way he's pitched makes you feel better about the entire situation," said Hargrove.

When asked how much ground does the "entire situation" cover, Hargrove replied, "It could be two weeks, or two months from now (that Shuey could be recalled). There are a lot of things floating around out there."

Said Shuey of his demotion, "It just burns another option. It is my last option, which means they'll have to keep me next year or put me through waivers."

And so, when the Indians returned to Cleveland for the opener, Shuey was on his way back to Buffalo.

NEWMAN TO THE BENCH

Another significant decision by Hargrove involved the switching of Jeff Newman from third base coach to bench coach, and the installation of newcomer Toby Harrah at third.

Harrah, a former teammate of Hargrove with Texas and the Indians, was added to the staff as a replacement for Buddy Bell, who'd served as bench coach in 1995. Bell left the Tribe to sign a two-year contract to manage Detroit.

In explaining the coaching switch, Hargrove insisted it was not a reflection on Newman's work at third base. "It is a natural progression for a coach who wants to become a manager eventually, to serve a term in the dugout," Hargrove said.

"It was a move Jeff and I both wanted to make. John Hart and I both thought Newman was the best third base coach in the American League. When you become a bench coach it's like getting your ticket punched to become a manager. You don't have to have it on your resume, but it helps."

Newman had been a candidate during the off-season to replace Tony LaRussa as manager of the Oakland Athletics before Art Howe was given the job.

Among the Tribe's final statistical leaders: Belle hit for the highest average of the regulars, .440 (37-for-84) with five homers and 17 RBI in 28 games, and Ramirez, who batted .346 (28-for-81) in 27 games, led the team with eight homers and 24 RBI, while Ogea, Clark and Lopez had the winningest pitching records, each with 3-0, though Nagy (2-1) had the best earned run average, 2.42, among the starting pitchers, followed by Hershiser (1-0), 3.46; Martinez (1-2), 3.60; Ogea, 3.60; and McDowell (1-2), 4.58.

The team batting average was .299, compared to the opponents' .265, and the pitchers' cumulative ERA was 4.50.

Defensively, the Indians committed 41 errors in 35 games, though Hargrove sloughed it off, saying, "Most of them came early in spring training before we got ourselves together. Of the chargeable miscues, Baerga had the most, seven, followed by Thome, who had six.

The final roster: Pitchers - Jack McDowell, Charles Nagy, Orel Hershiser, Chad Ogea, Dennis Martinez, Paul Assenmacher, Alan Embree, Jose Mesa, Eric Plunk, Jim Poole, Julian Tavarez; Catchers - Sandy Alomar Jr., Tony Pena; Infielders - Julio Franco, Carlos Baerga, Omar Vizquel, Jim Thome, Alvaro Espinoza, Scott Leius, Eddie Murray; Outfielders - Albert Belle, Kenny Lofton, Manny Ramirez, Wayne Kirby, Jeromy Bernitz.

OPTIMISM REIGNS SUPREME

On the eve of the opener there was, of course, plenty of optimism regarding the Indians' chances in 1996.

Virtually every scribe in town picked them to win the pennant again, although opinions were divided as to the likelihood they'd prevail in the World Series.

Paul Hoynes, Bill Livingston and Bud Shaw of the *Plain Dealer* all predicted another pennant, as did Jim Ingraham in the Lake County *News-Herald* and Lorain *Morning Journal,* and Sheldon Ocker in the Akron *Beacon-Journal.*

Atlanta was favored by Hoynes, Shaw, Ingraham and Ocker to win the National League pennant, with Livingston picking Los Angeles. But only Livingston expected the Indians to capture their first World Series in 48 years, since 1948.

USA TODAY's five baseball writers - Hal Bodley, Mike Dodd, Rod Beaton, Mel Antonen and Chuck Johnson - were even more impressed by the Indians.

They were unanimous, not only in their expectation that the Indians would return to the World Series, but also that, this time, they'd win it. Bodley, Dodd and Johnson thought the Tribe's opponent would be Atlanta, while Los Angeles and Houston were favored by Beaton and Antonen, respectively, to win the N.L. pennant.

Another who harbored great expectations was Sharon Hargrove, wife of the Tribe manager.

However, Mrs. Hargrove also confessed to some realism in one of her columns appearing in *Indians Ink.* "By this time next year I'll be writing about the '96 Cleveland Indians World Champions!! That's a promise!!!" she wrote.

Then this addendum: "Take it to the bank, because if we don't win it all in '96, I have a feeling the Hargroves will be talking about rebuilding another organization!"

2

'IT'S TIME TO
PLAY BALL'

April 2-April 11

Opening Day - April 1, 1996 - the beginning of what was expected to be an even greater pennant-winning season for the Indians, dawned bright and clear, but cold, along with five inches of snow that blanketed Jacobs Field.

Was the weather also a portent of something other than a second consecutive glorious Indian Summer in Cleveland?

Another incident that led to more speculation that 1996 would be fraught with controversy and travail occurred five days into the season when Albert Belle got himself in trouble again.

This time it was for throwing at, and hitting a *Sports Illustrated* photographer with a baseball, though that transgression wasn't reported until two weeks later, after which American League President Dr. Gene Budig took action against the enigmatic outfielder.

Belle, who would be eligible to become a free agent at the end of the season, also was in the news through the first couple of weeks in the Indians' ongoing - albeit unsuccessful - effort to sign him to a long term contract.

As for the Tribe's opener against the revamped and also-hopeful New York Yankees, it was postponed until the next day, which had been an open date in the schedule.

Highlighting the pre-game ceremonies on April 2 was the presentation by Dr. Budig and Indians owner Richard Jacobs of the 1995 championship rings to Manager Mike Hargrove, his coaches, the players and trainers, as well as front office personnel.

Dave Winfield, who played briefly for the Tribe in 1995, and for the Yankees from 1981-90, threw out the ceremonial first pitch and then Dennis Martinez took the mound.

Not only was Martinez hoping to get the Indians off and running as he did in 1995 when he went 9-0 in his first 16 starts, he also was trying to register the first of 12 victories he needed to tie Hall of Famer Juan Marichal as the winningest Latin American pitcher in baseball history.

However, David Cone and the Yankees spoiled the day for the Indians and Martinez - as well as the 42,289 fans who comprised the 53rd consecutive capacity crowd at Jacobs Field, dating back to 1995, and would be the first of 79 more to follow.

Cone yielded only two hits over seven innings, Julio Franco's single and Sandy Alomar's double, and three relievers held the Indians at bay in the eighth and ninth for a 7-1 New York victory that was much closer than the score indicated.

MARTINEZ: 2-14 VS. THE YANKEES

Martinez was almost as effective as Cone, allowing only two runs on five hits through the first seven innings.

But the Yankees took advantage of Alan Embree for three runs on Bernie Williams' homer in the eighth, and added two more in the ninth off Eric Plunk and Paul Assenmacher.

"I did the job I was supposed to do, I got people out," said Martinez, though he wasn't entirely correct. He served a solo homer to rookie Derek Jeter in the fifth when New York went ahead, 2-0.

"When you don't take advantage of the other pitcher when he's struggling, and the pitcher is the caliber of David Cone, you're going to be in trouble when he finds his groove," added Martinez, whose career record against the Yankees fell to 2-14.

The last time Martinez beat the Yankees was June 11, 1982 when he pitched for Baltimore.

It also was Martinez's sixth loss in 12 opening day assignments.

"Dennis was in and out most of the day," said Hargrove. "He was down real good in the strike zone one inning, and up a little the next. But he deserves credit for taking us as deep into the game as he did."

The Indians had ample opportunities to score against Cone, who walked six, including two in each the first and fourth innings, but were unable to come through with a hit in the clutch, a problem that would persist in 1996.

They stranded eight base runners, three in two different innings by Manny Ramirez, who didn't wait long to get into trouble off the field.

On the very first night the Indians were back in Cleveland, Ramirez was cited by the police for two traffic violations. He was clocked going 50 in a 25 miles-per-hour zone, and for running a red light. Both violations occurred on Ontario St. near Jacobs Field.

SECOND-GUESSING HARGROVE

Hargrove left himself wide open to criticism when he declined to have Embree intentionally walk Williams with first base open and two on and two out in the eighth.

Williams, a right-handed hitter, whacked a 2-and-0 pitch from Embree, a left-hander, into the left field bleachers.

Afterwards, callers to the area talk shows came down hard on Hargrove for his decision to pitch to Williams and, unlike 1995, was the kind of second-guessing of the manager that would persist most of the season.

"We thought about walking (Williams)," said Hargrove. "But Alan is a power pitcher and when he's on, it doesn't matter if he's facing a left-hander or right-hander.

"I also didn't relish the idea of bringing in Eric Plunk with the bases loaded for his first appearance of the season."

The Indians' only run was manufactured by Kenny Lofton, who was seeking his fifth consecutive A.L. stolen base crown. He singled off first reliever Bob Wickman in the eighth, stole second and third, and scored on an infield grounder by Carlos Baerga.

Martinez shrugged off the loss, saying, "There won't be too many games like that with this team. Fortunately, this is only the first game and we can go from here."

Unfortunately, however, the next two games were very similar, though separated by another postponement, and the Indians found themselves in the strange position of looking up - instead of down - at the rest of the A.L. Central Division with their 0-3 record.

First, the Yankees continued to torment the Tribe with a 5-1 beating on April 3, as Jack McDowell made his Cleveland debut, pitching well enough to win most games.

LOFTON TIES TERRY TURNER

The only positive note was that Lofton stole two more bases in as many attempts, giving him 254 in four-plus seasons, which tied the club record set by Terry Turner from 1904-18.

The Tribe's defensive problems - the same that surfaced in spring training when they were charged with 41 errors in 35 games - were a factor in McDowell's loss to the Yankees Andy Pettitte.

Lofton, Franco and Baerga committed errors, two of them resulting in unearned runs in the seventh and ninth innings that put the game out of reach.

Of the six hits off McDowell, one barely eluded Omar Vizquel's desperate lunge, another was an infield grounder that Jim Leyritz beat out, and a third was a pop fly that plopped to earth in front of Ramirez.

Something else that contributed to the damage - and to Hargrove's subsequent irritability - was a bases loaded walk by Julian Tavarez that forced in New York's run in the seventh.

It gave the Yankees a three-season, 8-2 record against the Indians at Jacobs Field.

McDowell didn't make excuses for his lack of success. "Obviously, I didn't pitch well enough to win the game, so I'm not happy about it," he said. "You've got to pitch better than the other guy. That's what it's all about."

More bad weather, rain and temperatures in the 30s - which might have been a factor in the Indians' problems - forced postponement of what would have been the series finale against the Yankees on April 4.

MORE DEFENSIVE PROBLEMS

The skies cleared the next day and Toronto came to Jacobs Field and kept the Indians winless in the opener of their three game series, beating Orel Hershiser, 7-1.

The loss, in which the Indians were held to one run, for the third straight game, and six hits by the Blue Jays Juan Guzman was another exercise in defensive futility. They mishandled - though no errors were charged - three plays in the field.

Belle slipped and was unable to catch what became a single by Otis Nixon, Franco waved at, but couldn't come up with a grounder by Carlos Delgado, and Jim Thome failed to pick up an Alex Gonzalez bounder.

What's more, on four occasions Indians batters failed to drive in runners in scoring position, leaving them 1-for-23 in that department.

And the usually reliable Hershiser uncorked three wild pitches, each of which helped the Blue Jays score runs.

The Indians averted a shutout in the eighth on a homer by Franco, though it served only to nullify a homer by Toronto's Ed Sprague off Embree. It was the second home run in two games - and two innings - off Embree, who'd been warned by Hargrove in spring training to "bear down or else."

The loss marked the first time the Tribe dropped three straight at Jacobs Field since June 24-27, 1994.

Bench coach Jeff Newman called the shots in this one, as Hargrove was home in Perryton, Texas with his father, Dudley, who underwent a knee replacement operation.

"Right now we're playing pretty ugly," Newman correctly assessed the situation that caused great consternation among Tribe fans, motivating many more to call the talk shows with their concerns.

Their recommendations ranged from firing John Hart and Hargrove to trading away half the team's players, and demoting the other half.

"We're not hitting, we're not playing good defense, and we're scattering our hits," added Newman, and again he was right.

Hershiser was philosophic. "The longer this goes on, people will get frustrated," he said. "But I don't sense frustration (among the players). This team has tremendous talent. It's early (and) we're going to be fine."

SHUEY ESCAPES INJURY

After the game the Indians revealed that pitcher Paul Shuey had been involved in an automobile accident two days earlier in Buffalo. His four wheel drive vehicle was totaled after it skidded on ice and rolled over twice.

Fortunately, Shuey was wearing a seat belt and was not injured seriously, but it was the only good news the Indians had received since leaving spring training.

Shuey's accident was similar to the one in which McDowell also escaped injury in Winter Haven, Florida, when his car skidded off a rain-slickened highway, rolled over and was totaled, but he was unhurt.

Another who was philosophic despite the negative start was Hart, who kept the Indians' troubles in perspective, including the defensive problems.

"I go back to the club I saw last year," he said. "I don't think that will change much. We'll be a solid defensive team. Not spectacular, but solid. We didn't build this club around Gold Gloves. I don't like the way we're playing now, but I'm not concerned."

Hart also zeroed in on Baerga, which was significant in view of what would happen later in the season.

"I think Carlos is playing heavy right now," Hart said of the second baseman whose weight reportedly was "down" to 227 from the 230-plus he'd weighed at the onset of spring training.

"(Baerga) has the kind of body type that is going to make it difficult for him unless he pays more attention to his conditioning.

"God gave Carlos great eye-hand coordination, and a great joy for the game. But Carlos will have to pay attention to himself physically if he is going to stay at this level. He's not 22 years old anymore. I hate to see his great skills erode because he's not paying attention to himself physically."

'INDIANS ARE CATCHABLE'

Whether Hart really was unconcerned after the Indians' mediocre play in spring training, and their 0-3 season-opening start, the problems to date recalled the comments of Jerry Reinsdorf, the outspoken owner of the Chicago White Sox.

Reinsdorf was quoted as saying that the Indians would be "catchable" in 1996 because, he said, their pitching was questionable. He named Hershiser, Martinez and McDowell as being suspect because of their age and previous injuries.

Reinsdorf was particularly caustic in his remarks about McDowell, who came to the major leagues with the White Sox and had ongoing troubles with the Chicago owner before he was traded to the Yankees in 1995.

"Jack hasn't had a good year since 1993 (when he won the A.L. Cy Young Award)," snorted Reinsdorf.

The Indians finally won their first game on April 6 and, though there was no great improvement in their offense, Charles Nagy didn't need much help.

Nagy scattered six hits over six innings and the relief corps, including Jose Mesa, did its job as the Tribe beat Toronto, 6-3.

TEMPERING THE THRILL OF VICTORY

But the thrill of victory was tempered by the pre-game incident involving Belle - though it wasn't immediately reported - that would cause more problems for the star outfielder, and another headache for the team.

During the Indians' warm-up exercises Belle was angered because photographer Tony Tomsic was taking his picture and threw two baseballs at Tomsic. The second one reportedly would have hit the photographer in the head or upper body. It was deflected by Tomsic and struck his left hand, which was cut in two places.

Tomsic, whose injury was treated in the Tribe's training room, said that, after he was hit, Belle yelled and swore at him for taking his picture.

"The players were on the ground in front of the tarp, maybe on the edge of the (outfield) grass, stretching," Tomsic was quoted by *USA TODAY* on April 23. "I popped a couple of head shots of Albert, and he shook his finger at me and said, 'No, no, no,' and I backed off.

"Then, (the Indians) started warming up playing catch. He (Belle) was in short left field. I was on the track near the tarp. At no time was I ever in this guy's face - before then or since then.

"I started shooting pictures as they were warming up because they were in these bright-red windbreakers. I heard some yelling from the players, and then I heard a ball hit behind me in the seats. I don't know whether it went over my head, next to me or what.

"Right after that, I was shooting Belle throwing, and it looked like something was coming at me and I put my (left) hand up.

"I heard a player yell, 'What the hell are you doing?' at Belle, and then I heard the word (expleted) and the ball struck me. Instinctively, I lifted my hand up - I guess I saw it coming - and caught it on the knuckle

"I yelled back at Belle, 'Would you please repeat that?' and he said, 'I told you not to take my picture, (expletive).' I said, 'I thought that's what you said.' That was it.

"Several of the players wanted to know if I was OK, but there was no apology. I really didn't want one."

NO FORMAL COMPLAINT BY TOMSIC

Still, Tomsic declined to file a formal complaint because, "I feel bad for the club ... I didn't want to cause trouble for (the Indians)." he said in a story by *Plain Dealer* sportswriter Paul Hoynes on April 21.

Tomsic also was quoted in *USA TODAY*: "The bad side of this is if something (involving Belle) happens two weeks, two months, two years down the road and somebody really gets hurt, I'm going to look like an ass. (But) I guess that's something I've got to live with."

Hart said he was unaware of the incident and would talk to both Tomsic and Belle to find out exactly what happened.

"No one filed a complaint with me," Hart was quoted as saying. "Albert is a grown man. He's going to have to take responsibility for his actions. The Indians can't be held accountable."

Belle would not comment.

The next day, according to the newspaper, Hargrove and several Tribe players - Hershiser, Vizquel and Alvaro Espinoza, but not Belle - inquired as to the condition of Tomsic's injured hand.

"Albert was castigated by his teammates big-time for doing it," Bob DiBiasio, Indians vice president for public relations, was quoted in *USA TODAY.*

Hargrove said he'd been told by Belle that he didn't intentionally throw at Tomsic. "Albert said he was playing long toss with Manny Ramirez and Tony (Tomsic) was standing right behind Manny when a ball got past him."

Though Tomsic did not file a complaint, A.L. President Budig and interim Commissioner Bud Selig promised an investigation into the incident.

And, later, after an HBO special, "Real Sports With Bryant Gumbel" in which he was interviewed by Spike Lee, Tomsic indicated that he might change. It resulted from Belle's admission that he did indeed intentionally throw at Tomsic, trying to hit him.

P.D. EDITORIAL BLASTS BELLE

Meanwhile, the *Plain Dealer*, in an April 23 editorial, expressed outrage:

"If Albert Belle can't behave like a normal human being, then Cleveland - and the Indians - don't need him.

"For too long the Indians, their loyal fans and even local news organizations have looked the other way or downplayed Belle's dangerous behavior.

For too long Belle's phenomenal offensive talents have been used as justification for an attitude that seems to say, 'He's worth the trouble.'

"Well, maybe he's not. and maybe it's time for Belle to take his act elsewhere when he becomes a free agent at the end of this season."

The editorial concluded:

"With or without Belle, the Indians will remain an outstanding team with a first-class organization. If Belle thinks he can find a more tolerant team and fan base elsewhere, he's in for a rude awakening."

The Indians victory over Toronto that followed wasn't pretty. They committed two more errors, by Belle and Baerga, and the Blue Jays connected for two homers, one of them a 420 foot shot by John Olerud off Nagy, the other off Mesa.

But, as Nagy commented, "I'm just glad we won a game so we could get people off our backs. We lost three straight and everybody is writing us off. The expectations are so high on this team that people expected us to go 162-0. That's unrealistic."

The Indians broke loose for four runs in the second inning, but needed considerable help to do it. Included were four walks, an error, wild pitch and a passed ball to go with two hits, one of them Belle's double.

"We gave (the Indians) six outs," grumbled Joe Carter. "That was the difference. We gave them life when they didn't have any life."

"A run is a run, no matter how you get it," countered Lofton.

On the other hand, a run the Indians didn't score angered Lofton. It would have been carried home by Ramirez, on the wings of what would have been a sacrifice fly by Lofton.

It didn't count because Ramirez remained on third, despite being instructed by coach Toby Harrah to tag up and score after the catch.

When Ramirez didn't, Lofton glared at him, then threw his bat and helmet in front of the Indians dugout.

"Manny was the only person in the ball park who thought he couldn't score," said Hargrove.

MESA GOES 'ON STRIKE'

As for Mesa, who many thought was the Indians' most valuable player in 1995 when he racked up 46 saves in 48 opportunities, he struggled but prevailed after being greeted in the ninth by Alex Gonzalez's home run.

Apparently shaken by the homer, Mesa followed by walking Otis Nixon. But then - after a finger-pointing lecture by catcher Tony Pena in a conference on the mound - Mesa retired the next three batters to close out the game and give Nagy and the Indians their first victory of 1996.

However, Mesa's first save of the season didn't do anything for his disposition as he told reporters after the game that he didn't want to be interviewed. "I'm on strike," he said.

The next day it was Martinez's turn to indicate again that he'd overcome the physical problems that plagued him in 1995 with a strong, seven inning performance for his first victory as the Indians beat the Blue Jays, 8-3.

But still, it took a remarkable catch by Lofton in the very first inning to keep Martinez in the game, as well as four homers - two by Albert Belle and one each by Ramirez and Baerga - as the Tribe came alive offensively.

Lofton stole what would have been an extra base hit, even a home run in many major league parks, from Joe Carter with a back-to-the-plate grab a foot or two in front of the center field fence, and turned it into a double play.

Another double play in the second inning also saved Martinez from an early shower. A walk and two singles loaded the bases, and the Blue Jays took a 1-0 lead when Shawn Green was hit by a pitch.

After a summit meeting with pitching coach Mark Wiley, Martinez induced Charlie O'Brien to ground to Jim Thome, who started a double play. and though another run came home, it could have been much worse.

Spared by the double plays, Martinez blanked the Blue Jays until he tired in the seventh when he gave up another run, but by then the Indians' bats had come alive.

They tied the score with single runs in the third and fourth, Ramirez solo homered in the fifth, Baerga and Belle hit back-to-back homers in the sixth, three singles and Carter's error produced two runs in the seventh, and Belle hit another homer with the bases bare in the eighth. Ramirez also tripled and singled.

FRANCO: 'I TOLD YOU SO'

"Didn't I tell you? It was just a matter of time before this team hit," chortled Franco, who shook off two errors in the Tribe's first three games, and played a solid first base in the Toronto series, evoking a similar comment from Hargrove.

"I knew as soon as (Franco) felt comfortable and felt that he fit in, that we'd see his true talents," said the manager.

It ended the Indians first homestand and left them in second place with a 2-3 record, a half-game behind Minnesota.

Another rain-out on April 9, the Indians' third of the young season, cost Chad Ogea his first opportunity since being anointed as the fifth starter in the rotation, beating out Mark Clark, Albie Lopez and Brian Anderson for the job.

In his favor was the fact that Ogea demonstrated in 1995 that he could do the one thing that fifth starters must do - wait.

As Hargrove said, "Everyone who competed for that fifth spot pitched well. It wasn't a case of anyone winning or losing the job, but of who was the better fit for the job.

"Chad showed last year he was able to endure long periods of idleness and still be able to pitch effectively."

Ogea admitted, "I'll be honest, at first (in spring training) I was worried about messing up and getting sent back down.

"Then I reached a point where I said to myself, 'Don't worry.' Life is too short for that. I just decided to go out and pitch. I just concentrated on getting people out," which he did.

McDOWELL FAILS AGAIN

And so, it was McDowell who went back to the mound for Game 6 in

Baltimore on April 10, but he fared no better than in his Tribe debut, though the 3-2, 10 inning loss to the Orioles was charged to Julian Tavarez.

The Indians' offense was shackled again as they were held to six hits over eight innings by southpaw David Wells, and relievers Roger McDowell and old friend Jesse Orosco.

The end came three batters after Jeffrey Hammonds opened the tenth with a double off Tavarez.

Paul Assenmacher replaced Tavarez and Brady Anderson was retired on a sacrifice bunt that send Hammonds to third. Roberto Alomar was intentionally walked, but Rafael Palmeiro spoiled the strategy. He lashed a 2-and-2 pitch into the right field corner for a single that drove in Hammonds and ended the game.

For Assenmacher, it was particularly distressing as he was informed moments after the game that his father, Leo, had died of a heart attack in Detroit earlier that night.

"One of Paul's brothers called during the game and told us not to tell Paul until after the game," said Mike Seghi, the Indians director of team travel.

It was the Indians' first loss in extra innings since July 30, 1994. They had won 14 straight, including 13 in 1995.

McDowell was staked to a 2-1 lead on Belle's third homer with the bases empty in the sixth, and appeared to be in control when he struck out two Orioles in the seventh around a walk to Tony Tarasco.

But he couldn't get past Brady Anderson. With Tarasco on second with a stolen base, Anderson lined a single to center, tying the score and ending McDowell's work for the night.

"The one thing I wish I had back was the walk to Tarasco," said McDowell, who was tagged for a solo homer by Chris Hoiles in the fourth. It nullified the Indians' first run that came home in the third on Lofton's single, his sixth stolen base, and Baerga's one out double.

Despite the loss, the Tribe's McDowell was "terrific," according to Palmeiro. "That's the best stuff I've seen him have since he won the Cy Young in 1993," the Orioles' first baseman said.

But Wells was every bit as terrific, though the victory was credited to Orosco. After the Indians took a 1-0 lead in the third, Wells retired 17 of the last 18 batters he faced. Belle's homer was the only blemish.

BELLE'S CONTRACT 'ON HOLD'

Upon re-joining the Indians in Baltimore on April 10 after a scouting trip to Class AAA Buffalo, Hart announced that contract negotiations with Belle and his agent, Arn Tellem, had been broken off.

"It doesn't look like we're going to get anything done," Hart said, giving rise to speculation that Belle would become a free agent at the end of the season. "Rather than having it be a distraction during the season, we just broke off while making it very clear we want to retain him."

Belle, still waiting for whatever disciplinary action would be taken against him for throwing at, and hitting Tomsic with a baseball, again declined to comment on the stalled contract negotiations.

The Indians' new offer to Belle reportedly was a five-year package worth an estimated $43 million. The average annual value of the contract was believed to be $8.6 million, with $1.25 million deferred each year.

"We gave it a very good shot ... we made what we consider a tremendous offer," said Hart, referring to the new proposal.

It represented an increase of about $6 million over the life of the contract they offered on March 8 that reportedly called for between $37 and $38 million over five years.

"We don't feel we have anything to apologize for," continued Hart. "We just couldn't get a deal done. The direction we were going, we felt it was best to back away.

"We parted on amiable terms. (Tellem) knows we're interested based on the offer we made. This doesn't mean we couldn't get something done later in the season, or after the season.

"How Albert plays could affect any further negotiations. But we expect Albert to play well no matter what.

"Right now things are on hold. It's time to play ball."

Tellem denied that, by rejecting the Indians' latest offer, Belle was determined to test the free agent market at the end of the season.

"That has not even been thought about," said the agent. "I'm not going to comment on what we've been offered and not offered, other than to confirm what John has said about talks being broken off. The process with the Indians has been very good and cordial.

"But that's all I want to say."

THE WORST SINCE 1993

The Indians did play ball the next night, as Hart said it was time to do - but again, they did not play very well

And the resounding crash that was heard throughout baseball on April 11 was the alleged best team in the American League falling into fourth place in the Central Division, ahead - by a mere half-game - of only Kansas City.

Again it was the Tribe's defensive problems that hurt, costing a 14-4 loss to the Orioles.

"We didn't field well," acknowledged Hargrove, "but then, we didn't pitch well, or hit well either,"

There could be no dissenters as Baerga, Thome and Hershiser were charged with errors; Hershiser struggled from the first pitch and, except for home runs by Belle and Jeromy Burnitz, the Indians were held in check by, first, Scott Erickson and, then, Arthur Rhodes.

Hershiser, in losing his second start, got through the first inning unscathed. But he was tagged for a two-run homer by Tarasco in the second, gave up four runs in the third when the Indians committed their three errors, and served a solo homer to Anderson in the fourth when Baltimore increased its lead to 7-1.

"Everything that could go wrong in the third inning, did go wrong," said Hershiser. "It just snowballed."

And again, there were no dissenters.

DAVE JOHNSON: 'IT WAS SAD'

It was so bad, even Orioles Manager Dave Johnson expressed sympathy. "It was sad," he said of Hershiser's effort. "He was really laboring. I admire Orel so much ... he's such a great pitcher, but I've never seen him struggle like that to keep the ball down."

Hershiser scoffed at Johnson's remark. "I had a bad day, that's all there was to it," he said. "I was pretty much a non-athlete. There are some days when you wake up and all your athletic ability leaves you. I am sure there are a lot of weekend warriors out there who can understand that.

But it didn't bother Hershiser. "We're friends," he said of Johnson. "We play golf three or four times during the winter. I appreciate him being sorry. He's a nice man and a great manager."

As for speculation that age might have caught up with him - Hershiser would turn 38 in September - he said, "I'm not worried about it. I'm throwing the ball better than I have in a long time."

Hershiser wasn't the only victim of the Orioles' onslaught. In addition to the two homers he yielded, Plunk also gave up two, to Anderson and B.J. Surhoff; Ogea one, to Hammonds; and Mesa one, to Palmeiro.

When Baerga was approached by reporters asking about the error he committed that started the trouble in the third, he shooed them away with one terse statement: "I don't want to talk."

Which pretty much summarized the attitude of the majority of the Indians in the wake of their most lop-sided defeat since May 3, 1994 when they lost to Chicago, 12-1.

The loss to the Orioles dropped the Indians' won-lost record to three below .500 at 2-5, their biggest deficit since 1993 when they finished the season with a 76-86 record

Afterwards, and before the Indians left Baltimore for Boston, Hargrove held a closed-door team meeting in which he reportedly came down hard on the players for what he called a "lack of mental preparation."

It was an appropriate message - and, based on subsequent events, was well taken by the Tribesmen.

Albert Belle versus the California Angels June 9, 1996

3

NO PLACE LIKE FIRST PLACE

April 12-April 28

To paraphrase an old bromide, the Indians hit rock bottom before they rebounded to the top - although, to be sure, rock bottom could have been much worse.

They were in fourth place in the American League Central Division with their 2-5 record, but were only a game-and-a-half behind Minnesota on the morning of April 12.

The Indians slunk out of Baltimore, continuing the trip that would take them to Boston for four games and Minnesota for two, before returning to the friendly confines of Jacobs Field where their record was a remarkable 54-18 in 1995.

Five consecutive victories ensued, the first two of which vaulted them on April 13 into first place, where they stayed the rest of the season, though they subsequently were tied for the top from April 18-21, and again from June 9-10.

The Red Sox were the first victim of the resurgence, 3-1, as Charles Nagy, who would become the Tribe's most effective pitcher, allowed five hits in eight innings, and Jose Mesa recorded his second save.

Nagy's teammates didn't provide a lot of support and the Indians failed to capitalize on two early opportunities, the first when Kenny Lofton reached on an error to start the game, and rambled to third on Julio Franco's ground rule double.

But Aaron Sele struck out Carlos Baerga and Eddie Murray, around a walk to Albert Belle, and retired Manny Ramirez on a force at second.

Was it going to be another one of those games in which the Indians would waste one golden opportunity after another?

It was a problem that would plague the Tribe most of the season.

Sele also escaped a major threat in the second when a walk and two infield singles loaded the bases with one out. But only one run scored as Franco grounded out and Omar Vizquel was caught trying to go home from second.

The situation brightened for the Indians in the fourth as they added two more runs on three singles and a sacrifice fly, and Nagy made them stand up.

A TEMPEST IN A TEAPOT

The only distressing note was that another error by Thome in the sixth inning - the Tribe's 12th in eight games - gave Boston its only run.

But, to Mike Hargrove's way of thinking, winning nullified any negative element.

"It was important that we showed up physically and mentally prepared to play, and we did," he said. "There have been times when I've felt we haven't prepared mentally as well as we can for a game."

In addition to the game on the field, a word battle seemed ready to erupt between Belle and Red Sox first baseman Mo Vaughn, though it subsequently was better described as a tempest in a teapot.

Vaughn, who beat out Belle for the A.L.'s Most Valuable Player award by the narrowest of margins in 1995, was quoted in the Boston *Herald* as being angry at his rival, accusing Belle of "dis-respecting" him.

"I've heard (Belle) doesn't respect my abilities as a player," said Vaughn. "What does his criticism stand on? Who is he to criticize me as a person?

"He took it personally against me that he didn't win the MVP award. (But) I didn't do the voting. I think he had a hell of a year. But all I hear is how he had 50 home runs and 50 doubles last year.

"Well, if I played in that park (Jacobs Field), I'd have 50 home runs and 50 doubles, too," grumbled Vaughn (obviously ignoring the fact that if Belle played in Fenway Park where the left field wall - the famed "Green Monster" - greatly favors right-handed hitters, his extra base production undoubtedly would have been even greater).

Belle didn't respond publicly, which was par for the course for him, but when he reached first base in the first inning of the series opener, he was seen talking to Vaughn.

Afterwards Vaughn said of the spat, "It's over. We had a nice conversation at first base. He's a good player and person."

HELLO PAUL, GOODBYE ALAN

It also was after the game that the Indians made their first roster move of the season, demoting Alan Embree, who had been the subject of several "bear-down-or-else" lectures by Hargrove.

Embree, who'd made three appearances, allowing five earned runs on two homers and a triple in the Tribe's seven games, was sent down to Class AAA Buffalo and Paul Shuey was called up from that team.

The next night the Tribe not only beat the Red Sox, but embarrassed them, 14-2, as well.

The victory boosted the Indians back to where everybody expected them to be, first place, though their margin was only a half-game over Chicago, Kansas City and Minnesota, all tied for second in the A.L. Central.

Reliever Jim Poole said of the victory, "This was typical Indians' offense from last year. A couple runs here, a couple runs there, and - bang! - just dump on them."

It was an appropriate description.

Among the Tribe's 14 hits were homers by Vizquel, Belle (his fifth), and slump ridden Jim Thome, who had only one hit in 20 at-bats (.050) prior to the game.

Thome was philosophical about his slump. "Sometimes (slumps) are good," he said. "They bring you down to earth and make you realize you have to keep working hard at this game."

The Indians scored single runs in the first, second, third and fourth innings, two in the fifth and three in the sixth for a 9-0 lead, making it easy for Dennis Martinez to raise his record to 2-1.

But still, it was not one of Martinez's best efforts. "Dennis struggled the entire game," said Hargrove. "If he threw 30 curve balls, he left 27 up in the strike zone."

Martinez yielded both Boston runs on solo homers by Jose Canseco and Troy O'Leary.

SHUEY IS 'AWESOME'

Shuey pitched the ninth inning and, in the opinion of Thome, was "awesome." Though he gave up two hits, Shuey went on to strike out the side. "That's the best stuff I've seen since Jose Mesa," said Thome.

A ninth inning error in right field by O'Leary opened the door to five Tribe runs. It was the Red Sox's fourth error of the game, giving them 17 in 10 games, most in the A.L and four more than the Indians committed in nine games.

It wasn't as easy for the Indians the next night, but the result was just as satisfying, a 7-6, 11 inning victory that took four hours and 42 minutes to complete.

It was achieved on the wings of Franco's second homer since returning from Japan, boosting their record to .500 (5-5) and their lead over second place Minnesota to one game.

For the Red Sox, it was their ninth loss in 11 games and the Boston media already were counting the Red Sox out.

Franco's homer wasn't a mighty blow - it barely sneaked into the seats near the right field foul pole, about 330 feet from the plate - but Hargrove called it "just right."

"That was not a cheap home run," said Franco. "It is very hard for a right handed batter to hit the ball down the (right field) line like that. As soon as I hit it, I knew it would stay fair. Right field is where my power is.

"I was determined to try and do something to help us win. We'd been here all day and the weather could not get any worse so we might as well win the game and get it over with."

The temperature was 47 degrees at game time, and got colder as the game progressed.

There also was nothing cheap about the two-run, two-out homer by Lofton, also to right field, that tied the score in the sixth after Ogea wasted the Tribe's 4-0 first inning lead.

Ogea was making his first start since a March 27 appearance in spring training and was knocked out in the fifth. He was replaced by Shuey who, this time, was no improvement. The Red Sox rallied for five runs on five hits, a walk, Belle's error, and Shuey's wild pitch and a balk, for a 6-4 lead.

Lofton stole two more bases, giving him 10 in as many games, although he was thrown out trying to steal home in the first inning.

"I don't know what made me do it," he said of the failed attempt. "All the guys on the bench were telling me to go. I think I would have made it if I had not hesitated."

Mesa needed only eight pitches in the ninth to register his third save, alleviating - at least for the present - any concerns about his ability to continue to be as dominating as he was in 1995.

GET OUT THE BROOMS!

Three straight late inning come-from-behind victories over the Red Sox at Fenway Park early in the season launched the Indians' pennant drive in 1995, and those who remembered were hoping the same thing might happen in 1996.

That optimism was ignited on April 15 when the Tribe completed a four game sweep of the stumbling, error-prone Red Sox, beating them, 8-0, as Jack McDowell won his first game in a Cleveland uniform.

"Black Jack" for the first time in three starts lived up to that which had been expected of him when the Indians signed him to a two year, $9.6 million guaranteed contract on December 14, 1995. McDowell scattered nine hits with a walk, and struck out nine.

"The biggest thing we got out of this series," said Hargrove, "is that we regained some of the confidence that was knocked out of us in the first seven games. I'm not talking about cockiness or arrogance, but confidence in this team's ability to win."

One whose confidence had to be inflated was Lofton, who batted .179 (5-for-28) through the first seven games, but went 8-for-17 (.471) with six runs and five stolen bases against the Red Sox.

"I figured I needed to get on base any way I could and help jump start our offense," said Lofton. "When I get on base everyone else seems to relax and hit."

That certainly was the case in this game as Lofton began it with a single, stole second, took third on a passed ball with one out and scored on an error, Boston's 20th in 12 games (with the 21st coming later).

Belle's sacrifice fly got another run home in the first, and Lofton singled again in the second when the Indians got three more runs for a 5-0 lead.

"It makes all the difference in the world when you get your leadoff hitter on base, especially when it's Kenny Lofton," said Hargrove.

The Indians added three more runs in the sixth, making it easy for McDowell, who struck out nine in pitching his 13th career shutout.

"When we started this season everything was 'Indians, Indians, Indians,'" said McDowell. "We had to just step back and relax."

NO NEED FOR SYMPATHY

The "relaxation" formula apparently worked as the Indians moved on to Minnesota where they beat the Twins, 7-2, behind Hershiser, and this time nobody felt sorry for the veteran right hander.

Though the Indians received big-time help from Twins' center fielder Roberto Kelly to take a 4-0 lead in the second inning, Hershiser, winning his first game, pitched seven strong innings. He faltered only in the fifth when

Minnesota scored twice to cut its deficit to 5-2.

Julian Tavarez blanked the Twins in the eighth and ninth for the Tribe's fifth straight victory.

Lofton continued his hot hitting with a home run and a single, and another stolen base, but it was Kelly who lost two fly balls in the gray Teflon ceiling of the Metrodome to give the Indians a running start.

With one out in the second inning, Ramirez flied to center. It should have been the second out, but Kelly couldn't find the ball and it fell for a double.

The very next batter, Thome, did essentially the same thing - and so did Kelly - except that Thome's was hit a little deeper. Instead of Kelly catching what should have been the third out, the ball flew over the center fielder's head for a run-scoring triple.

Then Sandy Alomar Jr., not needing anymore help from Kelly, homered, and one out later, Lofton did the same.

"It was real crazy," Thome said of Kelly's misadventures.

"Our team must have lost 15,000 balls against that roof," said Hargrove, exaggerating slightly. "But you usually don't see it happening to the home team."

Hershiser, who in his first two starts was tagged for nine earned runs and 14 hits in 10 1/3 innings, said, "This time I knew where my pitches were going, unlike my first two games.

"When that's the case, the hitters have to move the bats because they know I'm going to throw strikes. When I don't know where the ball is going, (the hitters) just sit there and wait for a fast ball."

'A GAME WE SHOULD HAVE WON'

The Indians' winning streak was short-circuited at five the next night, April 17, ending their eight game trip and sending them home with a 7-6 record and a half-game lead over Milwaukee.

The loss, 9-8, to the Twins, was the result of some unusually poor pitching by Nagy, and some not-so-unusual base running

And though Nagy grumbled to reporters when he was asked about what appears to be his inability to pitch well in a domed stadium, the fact is, the defeat was his fourth in four starts in the Metrodome, to go with an 0-5 record in Seattle's Kingdome.

Nagy has had slightly better success in Toronto's Skydome where his record was 4-3, though that might have been due to the fact the roof in that stadium is opened when the weather is good.

"I'm sick and tired of answering that question," Nagy snapped when asked if he has a problem pitching indoors. "I just didn't pitch well. the surroundings had nothing to do with it."

There was no doubt that Nagy didn't pitch well in the fifth inning after he'd been staked to a 7-2 lead. The Twins got to Nagy for three runs on three hits, cutting their deficit to 7-5.

Shuey came out for the sixth and was even worse. Marty Cordova greeted him with a homer, and before Hargrove could rush Eric Plunk to the rescue, the Twins scored three more runs on two walks and another homer for a 9-7 lead.

"It's disturbing that Shuey's had back-to-back bad outings," said Hargrove. "He couldn't throw strikes. He was behind on everyone."

Vizquel sat out a game for the first time in 1996, and though it was speculated that his ailing shoulder was the reason, Hargrove said it was nothing serious.

"I was only taking advantage of an opportunity to give Omar two days' off," said Hargrove, considering that the Tribe had an open date the next day.

It was after a three run homer by Ramirez in the third inning, giving the Nagy a 6-2 lead, that the mis-adventures on the base paths began.

Thome walked and tried unsuccessfully to go to third as Tony Pena grounded out for an inning ending double play.

Then in the fourth, after Lofton and Franco led with singles, they attempted a double steal. Franco was thrown out at second moments before Baerga doubled for one run instead of two. And then to compound the over-aggressiveness, Baerga was retired trying to stretch his hit into a triple.

"That was a game we should have won," lamented Hargrove, and again he was right.

NO. 200 FOR ALBERT BELLE

Back in Cleveland with an open date on April 18, the Indians, despite being idle, fell into a tie with Milwaukee for first place in the A.L. Central Division as the Brewers beat Kansas City, 8-2. It gave both leaders 7-6 records.

Hart took the occasion of a day off to address what he considered to be the Indians' only problem that had surfaced to date: "We have one unsettled spot in the bull pen ... one spot that's been hurting us."

It was an obvious reference to the fact that neither Embree, who had been demoted to Buffalo, nor Shuey, who replaced him, had pitched well in their long relief roles.

Still, Hart insisted, "I'm not going to put this team under a microscope at this point - 13 games - in the season. This is basically the same team we had last year. It is a team with a lot of talent. I am not going to make any judgments until 30 or 35 games into the season."

He also scoffed at those who second guessed the trading of Mark Clark the day before the season started.

"Mark Clark could not have pitched out of this (long relief) role," said Hart. "He's a starting pitcher, not a long guy."

The Indians continued their mastery over Boston as they opened a five game homestand against the Red Sox on April 19, and it was Belle who got them off and running.

Not only did Belle hammer his 200th career homer in a 9-4 victory, he also doubled and singled, making it easy for Martinez to hike his won-lost record to 3-1, though he gave up homers to Vaughn and Mike Stanley. He got eighth and ninth inning relief help from Poole and Mesa.

Hargrove was ebullient in his praise for Belle. "If Albert stays healthy, if he stays as consistent as he's been, he will put numbers on the board very few people can in the game.

"I have not seen anyone like him in a long, long time as far as putting together the package of power and hitting for average."

Martinez also spoke in awe of Belle's ability. "He is unbelievable. So powerful. He is never fooled by a pitcher over an entire game. I am very happy he is on my team," said Martinez.

Belle, as had become his custom since spring training, declined to be interviewed.

CLOSING IN ON THORNTON

Belle's homer, his sixth of the season, placed him fifth among the Indians' all time leaders, behind Earl Averill (226), Hal Trosky (216), Larry Doby (215) and Andre Thornton (214).

Belle's 200 homers are 6.91 percent of his 2,893 career at-bats - fourth highest in baseball history behind Babe Ruth (8.5 percent), Ralph Kiner (7.09 percent) and Harmon Killebrew (7.03 percent).

But it wasn't only Belle who sparked the offense, providing the Indians with a 41-13 edge in runs scored against the Red Sox in five games to date.

Lofton also was a major contributor, going 3-for-4, raising his average to .333, and stealing his 13th base as the Indians socked 13 hits of assorted shape and size.

"Kenny (Lofton) is our starter, and Belle is our buster," said batting coach Charlie Manuel after the Indians broke open the game with five runs in the sixth inning, but remained in a tie with Milwaukee, which beat Kansas City again, 8-2.

On April 21, the day the story broke in the *Plain Dealer* - 15 days after the fact - that Belle had intentionally hit free lance photographer Tony Tomsic who was shooting pictures for *Sports Illustrated,* with a baseball, the Indians squeezed out another victory over Boston.

This time the Indians beat the Red Sox, 2-1, with their gloves - especially Thome, who made two outstanding defensive plays - and some timely situational hitting against knuckleballer Tim Wakefield.

The Tribe's two runs came in the third when Pena coaxed a one-out walk, Vizquel dropped a perfect bunt down the third base line for a single, Pena took third on Lofton's fly to center, Vizquel stole second, and Franco delivered a single on a 2-and-2 pitch, scoring both runners.

"I was thinking bunt all the way," said Vizquel. "The way (Wakefield's) knuckleball was going, I had to get on base somehow."

Franco, who struck out in his first plate appearance, said of his hit, "You don't want to think too much in that situation ... I just wanted to put the bat on the ball."

McDowell got credit for the victory, his second in three decisions, but it was Tavarez who preserved it for Black Jack.

McDowell, who gave up Boston's only run on two singles and a walk in the sixth, couldn't make it through the seventh after Bill Selby led with a single. The next two batters were retired bringing Vaughn to the plate, and Hargrove replaced McDowell with left hander Paul Assenmacher,.

A FOURTH SAVE FOR MESA

But Assenmacher complicated the situation by walking Vaughn on four pitches, loading the bases.

That brought Tavarez to the scene and he promptly struck out pinch hitter Jose Canseco on a full count, and Mesa worked a one-two-three ninth for his fourth save.

The victory kept the Indians in a first place tie with Milwaukee, which beat Kansas City again, 12-4.

As for the incident involving Belle, A.L. President Dr. Gene Budig said he would investigate the charge and would take whatever action was deemed appropriate at a later date.

That "later date" would be four weeks down the road.

The Indians employed another new tactic to beat Boston for the seventh consecutive time in 1996, 11-7, on April 21, sinking the Red Sox deeper in the basement of the A.L. East Division with a 3-15 record, 8 1/2 games behind first place Baltimore.

The Tribe, which had previously beaten the Red Sox with the long ball and defense, this time took advantage of nine bases on balls issued by four of the six Boston pitchers in the game.

Four walks, three of them in a row, helped the Indians score five runs in the sixth inning when they overcame a 5-2 deficit.

Kevin Kennedy, the Red Sox manager, couldn't hide his disgust. "I've tried to be patient ... I don't want to slam anybody," he said - then he did.

"It's unbelievable. It really is. These are supposed to be quality big leaguers and they throw ball one, ball two, ball three, ball four. I've never seen anything like it in my 21 years in baseball.

"It's ridiculous. I was a (minor league) catcher my whole career. I guarantee you that you can throw the ball over the plate. I throw batting practice every day. So do my coaches. You can throw the ball over the plate," he said again.

While the Indians were patient enough to accept the walks, they still swung the bat, especially Ramirez. He homered twice, in the second and sixth innings, both off Roger Clemens, who walked three before he went to the showers in the sixth.

Hershiser started for the Indians but struggled again and was replaced in the fifth by Chad Ogea, who became the beneficiary of the Red Sox pitchers' generosity.

FRANCO QUIETS THE CRITICS

Franco, about whom there had been considerable doubt concerning his ability to play first base, quieted his critics on April 22 with two outstanding defensive plays that were major factors in the Indians' 6-3 victory over Baltimore.

It was the eighth straight time the Indians had beaten the Orioles at Jacobs Field, and their fourth consecutive victory, lifting them into undisputed possession of first place as a result of Milwaukee's 6-2 loss to Oakland.

Franco also stroked three singles, extending his consecutive game hitting streak to 10.

But it was Franco's defense that dominated the praise of Hargrove, who called the two defensive plays "huge," without which the Tribe probably would have lost.

"I've felt OK with Julio there (at first base) since the first week of the season," said Hargrove. "It was just a matter of letting him settle in."

The first of Franco's game-saving plays came in the fifth inning with the Indians clinging to a 2-1 lead. Chris Hoiles led with a single off Nagy and, on a run-and-hit play, Tony Tarasco lashed a liner toward right field.

Franco leaped for the ball, snared it and easily doubled Hoiles off first.

It took on added significance as Jeff Hammonds followed with a single and Brady Anderson walked before Roberto Alomar made the third out.

Franco said, "It was a case of nothing but reflexes. You either catch the ball, or you don't."

Then in the eighth, with Poole on the mound and the Tribe now ahead, 5-3, Roberto Alomar opened with a double, and would have scored as Rafael Palmeiro whacked another shot toward right.

Franco again snared the ball, saving a run as the Orioles again failed to score. "You always want to make a big play ... I'm glad I was able to do it in that situation," said Franco.

Nagy, of course, was "glad," too. He wound up with a victory that raised his record to 3-0, with Mesa pitching the ninth and picking up his fifth save in five opportunities.

Thome also played a key offensive role with a triple in the second inning when the Tribe took a 2-0 lead against Scott Erickson, and his second homer of the season in the sixth, broke a 3-3 tie.

LOPEZ COMES UP, SHUEY GOES DOWN

After the game the Indians announced that Albie Lopez was being re-called from Buffalo, where his record was 2-0 with a 1.26 earned run average, and that Shuey was being returned to that American Association team.

Lopez didn't have to wait long to see his first action - he assumed the fifth starter's role in place of Ogea and took the mound against Baltimore on April 23 - but didn't last long.

Ironically, Lopez needed to be rescued in the fifth by Ogea, and it was Ogea who was credited with the Indians' 9-8 victory, their fifth in a row and ninth in 10 games.

It was an impressive triumph for the Indians as it came against the Orioles' ace, and one of the best pitchers in the A.L., Mike Mussina. He was roughed up for 10 hits and all the Tribe's nine runs in 6 2/3 innings.

They were the most runs allowed in one game by Mussina in his five-plus years in the big leagues.

Belle ended Mussina's night with his seventh homer, a three run shot with two out in the seventh.

It came in the wake of a disputed, pivotal call by umpire Tim Tschida - that television replays proved was wrong - when Franco was credited with a single on a liner to right that actually had been caught by Tarasco.

It extended Franco's hitting to 10 games and, instead of ending the inning, kept it alive for Belle to unload his homer and account for the winning margin.

Ramirez also delivered a three run homer (No. 5) off Mussina in the fourth when the Tribe went ahead, 4-3.

Lopez gave up a two run homer to Bobby Bonilla in the fourth when the Orioles broke on top, 3-0, and was kayoed in the fifth, when the Orioles tied the score at 5-5.

Despite Lopez's problems, Tribe pitching coach Mark Wiley said, "I thought he threw outstanding. Albie wasn't getting his breaking ball over, but he will."

Wiley also said that Lopez would continue as the fifth starter in the rotation, with Ogea remaining in long relief.

"I wish I could have gone five (complete innings) to get the win, but maybe next time," said Lopez. "Now I can go out every fifth day and not worry. Once I get a regular routine down, I think I'll be all right."

Ogea, who was charged with three of the four runs the Orioles scored in the eighth when they came within one of the Tribe, said he wasn't upset about losing the starter's job he'd won in spring training.

"Whatever role I'm in, I'm going to work hard at," he said. "I have to stay ready. You have to do a lot of throwing on the side. There'll be spot starts down the road. I feel like I'm throwing the ball well."

Assenmacher and Tavarez bailed out Ogea in the eighth, and Mesa needed only 10 pitches to put the Orioles down in order in the ninth for his sixth save in six opportunities.

It ended the Indians' homestand with a two game lead over Milwaukee and sent them back on the road to New York and Toronto, where a couple of unwanted thrills awaited them.

'SCARED (EXPLETIVE)' IN NEW YORK

Arriving in New York in the early hours of April 24 for a two game series against the Yankees, the Indians were alarmed - several players said they were "scared (expletive)" - by a rough landing at LaGuardia Airport.

One Tribesman called it "the worst I've ever been through, and I've been flying for a long time. But don't say I said that."

As the plane was coming in for a landing, it was buffeted by a strong gust of wind and one wing dipped close to the ground. "I thought it was going to scrape the runway," the player said.

Fortunately, the rough landing was only a scare, and so was another frightening incident four days later. The Indians were awakened at 2:30 the morning of April 28 in Toronto by the fire alarm in their Westin Harbour Castle Hotel.

It turned out to be a false alarm, but also shook up the players and robbed most of them of their sleep before playing the Blue jays that afternoon.

"(The fire alarm) taught me one thing about my players," Hargrove made light of the incident later. "When the alarm went off, I jumped out of bed, put on my clothes and ran down to the lobby."

It was full of guests, but not many Indians. Coaches Mark Wiley, Dave Nelson and Luis Isaac were there, along with pitcher Eric Plunk."

"I guess that meant there are only five intelligent people on this club," said Hargrove.

MARTINEZ CAN'T BEAT YANKEES

The rough landing at LaGuardia might have been a factor in Martinez's performance against the Yankees that night, although he has had more problems against them than any other team in his 20 year major league career.

Martinez was hit hard in the first inning, giving up six runs on five hits which did nothing for his temperament, and he was ejected by umpire Gary Cederstrom before he retired anybody in the fourth.

The bottom line was a 10-8 loss that ended the Tribe's five game winning streak, and lowered Martinez's record against the Yankees to 2-15 with a bloated, cumulative 5.10 ERA.

What led to Martinez's ejection was a 2-and-2 pitch to Wade Boggs, the Yankees' second batter in the fourth, after Derek Jeter singled and stole second to start the inning.

Martinez thought the pitch to Boggs should have been strike three, but Cederstrom called it ball three.

Martinez walked halfway to the plate and shouted at the umpire. "The pitch was right down the middle," he said. Cederstrom listened for a few moments, then gave the thumb to Martinez., who was still steaming after the game.

"I couldn't hold it in anymore," Martinez said of his complaint to Cederstrom. "It wasn't the umpire's fault that I gave up those six runs in the first inning, but to me and my catcher (Sandy Alomar), he missed seven to 10 pitches.

"I asked him how I could adjust to his strike zone and he started squeezing me after that."

When asked what might happen the next time he pitches and Cederstrom is behind the plate, Martinez replied, "I'm not going to worry. I think I did what I was supposed to do. I don't think I was getting treated fairly."

The trouble, according to Martinez, was that, "Cederstrom took it personally. A lot of umpires will tell you if a pitch is down or up. But some umpires think you are showing them up.

"They have to understand it's OK for a pitcher to ask about a pitch. All we're trying to do is adjust. I don't think what happened was fair, but there are good and bad umpires in baseball just like there are good and bad players."

NOT THE SAME AS LAST YEAR

After Martinez was banished, Poole replaced him on the mound and, after throwing a third strike past Boggs, promptly complicated the situation.

Bernie Williams singled for the Yankees' seventh run, Paul O'Neill also singled, Williams stole third and, after Ruben Sierra struck out, Tino Martinez blasted a three run homer.

The Indians, who scored twice on three hits in the second, fought back in the sixth on Thome's three run homer, and almost caught the Yankees on another three run homer by Vizquel in the eighth.

"Last year we came back and won games like this because our bull pen came in and stopped the other team," said Poole. "That's what makes (Martinez's) homer so disappointing."

Poole, coming into the game, had not allowed an earned run in six appearances this season.

But Dennis Martinez and Poole weren't the only Tribesmen who had bad nights.

Ramirez, playing in front of another large contingent of relatives and friends in his home town, went 2-for-2 with two walks, but also made a critical throwing error in the first inning, and later lost a fly ball that fell for a double.

Belle, who was booed and taunted throughout the game by the New York fans in Yankee Stadium, met for 90 minutes with major league officials prior to the game.

They were investigating the April 6 incident in which Belle threw two baseballs at Tomsic, the free lance photographer, hitting him with one.

Belle, accompanied by his agent, Arn Tellem, Hart and Gene Orza, associate general counsel for the Players Association, was interviewed by Kevin Halliman, head of security for the commissioner's office, and Jim Murphy. Also in attendance were lawyers Bill Schweitzer of the A.L., and Louis Melendez of the Player Relations Committee.

Only Hart would talk after the meeting, though his comment was very general and non-committal.

"I don't know what the timetable is, but it was made clear that the investigation will be concluded as expeditiously as possible," Hart said.

MURRAY INJURES HIS SHOULDER

Though Belle had nothing to say, whatever anger he might have felt because of the ongoing probe and the heckling he was receiving from the New York fans, he took out on Yankees pitcher Andy Pettitte.

Belle blasted his eighth homer, a solo shot in the eighth inning, breaking a tie and giving the Indians a 4-3 victory, their first over the Yankees in four games.

"Albert Belle has feelings just like anyone else," Hargrove talked about the vocal abuse aimed at the Tribe left fielder for the second consecutive night.

"You know he has to hear things people say and yell. But he's one of those people who has the ability to focus completely on the task at hand. He can shut everything else out."

Belle's homer made a winner of Poole, who took over in the seventh for McDowell, who was making his second start against his former teammates.

"This time I followed the scouting report, and I didn't throw an 81 miles-per-hour fast ball right down the middle and put it on a tee," quipped Poole, who retired the only batter he faced in the seventh.

The Indians provided McDowell a 3-0 lead that he couldn't hold as the Yankees scored twice on four hits in the fifth, and pulled even on Tino Martinez's second homer in two games in the sixth.

After Poole put down the Yankees in the seventh, Tavarez blanked them in the eighth, and Mesa registered his seventh save in seven opportunities, though not without a last minute scare.

He retired the first two batters in the ninth, then walked O'Neill and Sierra lined a shot to right field that Ramirez hauled down with a nice catch.

"I lost my breath on that one," admitted Hargrove.

Murray, still looking for the first of the 21 homers he needed for a career total of 500, made a rare appearance at first base and suffered what was considered at the time to be a minor injury.

It occurred in the sixth inning after Tino Martinez's homer tied the score, and Tim Raines walked.

Jim Leyritz lined to Baerga, who threw wildly to first, trying to double Raines. Murray dived for the ball, attempting to keep it from going into the Yankees' dugout and hurt his left shoulder, but stayed in the game.

Raines reached third on the play, but McDowell induced the next two batters to ground out.

"I looked over from our dugout to see what happened, and all I saw was a cloud of dust and Eddie's legs and arms flapping around" as he went into the dugout, said Hargrove.

"When (Murray) came back to our dugout after the inning he had a scrape under his mustache and another above his eye. I think that tells a lot about the character of the man."

HERSHISER EVENS HIS RECORD

Murray's injury didn't hurt him the next night, April 26, in Toronto where his two hits - but not yet a homer - helped Orel Hershiser even his won-lost record at 2-2 as the Indians beat the Blue Jays, 6-3.

Murray's second single drove in two runs in the third inning when the Tribe took a 5-0 lead.

Ed Sprague solo homered off Hershiser in the fourth, and the Blue Jays - with what the Indians thought was help from umpire Larry Barnett - cut their deficit to two runs on Joe Carter's disputed two run homer in the sixth.

Television replays indicated that Carter's one on, one out shot to left hooked foul, though Barnett saw it differently. "He said the ball curved around the pole," said Hargrove. "I think he called it wrong, but his opinion is the one that counts."

Hershiser sloughed it off, pitched a one-two-three seventh and turned the job over to the bull pen, but wasn't pleased with himself.

"Any time you struggle, you're very mechanical," said Hershiser, always the thinking man's pitcher. "You're thinking too much. It's tough to know if your talent is just coming out of your body or you're still forcing things.

"It's not like I've been getting killed. I pitch good, give up a big crooked number, pitch good, and give up another big crooked number.

"But it will happen. I'll be all right. If I'm not, I'll get released or traded."

Plunk and Mesa were perfect in relief in the eighth and ninth innings, with Mesa racking up another save, giving him 8-for-8.

OGEA AND EMBREE TRADE AGAIN

Another large contingent of Tribe fans hooted and hollered in the Skydome, but this time it did no good as the Blue Jays exploded early against Nagy and waltzed to an 11-6 victory.

It was only the Indians' second loss in nine games, and third in 15, but cut their first place margin to one over Chicago.

Nagy, who has a history of struggling when he pitches in a domed stadium, was kayoed in the second inning after the Blue Jays had taken a 5-1 lead.

When Hargrove visited the mound to bring in another pitcher, Nagy slammed the ball into the manager's hand, instead of handing it to him.

But if it bothered Hargrove, he wouldn't admit it. "When the manager's hand hurts after the ball is handed to him, that's not always good," he said. "But I think Charlie was just mad at himself, mad at the circumstances and mad that I wasn't going to let him pitch anymore.

"I can appreciate that. I'd rather have him that way than to be looking into the dugout for help."

It probably was all that Hargrove appreciated on this night.

Nagy said: "I don't know if I could've gotten myself straightened out or not. It was Grover's decision. I lost my temper out there. I had no right doing that. I apologized. I was just mad."

Of his pitching, he said, "I left a lot of balls out over the plate, and I couldn't throw a fast ball in against a left hander." It was his first loss in four decisions.

Nagy's immediate successor was Ogea, who was no improvement and, after the game was put on the disabled list with tendinitis in his right shoulder.

The Indians' biggest blow was Franco's third homer in the fifth inning, a three run shot that cut their deficit to 7-4. But the Blue Jays bounced back with four more runs in their half of the fifth as Ogea served homers to Carlos Delgado and Charlie O'Brien.

Called up to take Ogea's place on the active roster was Embree, who made the team in spring training, but was demoted to Buffalo on April 12.

"I thought I could pitch through it," Ogea said of his sore arm, "But it got worse. I'll take four days off and slowly try to work the shoulder back into shape (at Buffalo)."

'MORE PLUSES THAN MINUSES'

The trip ended with an explosion against veteran left hander Frank Viola, whose nickname was "Sweet Music" when he won the A.L. Cy Young award in 1988, but now was trying to make a comeback from elbow surgery.

The Indians beat him, 17-3, and afterwards Viola conceded, "It was an ugly way to start," then vowed, "But I guarantee you I'll get better."

He could hardly have gotten worse.

The 17 runs and 20 hits represented the Indians' best offensive showing of the season, and the victory was their 15th in 20 games after losing their first three.

"It was just a matter of time for this team because we have so many .300 hitters," said Alomar, whose first inning homer was one of three by the Tribe. Belle hit his ninth, and Alvaro Espinoza his first. "When it all comes together it's fun because that's when you get games like this."

The Indians erupted for six runs in the first inning off Viola, added three more in the second and, for all practical purposes, the game was over.

"Every day somebody else hits, which is why this team is so good," said Baerga. "I think we are a much better team than we were last year. We all knew Sandy (Alomar) could put up the numbers if he stayed healthy, and look at what (Franco) did."

Franco went 4-for-4 and was hitting .315. "That Julio is really something," chortled Hargrove. "When he gets three hits, he wants four. Some guys, after getting three, will relax and consider it a good day. But not Julio. He always wants more."

Lopez got credit for the victory, his first, though he gave up nine hits and all the Blue Jays' runs in six innings, during which he made 117 pitches.

The Indians, with a one game lead over Chicago, returned home to face the White Sox in their first head-to-head confrontation of the season.

Hargrove said of the Tribe's performance to date, "If someone had asked me in spring training if I'd settle for a 15-8 record in April, I would have taken it in a minute.

"There have been some rough spots ... our starting pitching has been a little spotty, and I'd like to see a little more consistency by some of our hitters, but I'm satisfied it will all come around.

"All in all, there have been a lot more pluses than minuses."

A frustrated Jose Mesa during a game with the Chicago White Sox.

4

TAKING CHARGE IN THE A.L. CENTRAL

April 30 - May 16

The "pluses" that Mike Hargrove talked about in April, were even more prevalent in May.

The Indians went on to win five straight, six of seven and 12 of 16, giving them a 26-12 record (.684), best in the major leagues, and a 5 1/2 game lead in the American League Central Division on May 16.

But there also were some more anxious moments, including another threat to their personal safety - this time an earthquake that interrupted their game against Seattle in the Kingdome on May 2.

It was similar to the frightening experiences they'd endured a week earlier when their chartered airplane rocked and rolled in a rough landing in New York on April 24, and then they were roused from their sleep by a false fire alarm in Toronto on April 28.

The earthquake "scared the hell out of some of the guys," according to *Plain Dealer* sportswriter Paul Hoynes, but fortunately the only damage was to the players' psyche.

And though the game was suspended, everything returned to normal and action resumed the next night.

It was against Chicago in their first pivotal series of the season that the Indians' hot streak picked up a head of steam on April 30-May 1, though Hargrove said it would be inaccurate to call it "crucial."

Whatever, the Tribe took on a White Sox team that had won seven straight, closing to within a half-game of the idle Tribe after beating California, 4-3, on April 29.

But the Indians were equal to the challenge, sweeping the White Sox, 5-3 and 9-5, behind Dennis Martinez and Jack McDowell, inflating their margin to 2 1/2 games and counting.

Martinez pitched seven strong innings in the opener in his best performance since Game 6 of the 1995 A.L. Championship Series against Seattle.

BAERGA GETS HIT No. 1,000

Martinez was well supported in registering his 235th career victory that placed him within eight of Hall of Famer Juan Marichal, the winningest Latin American pitcher in baseball history.

Jim Thome homered and drove in three runs, Kenny Lofton went 3-

for-4, Albert Belle and Julio Franco each had two hits, Carlos Baerga doubled for his 1,000th major league hit, and Sandy Alomar Jr. singled.

But it was Martinez who received most of the plaudits after he shook off a first inning, 418 foot, two run homer by Frank Thomas, and a third inning run producing double by Harold Baines that put Chicago ahead, 3-0.

"I tip my hat to (Martinez); he pretty much shoved it down our throats after we had him on the ropes," said White Sox left fielder Tony Phillips.

"Dennis made only two bad pitches, both change-ups, then he used his fast ball more and it made everything effective," said Hargrove.

Martinez said the "turning point" of the game came in the wake of a 14 minute power failure at the end of the third inning at Jacobs Field.

"For some reason I started to pitch better after that," he said.

Then he joked, "But to tell you the truth, I wanted to go out and pitch with the lights off. I figured maybe I could get guys out that way. These days you do whatever you can to win ball games."

The game also had been held up in the bottom of the third to retrieve the ball that Baerga lashed over the head of right fielder Danny Tartabull for his 1,000th hit.

"A thousand hits in my seventh season means I'm doing a good job," said Baerga.

Franco's single, Baerga's double, a walk with two outs and Thome's single against Kevin Tapani cut the Indians' deficit to 3-2 in the third.

Then Thome solo homered to lead the sixth, after which Omar Vizquel's one out double, a walk and Franco's infield single scored a run that broke the tie.

"It was an important win," conceded Hargrove, "but to say this is a 'crucial' series for either team is untrue."

McDOWELL BEATS EX-TEAMMATES

Crucial or not, the Indians, behind McDowell pitching against his former teammates, beat the White Sox again the next night, hiking their first place margin to 2 1/2 games.

McDowell would have liked to sock it to the White Sox and their out-spoken owner, Jerry Reinsdorf, more convincingly. But he wasn't around to express himself afterwards, being called away for what originally was termed a "personal" emergency.

Later it was reported that McDowell had left the game and the clubhouse early because his back "tightened" up, although, the next day, he insisted it was nothing serious.

However, speculation would persist - despite denials by the pitcher and Tribe management - that McDowell was experiencing back problems similar to those that had affected his pitching in 1994 with the White Sox, and 1995 with the Yankees.

McDowell left the game with the bases loaded and nobody out in the eighth, after which Julian Tavarez gave up a three run double to Thomas.

By then, however, the Indians had built up an 8-2 cushion, large enough to withstand Chicago's late flurry.

But if McDowell wasn't around to gloat over the victory and the Tribe's two game sweep, Paul Assenmacher, another former Reinsdorf employee (1994) was - and did.

"The stuff Jerry had to say ... always interested me," said Assenmacher. "You're talking about one of the classic owners of all time. I guess he's become a baseball expert, too.

"I don't know if this win meant anything more to (McDowell) because he's always been such a competitor, but I would guess it means a little extra."

It also did to the Indians, who again roared back from an early deficit, this one 2-0 after two innings.

They tied the score in the fourth on Belle's two run homer, and took a 4-2 lead in the fifth on singles by Alomar and Vizquel, two walks and Baerga's sacrifice fly.

Alomar's hit extended to 15 his consecutive game hitting streak. He also drove in two runs with a double as the Tribe went ahead, 8-2, in the sixth when Franco also doubled for a run.

SHARK CARTILAGE HELPS ALOMAR

The big reason Alomar is hitting so well - his average climbed to .333 on 24-for-72 - was because his knees are no longer bothering him.

And one of the reasons for that, said Alomar, was because he's been taking medication composed of shark cartilage, which had been recommended by Eddie Murray.

"I started taking shark cartilage last year when I had a pinched nerve in my neck," said Alomar. "The muscles around my neck were kind of tight. Eddie Murray suggested, 'Why don't you try these pills. They might help you out.' (Murray) was taking them for a quadriceps strain.

"I took them and they helped me. I don't know if it was just psychological, but I've been using them for my knees for a year, and it seems to work."

Hitting instructor Charlie Manuel had another explanation for Alomar's resurgence at the plate: "Sandy is being aggressive and I think that's because he's having fun playing. He's healthy and he's relaxed."

Buoyed by the sweep, and comfortable with their lead in the A.L. Central, the Indians embarked upon a 10 game, 11 day, three city west coast trip that often in the bad old days - until last year - was disastrous.

The May 2 opener in Seattle was suspended by the earthquake in the seventh inning and was completed the next day for a 6-4 Indians victory. Then they beat the Mariners, 5-2, in the regularly scheduled game..

Tavarez was on the mound when the earthquake hit. "I was standing there when all of a sudden my hand began to shake," he explained. "I looked down at it and said to myself, 'Why am I shaking like that? Am I that nervous, or what?'"

Soon it became evident to the 30,211 fans - as well as the teams, officials and media - in the Kingdome that an earthquake measured at 5.3 on the Richter scale had hit the area. The tremors lasted about 10 seconds.

Though no injuries nor damage were reported, many in attendance, remembering that panels from the ceiling of the Kingdome had fallen during a game the previous season, rushed for the exits.

Umpire Jim McKean ordered the game suspended with two outs in the bottom of the seventh and the Tribe leading, 6-3.

"Sandy (Alomar) was the first to realize something was happening, that the earth was moving," said Baerga. "It felt like a snake was moving under our feet. Then I looked up to the third deck of the stands and people were running to get out."

Among them was Mariners' radio broadcaster Dave Niehaus, formerly a longtime resident in the Los Angeles area. He reportedly told listeners, "Folks, we're having an earthquake ... I'm getting outta here," which he did.

Hargrove, who had visited Tavarez on the mound moments before the quake hit, said he felt "dizzy" as he walked back to the dugout.

Then, "I felt the ground rolling and said to myself, 'I can't leave Julian out there by himself.' I turned around and was ready to go back to the mound, but Julian was already gone."

NEWMAN: 'IT WAS NO BIG DEAL'

Tribe coach Jeff Newman, a Southern Californian, also knew immediately that it was an earthquake. "I wasn't worried," he said, "because I've been through a lot of them that were worse, or at least worse than this one seemed to be."

Jim Poole also was unconcerned, but for a different reason. "It just goes to show you that left handers are off center," he said.

"For about 30 seconds, it felt like my whole world was straightened out."

Before the quake Belle homered for two runs in the first inning off Bob Wolcott who, as a rookie, beat the Indians, 3-2, in the first game of the 1995 A.L. Championship Series.

It would have been a three run shot but Lofton had been thrown out for the fifth time trying to steal, though he later swiped his 19th base.

The Indians added three more runs in the fourth, and another in the fifth, staking Orel Hershiser to a 6-0 lead.

The Mariners retaliated on a sixth inning homer by Jay Buhner. They scored two more on Edgar Martinez's homer in the seventh before Hershiser was replaced by Tavarez who blanked the Mariners in the eighth.

Jose Mesa pitched the ninth and locked up the victory, but not before Paul Sorrento solo homered with two out.

In the regularly scheduled game, Charles Nagy finally ended his jinx in the Kingdome where his career record had sunk to 0-5.

Perhaps it was the earthquake the previous night that changed his luck.

Whatever, Nagy hurled seven strong innings before giving way to Poole in the eighth, and the Indians prevailed for a fifth straight victory that hiked their lead to 4 1/2 games over Chicago.

"I knew I'd eventually win here," said Nagy, who had grown increasingly annoyed by questions about allegedly being "cursed" in a domed stadium.

Hargrove was, too. "I'm not going to talk about Charlie's so-called bad luck in a dome," said the manager. "It's better left alone. Charlie was aggressive, hit his spots and got a lot of ground balls.

"Forget about the damned jinx."

Not only did Nagy pitch well, his teammates hit well, too, despite leaving nine runners stranded - which would continue to be a problem for the

Indians most of the season.

They got an unearned run in the first, but the Mariners took a 2-1 lead on three hits and an error in the third, the only inning in which Nagy struggled until the eighth.

PENA: 'IT WAS EMBARRASSING'

One of Seattle's runs was waved home by umpire John Hirschbeck after catcher Tony Pena committed a grievous mental error. With Russ Davis on third and John Marzano on second, Nagy made a pitch that got away from Pena.

The catcher reached out and trapped the ball with his mask, which is against the rules. Seattle Manager Lou Piniella called the umpire's attention to the misdeed and the runners were allowed to advance, Davis going home with the first run of the inning.

"I've never done anything like that before," said Pena, a veteran of 15 years in the major leagues. "It was embarrassing. I thought I could get away with it, but somebody (Piniella) saw it."

Franco's homer leading the fifth tied it, and Pena atoned for his mistake by smashing a two run homer to give the Indians a 4-2 lead in the sixth. Lofton singled and Belle doubled for the final run in the ninth.

Then Mesa did it again, striking out two for his 11th consecutive save.

But the winning streak skidded to a halt in a 5-1 loss to the Mariners on May 4 as Albie Lopez continued his consistently inconsistent pitching.

As he'd done in his first two starts since being recalled from Class AAA Buffalo on April 21, Lopez threw his fast ball hard and often, and - this time - the Mariners hit it hard and often.

Of the 23 hits Lopez had given up to that point in 16 innings, seven were homers, including three in this loss. They were solo shots by Darren Bragg and Edgar Martinez in the first inning, and another homer, a two-run blow by Martinez in the sixth.

Franco homered in the third, but that was all the Indians got off Paul Menhart and three relievers. It was Menhart's first victory.

Alomar singled off Norm Charlton in the ninth, extending his hitting streak to 17, but it was small consolation as the Tribe's lead was cut to 3 1/2 games over the White Sox, who beat New York, 11-5.

Lopez had nothing to say after the loss, and Hargrove's only comment was the same he'd expressed after the pitcher's previous setback.

"It's like Mark (pitching coach Mark Wiley) and I have been saying all along," said Hargrove. "You can't win up here with only one pitch. No matter how good Lopez's fast ball is, he's got to be able throw his curve ball for strikes or he is going to get pounded."

ANOTHER GOOD GAME FOR MARTINEZ

Something else Hargrove said again was that the Indians needed a healthy Dennis Martinez. The veteran pitcher indicated that he was - at least that he was healthy at that point in the season - by winning his second game in a row, raising his record to 5-2 as the Indians prevailed, 2-0, in the series finale on May 5.

Martinez blanked the Mariners on two hits through the first six innings in recording his 236th career victory, tying him with Hall of Famer Whitey Ford in 50th place among baseball's winningest pitchers.

After Ken Griffey Jr. singled to start the seventh, Martinez retired the next two batters and turned the job over to Assenmacher, who combined with Tavarez and Mesa to complete the shutout.

"I'd say Dennis is back to where he was last year at the start of the season ... he was outstanding," said Hargrove.

But so was the Mariners' Chris Bosio after he was saved in the first inning by an outstanding catch by Griffey, who leaped up and reached over the 8 1/2 foot center field fence to rob Belle of a two run homer.

Bosio went on to shutout the Indians, also on three hits through the first six innings, until Manny Ramirez and Thome singled in the seventh.

Bosio was replaced by Bob Wells, who was greeted with another single by Pena for a 1-0 Tribe lead, before the next three batters were retired.

Then Murray provided an insurance run with his first homer of the season in the eighth off Mike Jackson.

Mesa didn't register his 12th save as neatly as he'd done so often in the past, yielding a single and a walk before slamming the door, but it extended his consecutive save-streak to 20 dating back to 1995.

Murray's homer, No. 480 of his career, alleviated - but didn't totally eliminate - fears that he had lost his long range power. Until then the veteran's only extra base hits were three doubles. He was batting a lowly .217 (23-for-106) with 14 RBI in 39 games.

"I don't know if (the home run) means Eddie is coming out of it or not," said Hargrove. "We could probably tell as much by looking at the leaves at the bottom of our tea cup.

"But the last few days he has been very sound mechanically in his swing. Eddie is too good a hitter for this (slump) to continue."

General Manager John Hart said of Murray's homer, "Hopefully, it will give him a boost. I've seen Eddie struggle before and come out of it. Right now the fact that he isn't hitting hasn't hurt because the ball club is winning.

"I've got to expect that, with an experienced veteran like Eddie, he's going to get some payback sometime," added Hart, in what would later prove to be prophetic.

In 1995, Murray hit five of his 21 homers in his first 119 official plate appearances, and went on to enjoy one of his best seasons with a .323 average and 82 RBI.

Murray's first homer of 1996 also was his 1,834th career RBI, moving him into 11th place in baseball history, ahead of former teammate Dave Winfield.

On the other hand, Vizquel's errorless streak apparently ended at 35, dating back to 1995, when he raced to the right side of second base to field a grounder by Luis Sojo, but dropped it in the process of making a throw.

Though Vizquel made no protest, Baerga disputed the call by the official scorer. "I don't think it was an error ... Omar had to go too far to reach the ball," said the second baseman.

The next day Baerga's complaint was addressed by the scorer and Vizquel's error was changed to a hit for Sojo.

Significant, too, was something else that Hargrove said after the victory that hiked the Indians' lead back to 4 1/2 games over Chicago, which had lost to New York, 7-1.

In the seventh, after Ramirez's and Thome's hits kayoed Bosio, Pena was due to bat against the right handed Wells.

It was anticipated that Hargrove would send up the left handed hitting Jeromy Burnitz or Wayne Kirby to bat for Pena.

Instead, Hargrove stuck with Pena.

"I decided to stay with what helps my pitcher (Martinez)," Hargrove replied when asked why he didn't employ a pinch hitter.

It was significant in view of the fact that, in spring training, Hargrove stressed that Alomar was the Indians' regular catcher. He said Alomar would be behind the plate when Martinez pitches - even though Martinez was outspoken in his preference for Pena.

HERSHISER-KIRBY: 'NO BIG DEAL'

Something else that transpired during the game in the Kingdome on May 5, but for the most part went unnoticed was what appeared to be a confrontation in the Tribe dugout involving the usually mild tempered Hershiser and equally-mild tempered Wayne Kirby.

It happened during the second inning, according to a report, when Hershiser suddenly rose to his feet and the two players began arguing. Hershiser finally walked away and went into the tunnel leading to the clubhouse. Kirby tried to follow Hershiser, but was restrained, first by Murray, then by coach Charlie Manuel.

Eventually Kirby went into the tunnel after Hershiser, later returned and sat alone on the bench, still obviously agitated. Coach Dave Nelson sat next to Kirby, apparently trying to calm him.

Later in the game both Hershiser and Kirby were seen in the dugout together, but kept their distance from one another. At one point Murray and Hershiser had a long conversation - Murray doing all the talking - at the end of the bench.

"They (Kirby and Hershiser) just had a disagreement about something. It was no big deal," said one witness.

It was later reorted that the disagreement between the players occurred because, "Hershiser was trying to give advice to Albie Lopez. Kirby was joking around, Hershiser took offense...(but) they were separated before blows were exchanged."

THE LONGEST HOMER IN OAKLAND?

The road trip that had such a promising start - five victories in six games in Chicago and Seattle - made an abrupt turn in the opposite direction the next two nights, May 6 and 7, after the Indians moved on to Oakland.

There they lost to the Athletics, 5-3, as the bull pen was unable to protect a one run, eighth inning lead, and 8-4, as Mark McGwire hammered what arguably was the longest home run ever hit in the Oakland Coliseum. It was struck off Hershiser.

The back-to-back losses, ending the Indians' 13 game winning streak over the Athletics dating back to July 21, 1993, cut the Tribe's first place margin to three over the White Sox.

In the opener of the series, the Tribe, behind McDowell, was leading, 3-2, after Belle cracked his 12th homer, a solo shot in the fourth. Baerga's two-out single, following hits by Vizquel and Franco, produced two more runs in the fifth.

McDowell, who was tagged for a homer by Terry Steinbach in the second and relinquished another run in the third, retired nine batters in order going into the eighth, when Ernie Young singled and was bunted to second.

With Jason Giambi, a left handed batter up next, Hargrove turned to his relief corps, which had allowed only one earned run in the previous 16 1/3 innings.

But it wasn't a good move this time.

Giambi said hello to Assenmacher with a double that tied the game. Then Eric Plunk, next on the mound, gave up a bloop single to McGwire that untied the score.

Two hits and one out later, Poole replaced Plunk and Geronimo Berroa, a former Tribe farmhand, singled for another run before the rally ended.

When asked why he replaced McDowell with Assenmacher, Hargrove pointed out that Giambi was hitting .185 (5-for-27) against southpaws, and .353 (30-for-85) against right handed pitchers.

"If Giambi didn't represent the winning run, I would have let Jack face him and finish the inning," he said.

The breakdown of the bull pen cost McDowell what would have been - should have been - his fourth victory. Instead, it was a loss charged to Assenmacher.

Alomar's consecutive game hitting streak also ended as he went 0-for-4 against four Oakland pitchers.

"It was fun, but it got hard to concentrate," said Alomar, whose average climbed to .326 (26-for-80) during the streak. "You come to the park every day and you think about it, and people ask you, 'Can you keep it going?'"

HARGROVE: 'JUST A DIP IN THE ROAD'

Oakland broadcaster Ray Fosse, a Tribe catcher from 1967-72 and 1976-77, was convinced that McGwire's homer was the longest ever hit in the Coliseum.

"I don't think the measurement that was announced (428 feet) was accurate," he said. "I've been out here a long time and it was the longest I've ever seen in this park."

Fosse estimated that the ball traveled "at least 480 feet, maybe 500 feet" into the center field bleachers.

Hargrove went a step further. "That might have been the longest homer I've ever seen," he said.

At the time McGwire was another of the many players who were upset with the media and would not express an opinion.

Whatever, rookie Doug Johns, who started on the mound for Oakland, said McGwire's tape measure shot pumped him up. It was delivered in the fourth inning and wiped out the Indians' 2-0 lead.

Hershiser was removed in the fifth, charged with four runs and 11 hits. The Athletics broke the game open with four runs in the eighth off Tavarez. He was tagged for a homer by Young and apparently was in the process of pitching himself to Buffalo.

"It was not pretty," acknowledged Hargrove of the way the A's battered Tavarez.

But the failure of the bull pen wasn't the sole cause of the two losses in Oakland. The Tribe's offense, which had been averaging more than seven runs a game for almost a month, was shut down by the A's.

Still, Hargrove insisted it was not a matter of great concern - at least not to him. "This is just a dip in the road," he said. "I've never seen this team take anyone (pitcher) for granted."

ANOTHER VICTORY FOR NAGY

Hargrove was right. The bats came alive the next night, salvaging the May 8 series finale, beating Oakland, 7-3. Belle hit his 13th homer, a three run blow in a five run fifth inning, making it easy for Nagy, who pitched seven strong innings.

When Giambi socked a two run homer in the eighth. Mesa took over in the ninth in what was a non-save situation. He was not as sharp as usual and was hit hard, giving up a run on a double and two singles before staggering out of trouble.

"I know I got hit, but that's the hardest I've thrown all year," Mesa claimed.

The difference between the Mesa of 1995 and the 1996 model to date, he said, was that, "Last year hitters read the scouting reports on me. They knew I was a hard thrower and that I had trouble throwing strikes. A lot of times they'd come to the plate and wait.

"This year they've changed their approach. They've had a year to study me on tape. Now they're swinging early because they know I throw strikes."

Alomar agreed. "This year (hitters) are swinging early because they know that's when Jose throws his fast ball. If they take his fast ball and get down in the count, he'll start sinking the ball, and then it's all over," said the catcher.

Also on the downside was a fifth inning error by Vizquel, and this time - though it also was a "tough" call - it was not reversed by the official scorer. It ended the shortstop's consecutive game errorless streak at 38, dating back to Sept. 24, 1995.

Vizquel ranged deep into the hole to field a grounder by Berroa. It was scored as a hit. But Vizquel's throw, which lacked velocity, probably because of his ailing shoulder, was in the dirt and bounced past Franco, allowing Berroa to take second.

"It was a tough error," acknowledged Vizquel, "but you're not going to go through the whole season without making one. It was just as well that I got it over with now."

MARTINEZ IS BAD; LOPEZ IS WORSE

The Indians' lead shrunk to 2 1/2 games over Chicago on May 10 after a horrendous performance by Martinez, and one that was even worse by Lopez resulted in a 13-8 loss to California.

Martinez was staked to a 4-0 lead in the first inning when Thome drilled his fifth homer, but couldn't hold it. The Angels retaliated in their half of the first with four runs, including Tim Salmon's homer.

The Indians made it 5-4 in the second, but again Martinez was hit hard and the Angels struck back in their half of the inning. J.T. Snow's three run homer put them ahead, 7-5, which finished Martinez.

It was the first indication that Martinez might be experiencing a return of the elbow problem he suffered the second half of 1995, though the company line was that his trouble was "not physical."

Ramirez solo homered in the third, and the Indians took an 8-7 lead in the fourth.

But then it became Lopez's turn to flop.

He was bombed in the bottom of the fourth for five runs, including homers by Jim Edmonds and Garret Anderson, and was gone before the fifth got underway.

"I can't say what's wrong," Lopez searched for answers. "I'm throwing the ball like I've always thrown it, but when I make a mistake the ball is taking off on me."

It certainly was. In 18 innings since being recalled from Buffalo on April 21, Lopez gave up nine homers.

"I've never given up home runs like this before," Lopez said. "When I get the fast ball up, they're jumping on it. It's frustrating, but I'll get things straightened out. I've just got to keep working."

Lopez's trouble, as diagnosed by Alomar: "When he has the good breaking ball, he's fine. But when he can't throw the breaking ball for a strike, he's got a problem."

HARGROVE: THE BALL MUST BE 'JUICED'

Hargrove had a different theory. "I didn't think the ball was juiced until (that game)," he said. "It's the first time I've seen what everyone else has seen around baseball. I've never seen the ball carry like it did.

"Every ball that was hit in the air, I was wondering, 'Is it going out?' And some of them just didn't sound right. The last homer (by Anderson) sounded like he hit it off the end of his bat."

All of which did nothing to help Lopez's status.

Asked if Lopez still figured to be the Indians' fifth starter, Hargrove said he didn't know. An answer would be forthcoming later.

As for Martinez's equally bad outing, Hargrove's only comment was, "He just left a lot of balls over the middle of the plate."

Martinez insisted he was not hurting. "I didn't feel anything (pain), I just never got into the flow of the game.

"But I've got to take this as a wake-up call," he said. "It doesn't matter how long you've been in this game, these things can happen. It's definitely a wake-up call for the rest of the season."

Something else that happened during the series opening loss to the Angels also raised questions about what appeared to be discord between Belle and Lofton.

Lofton was on third and Franco on first in the second inning when Belle grounded to Angels third baseman Jack Howell.

Lofton broke for home, then realizing Howell's throw would beat him to the plate, he stopped and got into a rundown. It was designed to allow Franco to go to third and Belle to second.

However, Belle remained on first and Lofton eventually was tagged out, after which he was obviously angry.

When asked about the incident, Lofton said he was mad at himself.

But later in the interview Lofton said, "Everybody watching on TV, and everybody in the ball park knew what should have happened. Albert should have gone to second base."

As for his display of anger, when he stared down Belle on the field, Lofton shrugged and said, "I do that a lot. If somebody doesn't get to a ball in the outfield, I do it. If somebody swings at a bad pitch. I do it. We all do."

Belle, of course, had no comment. He still was not talking to the media.

Relevant, too, was the fact that Hargrove benched Baerga - though it was explained at the time that the second baseman was only being "rested" - because of the slump that had reduced his batting average to an uncharacteristic .266.

"Carlos is struggling. He is tired, and I might give him some more time off ... then again, I might not," said Hargrove.

"Carlos is in a funk right now," hitting coach Charlie Manuel said of Baerga's problem. "He's not using his legs and he's chasing bad balls, especially with runners in scoring position."

Hargrove was tired, too, after the Indians - on the road for 21 of their first 32 games - had lost for the fourth time in six games in the wake of five straight victories.

McDOWELL WINS, BUT NOT EASILY

The next night McDowell was, for eight innings, the pitcher the Indians thought they had signed for big bucks as he breezed through six innings without allowing the Angels a run on May 11.

It was a game the Indians eventually won, 6-5, and a victory they needed to stay 3 1/2 games ahead of Chicago.

But it didn't come easily.

Coasting with a six run lead, McDowell gave up only his third hit, a single by Snow with one out in the seventh, and three pitches later Anderson cracked a homer.

McDowell got out of the inning and blanked the Angels in the eighth, but couldn't get past the first two batters in the ninth. Salmon singled and Chili Davis walked, and McDowell was banished.

Mesa took over but struggled again and the victory almost got away.

Snow fouled off seven straight pitches, then singled for one run. Anderson also singled for one, and the Angels' third run of the inning and fifth of the game came on a one out sacrifice fly by Don Slaught.

Then Howell, representing the tying run, flied deep to Lofton to end it for McDowell's fourth victory in five decisions, and Mesa's 13th save.

Murray, still the subject of speculation that he no longer had the ability to hit for power, delivered his second homer of the season and second in six games leading off the second inning - but he wasn't around at the end.

Murray was ejected by plate umpire Ken Kaiser after arguing a called strike in the eighth.

Thome's three run homer was the big blow in the Tribe's four run third inning off Scott Sanderson.

It also was Thome who triggered the fifth inning uprising that produced what proved to be the deciding run. Thome, Alomar and Alvaro Espinoza singled in succession to give McDowell the 6-0 lead he almost blew.

REMINISCENT OF 1995

The Indians had their long ball offense in gear again the next night with a ninth inning rally that was reminiscent of 1995, when they won 27 games in their final at-bat.

This one shaped up as a pitchers duel between Hershiser and the Angels' Jim Abbott as the teams battled through eight innings tied, 1-1.

Each scored in the fourth, the Indians on Vizquel's single, stolen base, ground out and Belle's single, and the Angels on Edmonds' leadoff homer.

But that was all either starting pitcher relinquished. Poole replaced Hershiser in the eighth, and Mark Eichhorn took over for Abbott in the sixth, Mike James came on in the seventh, and newly-anointed ace reliever Troy Percival stalked to the mound for California in the ninth.

Percival, a former minor league catcher, was 11-for-11 in save opportunities, and had not given up a run in 14 2/3 innings. During that time he'd struck out 20 batters and allowed only six hits.

Belle quickly changed all that.

As the first batter to face Percival, Belle swung and missed the first two pitches, both of them fast balls clocked at 95 miles per hour.

Percival's next pitch, another fast ball, this one clocked at 96 mph, went out even faster - off the bat of Belle. It was a laser shot over the center field fence, Belle's 14th homer of the season giving the Tribe a 2-1 lead.

But that was only the beginning of the end.

Murray and Ramirez went out, but Alomar and Thome also homered for a 4-1 lead that became the Indians' sixth victory, concluding the 10 game trip.

Mesa, winning a battle of the American League's dominant closers, blanked the Angels with 13 pitches in the ninth for his 14th save. and 22nd without failure dating back to 1995.

It was one of Hershiser's better performances, though the victory was credited to Poole. "I don't care about that," Hershiser said. "It's just good to be throwing well again." He allowed one run on five hits, struck out five and walked two.

Afterwards the Indians reveled in the clubhouse viewing television replays of the ninth inning uprising - especially the smile that split Belle's face as the camera caught him rounding the bases.

"That's the highlight of the year," Pena chortled. "It's the first time (Belle) has smiled in five years."

5

OFF AND RUNNING
BEHIND ALBERT

May 14-26

It was a long time coming - two days shy of six weeks, in fact - when American League President Dr. Gene Budig finally rendered a decision in the Albert Belle-Tony Tomsic case.

The Tribe slugger intentionally hit Tomsic, a free lance photographer working on assignment for *Sports Illustrated*, with the second of two thrown baseballs prior to a game at Jacobs Field on April 6.

On May 16, Budig ordered Belle to undergo "immediate and professional" anger counseling, though no fine or suspension was assessed.

"The answer was not another fine or suspension. That, in my judgment would not help the problem. Professional counseling is the answer," decreed Budig.

Interestingly, Budig handled the case instead of acting Commisioner Bud Selig because of the existence for the potential of a conflict. Selig owns the Milwaukee Brewers, a division rival of the Indians.

Belle, who also was ordered to perform community service with Cleveland youth groups, wouldn't comment on Budig's decision.

But his agent, Arn Tellem, did and obviously was relieved.

"There was no justification for a fine or suspension," said Tellem. "And with respect to community service, Albert has always been involved in local charities in Cleveland, so that's a non-issue."

As for counseling to curb Belle's anger, Tellem said, "While I don't believe it should have been ordered, this is something Albert has been working on with his own volition."

In his reprimand of Belle, Budig said in a written statement:

"Albert Belle has a problem, and the American League has a problem. This problem must be addressed in a forthright manner for the good of all concerned and to do less would be irresponsible.

"The commissioner and I believe Albert Belle must receive professional help, and the American League is directing him to participate in immediate counseling.

"Both the Cleveland Indians and the American League will monitor his participation and the session will be treated on a confidential basis.

"Failure on his part to comply will result in suspension.

"He will further be required to perform community service with youth groups in Cleveland, and that service will be determined by the Indians in consultation with the League. I believe Albert will benefit from and respond positively to these directives.

"My foremost concern is for Albert Belle the person and for the fans of major league baseball. It is time for those who care about Albert Belle to encircle him with genuine encouragement and consecutive support."

When asked what would happen if Belle failed to comply with the directive, Budig replied, "Albert Belle has the opportunity to make me look very good or very bad."

Tomsic, who had steadfastly refused to file an official complaint - which probably was a factor in Budig's decision to not suspend or fine Belle - had little to say.

"Something like this is not for me to pass judgment on," he said. "It is not for me to say."

Tomsic said he harbors no grudge against Belle, "though I guess he's upset with me," but admitted annoyance over one aspect of the incident.

"I never stuck a camera in his face like I see so many of the television guys do. Yet, I'm the one he throws the balls at. That does bother me."

Neither Hart nor Hargrove commented publicly on the action taken by Budig, but Dennis Martinez, always outspoken, did not mince words.

"It looks like they are picking on the man," he said. "Why don't they leave him alone? He's the best player in baseball."

Tellem was critical of the media. "It's time for the people in the media to give this man a break," he said. "They've got to call off the witch hunt."

Paul Hoynes of the *Plain Dealer* scoffed at the last remark. "Belle is left alone ... he is given more space by reporters than any other professional athlete in Cleveland. Still, he keeps making headlines."

Hoynes further stated in print that "the Indians have proven too many times that they are willing to look the other way regarding Belle."

WELCOME BACK, BUDDY BELL

It was two days prior to Budig's reprimand of Belle that Buddy Bell made his first return to Jacobs Field as manager of the Detroit Tigers for the opening of a nine game homestand on May 14.

But it was not an enjoyable reunion for Buddy with his former pals.

The pitching poor Tigers were swept, 5-1, 5-2 and 8-3 as Charles Nagy (6-1), Martinez (6-2), and Jack McDowell (5-1) picked up victories that boosted the Indians' first place margin over Chicago to a season high 5 1/2 games.

The Indians' return from their 10 game west coast trip also set the stage for a meeting between John Hart and Mike Hargrove with slump-ridden Carlos Baerga, who had been benched for the final two games in Anaheim.

Without revealing any of the cogent details of the meeting, there was little doubt about the Tribe's unhappiness with Baerga's performance to date - he was batting .266 with one homer and 23 RBI - and, perhaps more importantly, his physical condition and work ethic.

"Carlos is such a good kid," said Hart, "we just wanted to tell him we were still supporting him. We want to help him get through this."

Hargrove attributed much of Baerga's trouble at the plate to the fact that "he's jumping at the ball."

And when Baerga went 0-for-4 in the opener of the Detroit series, the manager said, "I didn't see Carlos swing at a strike."

Baerga didn't argue. "I've got to concentrate more, I know that," he said. "I don't walk that much, but I've got to be more patient. And I've got to keep videos of myself so I can see what I'm doing wrong."

In beating Detroit in the opener Nagy, off to the best start in his career, became the first A.L. pitcher to win six games. He hurled a route going, seven hitter.

"Charlie is pitching like he did before his (1993 shoulder) surgery," said Mike Hargrove. "He's really only had two bad outings since the All-Star break last year."

Encouraging, too, was Eddie Murray's performance. He delivered his third homer of the season in the fourth inning and scored behind Belle, who'd singled to extend his consecutive game hitting streak to 15.

"Eddie is getting closer and closer ... each at-bat is getting better," said Hargrove.

Manny Ramirez and Jim Thome also homered, Thome for the fourth time in four games.

Naturally, Bell was impressed and didn't mind saying so: "I've seen that team do some unbelievable things offensively. They're extremely confident, very talented and make great adjustments. It's a great team."

The former Tribe coach added, "It's a heck of a lot scarier watching (the Indians) from this side of the field."

After the game the Indians announced another roster change. They sent Albie Lopez, who had been hit hard while trying to fill the fifth starter's role, back to Buffalo. Recalled was Joe Roa, who was 1-1 in six appearances with the Bisons.

MARTINEZ: 'I NEEDED THAT'

Martinez was the winner the next night and attributed much of his success to the "wake-up call" he'd received in his previous start, when he blew a 4-0 first inning lead against California.

There was something else that helped even more, Martinez said.

He studied film of the perfect game he'd pitched for Montreal on July 28, 1991, against Los Angeles. "I wanted to see something positive," he said. "I wanted to see what I was doing then and compare it to what I am doing now."

Whatever Martinez saw, it helped, if not immediately.

The Indians staked him to a 2-0 lead in the first inning, but the Tigers retaliated with two runs in the second when they slapped four of the six hits Martinez allowed.

Perhaps that also proved to be a wake-up call for the Indians. They broke the tie with a run in their half of the second, Ramirez homered again in the third, and Julio Franco's walk, stolen base and Baerga's double in the sixth provided a three run margin.

Martinez did not allow another hit until John Flaherty doubled with two out in the seventh, but was stranded. Julian Tavarez blanked the Tigers in the eighth, and Jose Mesa did the same in the ninth, striking out three for his 15th consecutive save.

It also was significant that Tony Pena was reinstalled as Martinez's personal catcher. In doing so, Hargrove countermanded his spring training decision that, because Sandy Alomar was the Indians' regular catcher, he would work with Martinez, regardless of the pitcher's preference.

"It's very simple," said Hargrove. "Dennis is more comfortable with Tony. I talked to Sandy about it and he's comfortable with it. So we're going to go this way from now on.

"It also fits in with not wanting to overwork (Alomar). It has nothing to do with Sandy's abilities as a catcher. He's still our No. 1 catcher."

However, the move probably was based on the fact that, in his previous start, Martinez was ripped for seven runs and seven hits in two innings - with Alomar behind the plate.

It was that game that Martinez said was his wake-up call.

In Martinez's six starts with Alomar catching his record was 3-2 with a 6.82 ERA. When paired with Pena in three starts, Martinez was 3-0 with a 1.77 ERA.

Martinez said he always had a desire to pitch to Pena. "Even before I came here I always thought I'd like to pitch to Tony," he said.

"Now we're both here and we've got the chance to do it. It's good Sandy isn't taking it personally. The bottom line is that you just try to do what will make the pitcher pitch the best he can each day."

Belle doubled twice to extend his consecutive game hitting streak to 16, and Baerga's hit was his second of the game, ending a 7-for-43 (.163) spell that dated back to April 30, when he got his 1,000th career hit.

The game represented a double milestone for the organization as the 42,259 fans in Jacobs Field, comprised the 66th consecutive sellout, an ongoing A.L. record.

The victory also was the Indians' 100th since the 1994 opening of Jacobs Field where they'd lost only 37 games in two-plus seasons.

McDOWELL MAKES IT 12 STRAIGHT

McDowell completed the sweep over the Tigers, giving the Tribe 12 straight victories at home and 24 of 31 overall, scattering seven hits in a route going performance.

Belle, obviously unperturbed by the slap on the wrist he received from Budig, drove in five runs with two homers, giving him a 17 game hitting streak.

"It shouldn't surprise any of us what Albert does," said Hargrove. "He has the ability to block everything out except what he's trying to do."

When asked the obvious question, Hargrove replied, "Yes, I think Albert could hit 60 runs. Other guys like Frank Thomas, Barry Bonds, Ken Griffey and Matt Williams could, too.

"But if my life depended on somebody hitting 60 homers, I'd bet on Albert."

Buddy Bell also spoke of his respect for Belle's ability. "I don't know about the other league," said the Detroit manager, "but in this league he's probably the most awesome, the most feared hitter."

Belle, as usual, had nothing to say, which elicited a comment by Omar Vizquel. "That's OK ... he doesn't talk to me, either," quipped the shortstop.

Despite the Indians' five run margin that made it appear to be an easy victory, McDowell almost didn't survive the first inning. Four of the first five

Tigers reached safely on three hits and a walk, two of them scoring.

"I thought it might be one of those games," acknowledged McDowell, "but I got my rhythm going."

So did Belle, whose first homer was a three run blow in the third inning when the Tribe took a 5-1 lead. His second homer came with two out in the seventh. Scoring ahead of him was Baerga, who had struck out but reached first base when the third strike was a wild pitch.

It gave the Indians a season high 5 1/2 game lead over the White Sox, who lost to Milwaukee, 3-2, and sent the Tigers home with a 1-15 record in games at Jacobs Field.

OVERCOMING A SEVEN RUN DEFICIT

The Tribe's winning streak climbed to six the next night, May 17, in another game that was reminiscent of the 1995 season when they scored 48 come-from-behind victories.

This time, against Texas, the Indians overcame a seven run deficit to beat the Rangers, 12-10. Ramirez blasted a 405 foot grand slam, sending into near-hysteria the 68th consecutive sellout crowd of 41,225, which broke Colorado's major league record.

"I wasn't thinking home run," said Ramirez, who hit a 3-and-0 pitch from reliever Gil Heredia. "I was only thinking about taking the ball up the middle. I know I'm not hitting the ball the way I want to."

At least not until he uncorked the homer in the seventh inning, highlighting a six run uprising.

Heredia did not expect Ramirez to swing. "That's why I tried to throw a strike right down the middle of the plate," he said. "I didn't want to walk him."

It also was a big night for Murray, who hammered his fifth homer and singled three times in five trips to the plate.

Murray's seventh inning single drove in the Tribe's seventh run and was his 1,839th career RBI, moving him into 10th place on the all-time list, one ahead of Hall of Famer Ted Williams.

"There's only one Eddie Murray in this game," said Hargrove. "Even when Eddie was struggling he drove in big runs here and there. It's been my experience as a player, coach and manager that if you give the great ones enough time, they'll come around.

"Sure, there comes a time when everyone reaches the end of the line. But I never had that thought about Eddie."

The offensive explosion made a winner of Alan Embree, and took Orel Hershiser off the hook. He was kayoed in the fourth inning when he gave up six straight hits without retiring a batter, and the Rangers took a 7-2 lead.

It was Hershiser's worst outing of the season. Nine of the 18 batters he faced reached base, via a home run, five doubles, two singles and a walk.

"That's baseball," said Hershiser. "To tell you the truth, that's the best I've felt warming up in a long time.

"But my pitches straightened out on me. They (Rangers) got their regular hits, and some others that were in the right spot."

ANDERSON: 'IT WAS NERVE-WRACKING'

The search for a consistent fifth starter continued when Brian Anderson's first opportunity was unsuccessful in a 6-3 loss to the Rangers on May 18. It ended the Indians' winning streak at six and was their first setback in 14 home games.

Chad Ogea, who was on the disabled list with a sore shoulder, and Lopez both had beenunable to capitalize in earlier chances.

Though Anderson was neither very good nor very bad, Hargrove was non-committal in his evaluation of the southpaw.

He said, "Brian was outstanding, everything we could hope for," but stopped short of announcing Anderson would get another start.

"Right now we're studying our options."

Anderson also was unsure of his status. saying, "I really don't know what's going on," after being charged with the defeat. He gave up seven hits and four runs in seven innings, and admittedly was nervous after his fourth pitch of the game was drilled into the right field stands by Darryl Hamilton.

Anderson obviously also was still jittery in the second inning when he threw wildly on an attempted pickoff at second base, enabling Damon Buford to reach third and score on a sacrifice fly.

"It was nerve wracking," Anderson said of pitching in front of his family and friends. "This was one of the longest days of my life. I'm glad it wasn't a night game. I'd have been in a straitjacket if I'd had to wait all day."

Belle solo homered - No. 17 - in the bottom of the second, extending his hitting streak to an A.L. high 19 games. The Indians boosted their lead to 3-2, in the third, on three hits and a walk, but were shutout thereafter.

The Rangers got to a tiring Anderson for two runs in the seventh to go ahead, 4-3, and Alvaro Espinoza's throwing error gave them two unearned insurance runs against Paul Assenmacher in the eighth.

Baerga also committed two errors, giving him eight (compared to 19 all of last season) and running the Indians' season total to 34, second most in the A.L.

When asked for a comment after the game Baerga told reporters, "I don't feel like talking," which was unusual for him.

Of Baerga's problems - he went 1-for-4 and was batting .256 with one homer and 26 RBI - Hargrove said, "Let's don't bury him after one day. He's been awfully good for this team and this city for a long time. We've been patient with a lot of people and gotten them through rough spots."

THANK YOU, JOHNNY OATES

Then it became the Rangers' turn to help the Indians who capitalized on third inning errors by Dean Palmer and Bobby Witt that led to four runs and an 8-5 victory on May 19.

And an inning later it was Johnny Oates, the Texas manager, who committed an error, or at least a mistake in judgment.

After Alomar led off with a homer, and with Vizquel and Kenny Lofton on third and second with two out, Oates declined to have Witt intentionally walk Belle, who was hitting .359, and pitch to Murray, whose average was .255.

Belle promptly singled for two more runs, extending his hitting streak to 20.

"At that point I felt more comfortable pitching to Belle with a base open than to Murray with the bases loaded because Eddie's done it so many times," Oates tried to justify his strategy.

It also was a big day for Lofton, who reached base five times in five at-bats on three walks, a double and a single.

Lofton stole his 28th and 29th bases - he'd been caught nine times - putting him on course for 119 by season's end, which would exceed Rickey Henderson's A.L. record 108 set in 1983.

Lofton scoffed at the suggestion. "I am not going to steal 100 bases," he said. "There is too much attention being paid me. Stealing 100 bases does not even cross my mind."

Lofton, who has led the A.L. in stolen bases in each of his four seasons with the Indians, admitted that he has a goal, but is keeping it a secret.

"If I did say what it is," he said, "you guys in the media will make a big deal out of it. Then if I didn't make my goal, I'd be called a failure."

For Nagy, it was mainly a case of persevering to pick up his seventh victory in eight decisions. "It was one of those days when you keep the team in the game, and if you stay in long enough you get the win," he said.

He got the win after Jim Poole, Tavarez and Mesa each pitched perfect seventh, eighth and ninth innings in relief. Mesa closed the game with 12 pitches for his 17th consecutive save and 25th over two seasons.

THE BREWERS ARE COOLED OFF

The Milwaukee Brewers, the hottest team in the A.L. with 11 victories in their previous 14 games, were next to challenge the Tribe, but were cooled off in the opener of a three game series on May 21.

Franco's solo homer with two out in the ninth won it, 6-5, capping a game of long ball for the Indians, who prevailed for the 15th time in 16 games at Jacobs Field.

Thome unloaded two king sized homers, and Baerga one before Franco ended the game, making a winner of Tavarez. He was the second reliever to follow Martinez, who had sought his seventh victory.

Thome's second inning blast off Ben McDonald flew 445 feet into the stands and was said to be the longest homer in Jacobs Field history. He also delivered a 435 foot shot off Ramon Garcia in the seventh when the Indians scored three runs to forge a 5-5 tie.

The four homers did not include one by Belle, but he extended the A.L.'s longest hitting streak to 21 with a fourth inning single off McDonald, his former Louisiana State University teammate.

But it was Thome who commanded most of the post-game attention after he raised his home run total to 10.

"Jimmy (Thome) doesn't really know how strong he is," said Hargrove. "Those were his two shortest swings this year. The ball just jumps off his bat."

Thome wasn't sure. "I just think I'm learning more as a hitter," he said. "I like to watch the way Albert (Belle) hits. You can tell how intelligent a hitter he is the way he adjusts to the situation.

"I'm trying to concentrate on situations. I've gotten better with more experience, just in learning about pitchers."

The ball jumped off Franco's bat, too. "Yes, I was trying to hit one (a home run) in that situation with two outs and a tie game," said Franco. "You've got to try for the home run then."

Baerga's homer, only his second of the season, gave the Tribe a 1-0 lead in the first inning, and Thome made it 2-0 in the second. Martinez, however, couldn't hold it.

"That is the sort of thing that could get Carlos going," Hargrove said of Baerga, who had averaged 19 homers in each of his previous four seasons. "He had some good at-bats. They should help his confidence."

Greg Vaughn homered for Milwaukee in the fifth and the lead changed hands three times until the Brewers tied the score with a run off Poole in the eighth. That set the stage for Franco to deposit his game winner in the left field bleachers.

BELLE'S STREAK ENDS AT 21

The Indians and Brewers split the next two games, May 22 and 23, Milwaukee winning, 10-8, and the Tribe taking the series finale, 5-1, as Hershiser rebounded from his worst outing of the season six days earlier.

McDowell struggled in the loss to the Brewers and couldn't get through the fourth inning, and Belle's hitting streak ended at 21.

Still, the Indians almost pulled out a victory - one that would have again rekindled memories of all the late heroics that took place in 1995.

They had the potential tying runs on second and third with two out in the bottom of the ninth with Belle, the A.L.'s best RBI man at the plate against the Brewers' ace closer, Mike Fetters.

The 41,027 fans in the capacity crowd rose to their feet as the count went full, but Belle took the next pitch and umpire Terry Craft called it strike three, ending the game and the hitting streak.

"It was a sinker on the inner half of the plate," said Fetters. "That was exciting. It's what you live for as a closer. Some day he might get me, but tonight, I got him."

Hargrove said of the last minute drama, "That's all you can ask for. We had the winning run at the plate, but it just didn't happen tonight."

Belle batted five times. He flied out in the second inning, walked in the fourth, hit a sacrifice fly in the sixth, and grounded out in the seventh before striking out in the ninth.

The Brewers roughed up McDowell for three runs in the second, another in the third and knocked him out in the fourth, taking a 7-2 lead.

That also was the inning Hargrove was ejected by Rich Garcia for the first time this season. He argued that the umpire was wrong in calling Belle out for runner's interference in attempting to break up a double play.

"Richie said Albert intentionally got in the way of the throw," said Hargrove. "I disagreed. He won."

Later in the game plate umpire Craft also won an argument with Lofton, who was ejected in the ninth.

The Brewers' lead soared to 10-3 off Embree in the fifth before the

Indians retaliated with a run in their half of the inning, and five in the sixth on six hits.

One of the hits was struck by Ramirez, and it should have been at least a double, but was only a single because he failed to run hard to first.

It happened after four singles produced two runs and left two runners aboard. Ramirez then lofted a drive along the right field line and stood at the plate watching the flight of the ball, thinking it would either be a home run or a foul.

But it was neither. The ball landed near the base of the wall in fair territory and Ramirez was lucky to reach first base.

"I talked with Mr. Ramirez ... the situation has been clarified," Hargrove said after the game.

As for McDowell, he said, "I never felt out of whack, but I never felt comfortable either."

In his victory over the Brewers the next night, Hershiser (4-3) squirmed out of one crisis after another through the first five innings, and breezed through the next two before Jose Valentin led off the eighth with a homer.

By then the Indians were ahead, 5-0, all their runs coming in the first three innings. When Vaughn singled after Valentin's homer, Tavarez bailed out Hershiser and blanked the Brewers through the ninth.

Asked about his performance, Hershiser, the thinking man's pitcher, replied, "There's all kinds of things I'm working on. There's a lot of cause and effect in a pitching delivery. I've just been real inconsistent with my pitches and my delivery."

'A MINI-NUCLEAR REACTION'

Then the Tribe happily paid a visit to old friend Buddy Bell - though the feeling probably wasn't mutual.

Not only had the Tigers been beaten up by the Indians in Cleveland a week earlier, they also were in the midst of an eight game losing streak that soon would climb to 11.

But first, another problem developed when the Indians' chartered airplane was grounded and they had to ride a couple of buses to Detroit, not arriving at their hotel until about 2 a.m.

"Everything was fine after a mini-nuclear reaction by Mike Seghi (director of team travel)," quipped Hargrove.

Then, in front of more of their fans than those cheering for Detroit in Tiger Stadium, the Indians continued their domination of Buddy's team, They beat the Tigers three straight - 6-3, 7-6, and 5-0 - keeping their first place margin at four over Chicago.

Still, those who rooted for the Tigers roasted Belle with their boos, though they obviously did not affect the Tribe slugger.

He blasted two homers, his 18th and 19th of the season, the second in the eighth inning breaking a 3-3 tie.

The Indians went on to score two more runs that inning. Eric Plunk, working in relief of Anderson, was the winner when Mesa set down the Tigers one-two-three with only 14 pitches in the ninth for his 18th save.

"There were some fans right on top of our dugout that were on Albert unmercifully (in the fourth inning)," said Hargrove. "But he never blinked, never reacted, never turned around. He just went up and hit a home run.

"If it was me, I would have had to go up and visit those guys. But Albert didn't say a thing.

"I'm sure those fans were there in the eighth, but I couldn't hear them. I moved to the other end of the dugout because I couldn't stand it anymore."

Then Hargrove offered more praise for Belle. "He is a very special hitter. His concentration, intensity and focus during a game is amazing to me. That's why I think he's one of the best right handed hitters in the game today."

In addition to Belle's two homers, Ramirez and Lofton also hit for the circuit.

"That's the one thing about this offense," said Anderson, who surrendered the Tigers' three runs on six hits in five innings. "You might hold (the Indians) down for their first two or three at-bats, but after that they can explode.

"That's why it would have done me some good to stick around an inning or two longer."

NAGY: THE A.L.'s WINNINGEST PITCHER

Nagy stuck around a couple of innings longer the next day and became the A.L.'s winningest pitcher with an 8-1 record, despite giving up, on May 25, a monster home run by Melvin Nieves. It was measured at 478 feet.

"Orel (Hershiser) is happy because I got him off the hook for giving up the longest homer of the season," chortled Nagy.

It was a reference to a shot by Oakland's Mark McGwire off Hershiser on May 7, although that blow was said by some to have traveled "between 480 and 500 feet" in the Oakland Coliseum.

"I didn't look at it at first," Nagy said of Nieves' homer. "But about five seconds later I took a look and it was still out there."

Baerga homered in the first inning for the Tribe, but it was nullified when the Tigers clawed back with four runs in their half of the first, highlighted by Curtis Pride's homer.

But again Nagy persevered.

The Indians tied the score in the fourth when Lofton whacked a three run homer, only to have the Tigers go ahead again in the bottom of the fourth, 5-4, on another homer by former Tribesman Mark Lewis.

Two walks and two hits, the second a pinch double by Vizquel, enabled the Indians to regain the lead, 7-5, in the seventh, and also saved Nagy when Nieves homered in the eighth.

After Nagy issued a walk to Raul Casanova with two out, Tavarez came on and pitched out of the inning, despite another single by Lewis that complicated the situation.

Then Mesa stalked out of the bull pen in the ninth and ended it to register his 19th consecutive save and 27th dating back to 1995.

Belle, who was held hitless only seven times in the Tribe's first 46 games, exploded a three run homer the next day, May 26, completing the sweep over the hapless Tigers and handing them their 11th straight loss.

More than 107,000 fans attended the three game series, and Tiger officials estimated that about 70,000 of them were Clevelanders following the

Indians.

It was a big game for Martinez, who scattered eight hits in his first complete game victory of the season, raising his record to 7-2.

It also was the 238th victory of his career, only five fewer than Juan Marichal.

Even more important to the Indians was the performance by Martinez, who had observed his 41st birthday 13 days earlier.

Martinez made 119 pitches, striking out five and walking one, providing a strong indication that he was over the physical problems that plagued him the second half of 1995.

"That was a vintage Martinez game," said Hargrove. "He kept the ball out of the middle of the plate, he hit the corners and changed speeds. When a pitcher does that he can make it tough on young hitters like the Tigers have."

Belle also made it tough on the Tigers, especially Bell, their rookie manager who was enduring his first season as Sparky Anderson's successor.

The turning point in the game came in the eighth inning when Bell was faced with a critical decision - just as Johnny Oates, the Texas manager, had been exactly a week earlier.

The Indians were leading, 2-0, with two out, runners on second and third and Belle at the plate.

Should the league's leading home run hitter be intentionally walked?

Or let Brian Williams, who had pitched a strong game to that point, face Belle, who in three previous at-bats had struck out twice and grounded into a double play?

Bell chose the latter and Belle - just as he'd done to Oates - proved the strategy wrong. He walloped a 1-and-0 fast ball from Williams into the lower left field stands for his 20th home run.

"Looking back on the situation," said Bell, "pitching to Albert was not real smart. I don't know how it would have come out the other way, but I don't think you should let the best offensive player in the game right now beat you."

The homer was Belle's fifth against the Tigers in the last six games, all of which also made a believer of Williams.

"We've watched Belle for two series," said Willaims, "and when anyone makes a mistake against him, he doesn't miss it. He hits good pitches, too, but he doesn't miss mistakes."

Williams, who previously pitched in the National League, was asked to compare the Cleveland slugger with Barry Bonds of the San Francisco Giants.

"I think Albert is better," he replied. "You can get away with some mistakes to Barry, but if you throw 10 to Albert, you might get away with one. If you throw 10 mistakes to Bonds, you might get away with five."

Williams' "mistake" to Belle gave the Indians three more runs and, ultimately, their fourth straight victory and 13th in 16 games.

It also maintained their four game margin over Chicago in the A.L. Central, and sent them on to Arlington, Texas to face the Rangers, who were leading the A.L. West by 3 1/2 lengths over Seattle.

It would not be a pleasant trip.

Carlos Baerga in action at second base against the Kansa City Royals.

6

BACK TO EARTH
WITH A THUD

May 27-June 9

It was too early to start taking orders for the post season playoffs, but there didn't seem to be much doubt that the Indians were in the driver's seat in the American League and were headed for another trip to the World Series.

They had taken over first place in the Central Division after winning 31 of 39 games since April 11 for the best record - 33-14 (.702) - in baseball which, at that rate, would give them an A.L. record 113 victories.

They were leading the Chicago White Sox by a comfortable margin of four games, Albert Belle was hitting home runs at a pace that would give him 69 over the course of the season, Charles Nagy was on track to win 21 games (and probably the Cy Young Award), and Jose Mesa continued to be unbeatable with 19 saves in 19 opportunities, and 27 in a row dating back to September 3, 1995.

As Julio Franco was quoted in *Baseball Weekly:*

"I've played with a lot of teams, good and bad, and I think the only team that can beat the Cleveland Indians is the Cleveland Indians. We've got great ability. All we've got to do is concentrate on the mental part of the game and we'll be all right."

Or as Jim Ingraham wrote in the Lake County *News Herald* and Lorain *Morning Journal:*

"The Indians should have things pretty much taken care of by Labor Day, which, like last season, will give them most of the month of September to rest the warriors in preparation for the October post season pressure cooler.

"We can say this about the Indians because their talent level is so overwhelmingly dominant that almost nothing else matters."

Then a funny thing happened in The Ballpark in Arlington, home of the A.L. West leading Texas Rangers - and some more funny things would happen to the Indians in the next two weeks.

They'd go on to lose seven of 13 games and fall into a tie with the White Sox.

MORE TROUBLE INVOLVING BELLE

And Belle would be involved in a couple more controversies, one of a minor nature with a fan in Arlington, the other a major confrontation with

Milwaukee Brewers infielder Fernando Vina. The latter would result in more trouble for the slugging left fielder.

It all began with three consecutive losses to the Rangers - 3-2, 11-3, and 5-4, May 27-29 - in the wake of another travel near-snafu, which some would consider a portent of trouble ahead.

Upon leaving Detroit after sweeping a three game series from the Tigers, the Indians sat in their Champion Airlines chartered airplane and waited almost six hours on the runway while a minor mechanical problem was corrected.

Jack McDowell was the loser in the first game in Texas when he was unable to hold a 2-1 lead in the eighth.

First, he served a two out, solo homer to Dean Palmer that tied the score in the bottom of the eighth.

Then McDowell gave up the winning run in the ninth when Lou Frazier singled with one out and Darryl Hamilton doubled with two out.

"It was poor pitch selection, and even poorer execution," McDowell said of Palmer's homer. "I threw him a splitter (split-finger fast ball) that hung there.

"The pitch to Hamilton wasn't that bad, but I never should have been in that situation to begin with.

"This is the kind of game I've got to win."

McDowell might have, but for a base-running blunder by Belle in the top of the ninth that displeased Manager Mike Hargrove.

Belle lined a two out shot off the left field wall against Roger Pavlik, who won his seventh game in nine decisions. It should have been a double, but Belle failed to slide into second and was tagged out on a perfect throw by Frazier to second baseman Mark McLemore.

"Albert should have slid," acknowledged Hargrove. "I talked to him about it and he told me, 'I should have slid. I don't know why I didn't.' It wasn't that he didn't run hard. He ran hard all the way. He just didn't slide."

Until the eighth the game belonged to the Indians - and especially to Kenny Lofton.

First, he made an outstanding catch of a sinking liner by Hamilton to end the seventh with a runner on second, preserving a 1-1 tie that resulted from solo homers by Carlos Baerga in the first inning and Mickey Tettleton in the second.

It was Baerga's fourth homer of the season and third in seven games. Tettleton hit a pitch that McDowell said he "grooved."

HERSHISER: CONSISTENTLY INCONSISTENT

The next night was even worse. The victim - or culprit - this time was Orel Hershiser, who allowed six runs on eight hits in 1 2/3 innings, his shortest stint since Aug. 16, 1991, when he pitched for Los Angeles.

Actually, it was an embarrassment, and the loss enabled the White Sox to cut their second place deficit to three games.

When it was over, Hargrove was steaming, though most of his anger was directed - again - at reliever Alan Embree, who replaced Hershiser in the second inning.

"It's safe to say I was not happy," confirmed Hargrove. "To me, (Embree) wasn't throwing. He was just guiding his pitches, trying to get through it."

Hargrove delivered a finger-pointing lecture to Embree on the mound in the fifth inning. "I felt like Alan was not giving it his best shot, and I told him so," said the manager.

When Embree was asked how he responded to Hargrove, he replied, "All I said was, 'Yes sir.'"

The Rangers sent 10 batters to the plate in the first inning, scoring five runs, and Hershiser was excused in the second after Ivan Rodriguez homered, and Tettleton and Warren Newson singled.

Embree got out of the inning, but gave up a run in the third on Kevin Elster's homer, two in the fourth on a walk and Palmer's homer, and two more in the fifth on Rodriguez's second homer.

It was a sobering experience.

The Indians' only runs came on Belle's 21st homer, a solo shot in the fourth, and two in the eighth - when the issue no longer was in doubt - on four singles and a walk.

As for Hershiser's performance, coming on the heels of a splendid outing against Milwaukee five days earlier, Hargrove said, "I've never seen anyone be this consistent being one game off and one game on. I don't know what to make of it, but it certainly has me concerned."

Something else that concerned Hargrove was that Omar Vizquel got picked off base for the third time this season. It happened with the Indians trailing by six runs. Hargrove was fed up.

"Three is the charm for me," he said. "Omar is very conscientious about the way he plays baseball. Fines and taking money from him isn't the answer. I told him, 'Omar, that's not you. You don't do things like that in a situation like that.' I'm satisfied it won't happen again."

CAREER HOMER No. 215 FOR BELLE

It was after the game that Belle got into a squabble with Ken Logan, a Rangers fan who caught the home run Belle hit off Darren Oliver.

It was Belle's 21st of the season and 215th of his career, moving him ahead of Andre Thornton and into a tie with Larry Doby for third place among the Indians' all-time home run hitters. Belle wanted the ball for his trophy case.

Logan alledgedly requested in return an autographed ball from Belle, who refused. Belle's objection was that he claimed Logan had been one of the fans in the left field stands booing and taunting him during the game.

The incident made the newspapers, of course, further tarnishing Belle's public image. The A.L., however, did not get involved.

"We regret it happened, but we will not look into it," said Phyllis Mehridge, vice president of administration and media relations.

A few days later reporters received a fax from an unknown source, though Belle's twin brother Terry was thought to have sent it. Belle was quoted as giving his version of the incident.

A headline at the top stated: "Would the media, please, settle down and come to their senses."

It went on to say: "A few days ago I hit a home run in Texas. After having been taken out of the ball game, I requested if someone could retrieve the ball for me. Shortly thereafter two security guards brought a fan into the clubhouse with a ball in his hands. I immediately recognized this man as being among a group of fans who had been abusively heckling me throughout the game. Whether this man participated in the heckling I could not say for sure since my back was turned to that part of the stands during the game. The mere sight of him reminded me of all the heckling, and so I determined not to deal with him. I told him so and walked away. End of story. I believe my actions were reasonable and justified."

When Bart Swain, the Indians manager of media relations, was asked about the fax, he said Belle had no knowledge of it.

When asked if it came from Belle's brother, Swain said, "I talked to Terry and he said that Albert didn't send it. Terry beat around the bush - (but) he never said, 'Yeah, I did it.'"

ANOTHER BULL PEN BREAKDOWN

It was more of the same the third night, May 29, though the score was much more respectable.

The Rangers rallied again with three runs in the eighth against Tribe relievers to overcome a 4-2 deficit. It spoiled an otherwise good performance by Brian Anderson, who yielded two runs on five hits through six innings in his second opportunity as the Indians' fifth starter.

Both runs off Anderson came in the first inning on Rodriguez's single, a walk and Tettleton's double, after the Tribe broke on top on Franco's homer.

Belle's single, Jim Thome's triple and Jeromy Burnitz's two out single regained the lead, 3-2, for the Indians in the sixth, and singles by Vizquel and Franco around a stolen base upped their margin to 4-2 in the seventh.

But then the bull pen failed again.

Julian Tavarez blanked the Rangers in the seventh, but couldn't in the eighth. Rodriguez singled with one out, took second on a wild pitch, scored on Tettleton's two out single, and was replaced by Paul Assenmacher when Palmer singled.

But Assenmacher was not the answer. McLemore greeted him with a single and, first, Frazier walked, loading the bases, then McLemore scored on Sandy Alomar's passed ball.

After another walk, Eric Plunk replaced Assenmacher and got the third out, but by then the damage was done. The Indians could not retaliate against Mike Henneman.

In an attempt to bolster the Tribe's offense, Thome was moved up into the fifth spot in the batting order behind Belle, and Eddie Murray was dropped to sixth.

"We moved Jimmy up to give Eddie a chance to catch his breath," said Hargrove.

Murray, who was batting .250 with five homers and 20 RBI, singled and walked in four plate appearances, but other than Thome's RBI triple, the shake-up did not play a role in the scoring.

The only saving grace in this one was that the White Sox also lost, 6-5, to Toronto, so the Indians' lead stayed at three as they left Arlington and moved on to Milwaukee for a four game series against the Brewers.

NAGY IS TRIBE'S STOPPER AGAIN

In an otherwise ugly game on May 30, Nagy righted the ship in the opener as he collaborated with three relievers for a 2-0 victory, his sixth in a row, raising his record 9-1 and establishing him as the winningest pitcher in the A.L.

It also was the fifth time Nagy stopped Tribe losing streaks this season.

But it didn't come easily, as nothing had for the Indians at that time, perhaps because they'd been lulled into a sense of complacency based on their success earlier in the season.

Nagy and the Indians seemed to be coasting with their two run lead going into the eighth inning when trouble reared its ugly head.

Mike Matheny doubled and David Hulse walked, Plunk replaced Nagy and the Indians immediately caught a break. Alomar picked off Matheny when Kevin Seitzer attempted to bunt and missed the pitch.

(Yes, the same Kevin Seitzer who would later be acquired by the Indians and spark their drive to the post season playoffs.)

Quickly, however, the Indians found themselves back in trouble as Plunk hit Seitzer with a pitch, bringing Jose Valentin to the plate with the potential tying runs on base. The situation worsened when Valentin walked.

But Greg Vaughn fouled out and Assenmacher, after falling behind in the count, 3-and-1, struck out Dave Nilsson, ending the threat.

Mesa gave up a hit in the ninth, but prevented further damage and remained perfect in save opportunities with his 20th.

Hargrove, relieved that the Indians hung on to win the game, talked about the eighth inning histrionics.

"When you're going through something like we're going through right now," he said, sounding a little like Casey Stengel, "that's how things go.

"We took them out of that inning with the pickoff, and then put them right back in it. I guess we'll call it even."

Of Nagy's performance, Hargrove said, "That might have been the best stuff Charlie has had all year. He made only one bad pitch all night."

Hargrove also was relieved that Baerga was not seriously injured when he was hit on the right wrist by a pitch from Ricky Bones in the first inning. Baerga left the game in the fifth for X-rays that were negative.

The Indians got both their runs in the second on a walk, singles by Murray and Manny Ramirez, and Alomar's double all with one out - though Lofton thought they should have scored more.

With the two runs home, Ramirez was on third when Vizquel lofted a fly to left. Ramirez broke for the plate, but then retreated and held the base. Lofton was seen angrily kicking over a bucket of sunflower seeds in the dugout.

Though Lofton had nothing to say later, Hargrove explained, "Manny left (third base) too early. (Coach) Toby Harrah saw it and called him back."

BELLE IS HIT TWICE BY PITCHES

The next night's game was even uglier, but for a different reason.

The Indians prevailed, 10-4, but not before trouble began when Belle was hit by a pitch from Milwaukee reliever Marshall Boze in the eighth inning.

A few minutes later Belle leveled Vina, the Brewers second baseman with a forearm smash to the face, as he tried to start a double play by tagging the Tribe runner.

Belle was hit by a pitch a second time in the ninth, by Terry Burrows, and Tavarez set off a benches-clearing brawl when he threw a "message" pitch behind the head of Matheny, leading off the bottom of the ninth.

Belle, who had been booed and taunted by Milwaukee fans throughout the game - as well as the ones before and after - said later in one of his rare interviews, "We've decided that if anybody throws at me, we're going to throw back at them. We're not going to be pushed around this year."

Actually, the ugliness had its basis in the third, after Belle singled for a 3-0 Tribe lead, and became the lead runner tagged out on a double play grounder by Murray that ended the inning.

The ball was fielded by Vina who, instead of flipping the ball to Valentin for a force at second, elected to tag Belle in the base path, then threw to first to double Murray.

Afterwards, according to testimony that surfaced more than three months later in a television special, Tribe first base coach Dave Nelson scolded Belle for not tying up Vina, preventing him from getting off a throw to first base.

Thus, Belle found himself in a similar position - he was on first base after being hit by a pitch leading off the eighth inning - and Murray again grounded to Vina.

This time, heeding Nelson's advice, Belle crashed into Vina, knocking him to the ground before he could throw to first to double Murray.

"(Vina) got away with it (tagging Belle to start a double play) once, but not a second time," said the Tribe outfielder. "A second baseman has no business trying to turn a double play like that. Throw to second and then to first. It was a good clean hit."

The Brewers and their fans thought otherwise, of course.

After the Indians scored another run in the eighth for a 10-3 lead, Belle was hit on the left shoulder by a fast ball from Burrows with one on and one out in the ninth. The crowd of 24,050 loved it.

As he stalked to first base Belle could be seen shouting at Burrows.

'HE KNEW WHAT HE HAD TO DO'

And when the inning ended, Belle also was noticed yelling at Tavarez, who had replaced starter and winner Dennis Martinez.

"He knew what he had to do," Belle said of Tavarez. "They (the Brewers) started it, and we finished it."

When Tavarez's first pitch sailed behind Matheny's head the Milwaukee catcher threw down his bat, charged the mound, and players from both dugouts raced onto the field where numerous fights broke out.

Seitzer, playing first base for the Brewers in that game, was in the midst of that brawl, of course, although he later said. "I got wrapped up by Thome and neither of us really got involved."

Seitzer also said of Belle's vicious hit on Vina that it was "totally uncalled for ... he could have just run into (Vina), he didn't have to bring his forearm up like he did," the situation being what it was.

The Indians were ahead, 10-4, in the ninth and, as Seitzer said, "If it had happened in the third or fourth inning, when the game was still close, it might have been different. But not in the ninth with a big lead like (the Indians) had."

Umpire Joe Brinkman, trying to restrain Tavarez, got thrown to the ground by the pitcher, as TV replays later confirmed.

Though it was unintentional - Tavarez did not see who was attempting to pull him away from one of the Brewers - he was ejected and subsequently disciplined, as were Belle and Matheny.

Hargrove had nothing to say about the pitch Tavarez threw behind Matheny's head, but he absolved Belle of blame in his collision with Vina.

"That play was a good, hard play," said Hargrove. "I don't understand the reporting on that as being some dark and evil thing. It was a good baseball play."

McDowell was even more outspoken in his defense of Belle - and his criticism of the Brewers. "It seems like 90 percent of the fights in the American League are in Milwaukee ... (and) it's been like that for years," he said.

"Albert let Vina get away with that double play in the third inning. The second time Albert wasn't going to let him get away with it again. There was nothing wrong with what Albert did.

"If (the Brewers) play the game the right way, we'll play the game the right way. It's not that tough."

Though Brinkman said he put everything in his report to Dr. Budig, the A.L. president, it was significant that the umpires did not accuse Belle of interference and rule a double play - nor in any way reprimand him at the time - for his hit on Vina.

Three days later - unlike the Belle-Tomsic incident that took nearly seven weeks to adjudicate - Belle, Tavarez and Matheny each was suspended for five games, although all three immediately filed appeals.

It meant they could continue to play until Budig, acting as prosecutor, judge and jury, issued a second ruling in each case.

Hargrove said he was "absolutely, totally stunned" by Budig's decision.

Belle and Tavarez were scheduled to present their cases during the Indians next trip to New York, June 13-16.

BELLE: 'NO HARM INTENDED'

In an HBO television special, "Real Sports With Bryant Gumbel," Belle told interviewer Spike Lee, "I definitely had no intention of trying to hurt (Vina) or end his career or knock him out for the rest of the season."

Belle said, "From the way the collision looked, everybody thought I'd tried to hit him across the nose and break his nose, and that I'd tried to take a cheap shot at him. But if you watch it over and over again in slow motion, you'll see where I hit him and broke up the double play."

Belle admitted in the interview that his hard hit on Vina came on orders from Nelson. "I was going to make sure the next time it happens I wasn't going to be as lenient," he said.

General Manager John Hart also was interviewed by Lee and said, "Early in (Belle's) career a lot of the problems we had with Albert were that Albert could not accept failure and, therefore, he would do things ... out of frustration.

"In this era of political correctness, Albert is not baseball politically correct, and that doesn't wash real well."

As for the game itself, the victory was credited to Martinez, raising his record to 5-0 in his last seven starts and 8-2 overall. It gave him a career total of 239 - five fewer than his avowed goal, the number of games won by Hall of Famer Juan Marichal.

The biggest blow (other than the one Belle delivered against Vina) was Ramirez's 11th homer, a two run shot in the second inning. He also singled and doubled, and Tony Pena went 4-for-5 as the Indians rapped 18 hits.

The victory also raised to 5-0 Martinez's record with Pena behind the plate.

GAMMONS: 'TRIBE IS OUT OF CONTROL'

In the wake of the brawl in Milwaukee the Indians were severely criticized by Peter Gammons, the national baseball correspondent for ESPN.

Gammons, a former baseball writer for the Boston *Globe*, said the Indians were "out of control" and in danger of not getting back to the World Series. The report angered Hargrove.

"That kind of reporting really bothers me because the people doing it don't have the facts," he said. "That's a very biased report. I don't know where it comes from (but) this team is not out of control.

"Our image doesn't bother me ... or at least it didn't until that ESPN report. I don't have any complaints about the media's coverage of our team, as long as the facts are presented right."

When asked if the almost constant controversy surrounding Belle is a distraction to the rest of the team, Hargrove replied, "I don't think so because we have been playing fairly consistently. With Albert on the team you realize it's going to be the way it is, so you just go about your business."

There was more antagonism between the two teams - though no blows were struck - the next night, June 1, when the Brewers retaliated this time with their bats and gloves, beating the Indians, 2-1.

The hostility started almost immediately, following Lofton's double leading off the game. Brewers pitcher Angel Miranda attempted a pickoff and Lofton, scrambling back to second, collided with Vina.

Words were exchanged and the dugouts emptied again, but peace - if not harmony - was quickly restored.

Lofton testified, "(Vina) told me, 'You better be careful.' I told him, 'If you want a piece of me, come and get it.'"

Vina confirmed, "Yeah, I was still mad. The throw (from Miranda) was across the bag and I went into (Lofton) to try to catch it. I was playing hard, making a hard tag, just as Albert Belle plays hard."

BRINKMAN LAYS DOWN THE LAW

Then Brinkman, crew chief of the umpires working the game, said, "I told them if there was any more pussy-footing the innocent and the guilty would all go at the same time."

That was it.

Lofton never got off second base in that first inning, and the Indians didn't score until the sixth when Ramirez walked, Murray singled, Alomar sacrifice bunted, Scott Leius walked, Vizquel fouled out, and Lofton also walked, forcing in the Indians' only run.

Lofton doubled again in the third inning, and this time the Brewers' pickoff attempt was successful. The Indians stranded 13 runners and went 0-for-11 with men in scoring position.

"When you drive in some of those runs, your pitcher doesn't have to make a perfect pitch all the time," said Jeff Newman. He was the Tribe's acting manager as Hargrove was back in Strongsville attending the high school graduation of his daughter Melissa.

The Brewers got the run back, plus one, off McDowell in the seventh on Vaughn's single, Valentin's two out triple, and another single by Hulse.

The game ended with Ramirez being thrown out at second trying to stretch a single. "I thought I could make it," he said.

"I told him I thought it was great that he got a base hit in a clutch situation," said Newman. "But I also told Manny that we never want to make the third out on the base paths. It was just another cumulative mistake that we made. It was glaring because it was the final out."

The loss was the third straight for McDowell by a total of four runs. In his 12 starts to date, the Indians supported him with an average of 3.8 runs when he's been in the game. He left two starts with the score tied, two with a one run lead, and one while trailing by two runs.

In McDowell's previous two starts he pitched complete games, but lost, 2-1 and 3-2.

"Jack pitched a great game," said Alomar, "but sometimes when he gets a guy 0-and-2 he tries to be too nasty. It's like he's throwing a 3-and-2 pitch."

It cost the Indians only a half-game in the standings as Chicago's game against Detroit was rained out, leaving the White Sox 2 1/2 behind, but only two in the loss column.

TRIBE LEAD SHRINKS TO TWO GAMES

Even though the Indians won - and won big, 11-6 - the next day, June 2, the White Sox whittled another half game off their deficit by sweeping a double header from Detroit.

But, not to worry, as Alvaro Espinoza quipped, "We're like the Energizer bunny ... we just keep going and going."

They did this time as Espinoza hit a home run, his first, as did Franco and Ramirez to help the Indians overcome another inconsistent outing by

Hershiser, who gave up 10 hits, five walks and all Milwaukee's runs in only four innings.

Nevertheless, Hargrove said he was encouraged by Hershiser's performance. "He got through the first inning. I know he gave up four runs in the second, but one of the hits bounced off first base, another run came on a balk, and a couple of hits were off the end of the bat.

"The thing was, he made adjustments. In the last couple of starts I haven't seen Orel's good sinker (but) we saw it a couple of times today."

But Hershiser wasn't so positive. "Progress is one thing ... we need results, "he said.

Hershiser left in the fifth inning with the score tied, 5-5, runners on first and third and nobody out. Jim Poole took over and retired the first batter on a double play, enabling the Brewers to break the tie, and got the next to ground out, too.

Espinoza, who played shortstop to give Vizquel and his aching shoulder a rest, hit his homer, a two run shot, in the sixth, putting the Tribe ahead to stay.

It concluded a 6-4 trip that started with a three game sweep of the Tigers in Detroit, continued in Texas where the Indians were swept in four games by the Rangers, and finished with three victories in four games in Milwaukee.

But it didn't get any better - in fact, it got worse - back at Jacobs Field.

BELLE AND TAVAREZ SUSPENDED

It was upon their return to Cleveland that the Indians were notified of Budig's decision to suspend Belle and Tavarez.

Of Belle's reprimand the A.L. president said in a written statement:

"The American League will not tolerate an act that puts in serious jeopardy the safety of a player. The physical well-being of our players must be of paramount importance to all responsible individuals associated with the game."

Vina seemed pleased that Belle was suspended, saying he wasn't surprised. "If they look at the film it's pretty much etched in stone. I don't mind (Belle) running me over, but everybody could see that he hit me in the face with his elbow.

Hargrove wouldn't comment, but Gene Orza, an official of the Major League Baseball Players Association, said Belle's suspension was unusual "because he wasn't thrown out of the game or issued a warning."

And, as expected, Arn Tellem, Belle's agent, was "outraged."

"Albert had no intention of hurting Vina. His only thought was to break up the double play. I'm outraged by this ruling. This continues a pattern by the commissioner's office and the league office that holds Albert to different standards than any other professional athlete," said Tellem.

"The only malicious intent in this is by the league office in its treatment of Albert. The two pitchers that hit Albert get nothing. The man is under a magnifying glass. Anything he does, even when it's legitimate, is viewed as improper."

Budig also said that what Tavarez did was "inexcusable," in flipping Brinkman off his back. "Umpire Joe Brinkman was attempting to restore order when he was slammed to the ground."

Also, as expected, Richie Phillips, head of the umpires union, called Tavarez's suspension "woefully inadequate," saying, "I thought it should have been a minimum of 30 days."

The suspensions, if upheld, would cost Belle about $156,000 in salary, and Tavarez about $11,600.

FIFTH SUSPENSION IN SIX YEARS

It also would be Belle's fifth suspension in six years. He was suspended for intentionally hitting a fan with a thrown baseball in 1991; charging the mound in 1992 and 1993; and being caught with a corked bat in 1994.

He was not suspended in 1995, but he was fined $50,000 for his obscenity-laced outburst against television commentator Hannah Storm prior to Game 3 of the World Series.

The Indians opened a nine game homestand on June 4 and, with the White Sox in the midst of an 8-2 hot streak, proceeded to blow the Central Division lead they'd held since April 22.

It also was the beginning of great concern regarding Mesa, their ace closer who had - until now - shown no sign of losing the mastery he'd built up while registering 46 saves in 48 opportunities in 1995.

Since September 3, 1995, Mesa had logged 28 consecutive saves, including 20 this season.

In the first game of the home stand against Seattle on June 4, Mesa was called upon to protect a 7-6 lead in the ninth inning, but promptly gave it away.

Mesa was unable to retire any of the six batters he faced, walking four of them, and before Assenmacher could put out the fire, the Mariners scored four runs and won, 10-7.

It was only the third time in 69 save situations over two years that Mesa failed.

It also was the Indians' fifth loss in eight games - and their first in 119 games since August of 1994 in which they'd led after eight innings.

"Pena said his ball had so much movement (Mesa) couldn't keep it in the strike zone," said Hargrove.

"They didn't beat me, I beat myself," lamented Mesa. There were no dissenters. "I think I was trying to throw too hard.

"But, hey, I'm human like everyone else, and blown saves are going to happen."

Before Mesa beat himself, the Indians had fought back from 3-0 and 6-3 deficits, as Brian Anderson was bombed by Seattle through the first four innings.

BELLE HAMMERS HOMER No. 216

Belle hammered a two run homer, his 22nd of the season, in the seventh when the Indians tied the score, 6-6. It was Belle's 216th career homer, moving him into a tie with Hal Trosky for second place among the Indians' all-time home run hitters.

The Tribe went ahead by one in the eighth on singles by Alomar and Vizquel around a walk by Thome.

But then Mesa did the unexpected and the Indians' lead shrunk to one game over the White Sox, who beat Boston, 6-4, for their 14th victory in 16 games.

The White Sox continued to win the next night, June 5, beating the Red Sox, 8-6, in 12 innings, but the Indians clung to their one game lead, thanks in part to the generosity of the Mariners.

The Tribe took advantage of seven walks by six of the seven Seattle pitchers, scored seven runs when 11 batters went to the plate in the 61 minute seventh inning, and prevailed, 13-5, as Belle hit another homer, his 23rd.

It gave Belle a career total of 217, boosting him ahead of Trosky and into second place among the Tribe's all-time leaders, only nine behind Earl Averill's club record 226.

It would have been - should have been - Nagy's 10th victory and seventh in a row. But he also stumbled in the seventh, allowing the Mariners to tie the score at 3-3, before Poole could rush to the rescue.

Instead, the victor was Plunk after Alan Embree - not Mesa - blanked the Mariners one-two-three in the ninth, striking out two of them.

"Maybe this can get us going again," said Vizquel. "We have not been playing good ball collectively. I think it's good Chicago is playing well. That will put some pressure on us. Make us concentrate."

MARTINEZ CAN'T HOLD THE LEAD

Twenty-four hours later the Indians were back in the dumper, whether it was a lack of concentration or whatever, although, for the first time in two weeks, the pressure being applied by the White Sox had eased off slightly.

While the Tribe was losing again to Seattle, 5-2, Boston also was beating Chicago, 7-4, keeping the White Sox a game behind.

There wasn't much to second guess about the Indians' setback; they got two runs in the first inning on Baerga's homer, but Dennis Martinez let it slip away. The big blow was Edgar Martinez's two run homer in the third inning that put Seattle ahead, 3-2.

"We had our chances," said Hargrove, referring to eight runners the Tribe left stranded. "That's been the story of our games too often in the past couple of weeks." He was right. In the three games against Seattle the Tribe left 27 runners on base.

It's something the White Sox also had noticed.

On May 17 the Indians held a 5 1/2 game lead over Chicago. Since then the White Sox won 14 of 17 games while the Indians were going 10-8.

"We lost (to Boston), but we're right there with the Indians, and they know it," said White Sox pitcher Wilson Alvarez.

"And when Albert (Belle) serves his suspension, we'll have a good chance to get ahead of them."

Dave Martinez agreed. "When we step on the field we feel we can win every game. It's too early to watch the scoreboard, but it's not too early to win games."

McDOWELL HALTS THREE GAME SKID

Any fears that had developed concerning McDowell, as well as Mesa, were shunted aside, if not eliminated as the Indians continued their homestand, and clung to a one length lead over Chicago on June 7.

McDowell halted a personal three game losing streak, with Mesa's help, in a 4-3 victory over California, while the White Sox were beating Baltimore, 8-2.

As Pena said before the game, "It's too early to be watching the scoreboard ... all we can do is worry about ourselves."

Thome and Vizquel provided most of the support; Thome smashing a homer and double, and Vizquel driving in two runs with two singles.

The Angels seem to bring out the best in Thome who, in four games against them, was hitting .562 (9-for-16) with four homers.

As for McDowell, Hargrove said, "He lost three straight, but he was still pitching well. Tonight, we scored early, gave him some breathing room and he did the job."

It was California's fifth straight defeat, during which they've been outscored, 46-13.

Mesa, whose string of 28 saves in 28 opportunities dating back to September 3, 1995 was snapped three days earlier, started a new streak in the ninth inning, but it wasn't pretty.

He gave up a run on a hit and a walk, but fortunately had a cushion and staggered home free.

The crowd of 42,260, the 77th consecutive sellout at Jacobs Field, pushed the Indians' season attendance to 1,038,613 in 25 openings, the earliest the club has passed the million mark.

The Indians had a newcomer in uniform and another waiting in the wings, which some interpreted as an indication they were panicking, though Hargrove denied that speculation.

First baseman Herbert Perry was recalled from Class AAA Buffalo because of a strained right hamstring that hampered Murray, though it was Scott Leius who was placed on the disabled list to open a spot on the roster.

Leius, who had been signed as a free agent during the winter to serve as a utilityman, had a sore back - and also a sore bat. He was batting .033 on 1-for-30 after going hitless in his first 19 at-bats.

Perry was leading the American Association with a .338 average when he was recalled for the fourth time in three seasons.

"We are going to be cautious with Eddie (Murray)," said Hargrove. "If Albert (Belle) has to serve his suspension, we don't want two guys out at the same time."

SWINDELL IN WAITING

Also on hand was former Tribesman Greg Swindell, the left handed pitcher who'd been their No. 1 pick (second overall) in the 1986 amateur draft. He was traded to Cincinnati in November 1991, at which time he expressed great pleasure in getting out of Cleveland.

Swindell wound up with Houston, which released him with an 0-3 record and 7.83 ERA, and $3 million left on his $4.5 million salary this season.

"When I left here I didn't feel the team was going anywhere," Swindell said of his departure under strained circumstances five seasons ago.

"This is a no-lose situation for us, and we fully expect to sign (Swindell)," said Hart, which the Indians later did for about $72,000, based on the pro-rated $109,000 major league minimum salary.

"I'd like to be a starter (but) I'll pitch batting practice, if that's what the Indians want," said Swindell.

Hershiser, whose consistent inconsistency had worried Hargrove, followed the lead of McDowell and combined with Tavarez on a six hitter to beat the Angels, 5-0, on June 8.

It kept the Indians one game ahead of Chicago, which beat Baltimore, 2-1.

"When you're going good, you still have to take inventory so you can re-create what you are doing," said Hershiser.

"But I haven't been going good long enough this season to re-create much. It was just nice to throw the ball today and say, 'Oh, yeah, that's how you do that.'"

Franco, who reached base five times, scored twice and drove in a run, talked about what had become a "roller coaster season" for the Tribe.

"A lot of people thought this season would be like last year, but that's over rated," he said. "Every season is different. Some guys start hot, some guys start slow. Last year was great. I'm not taking anything away from it, but it's over. It's time to get back to reality."

Baerga offered similar reassuring advice.

"I know this team hasn't played as well as it can," he said. "We haven't scored the seven or eight runs a game like we did last year. But this team is going to explode. The second half will be different."

Ramirez homered leading off the second inning and Hershiser was staked to a 4-0 lead after four. The rest was easy as he allowed four hits over seven innings, and Tavarez two in the last two.

The Indians also made another roster change, recalling Chad Ogea from Buffalo, and sending Embree down again.

STILL IN THE LEAD, BUT TIED

The troubles that had befallen the Indians in the past two weeks - inconsistent pitching, wasted opportunities on offense, physical and mental errors, and fundamental mistakes - finally cost them their undisputed hold on first place in the Central Division on June 9.

They were beaten in the 13th inning, 8-6, by California, which ended a six game losing streak, and fell into a tie with the White Sox, who beat Baltimore, 12-9.

The extra inning loss was the Indians' second in three games this season after going 13-0 in overtime in 1995.

It also was the first time the Tribe did not have sole possession of the top rung in the division since April 22.

Over the past 13 games the Indians had gone 6-7, while the White Sox were 10-3, and 17-3 since May 17.

Still, the Tribesmen talked bravely. "It's not like we're 10 games out," said Poole. "Chicago is playing great baseball. When it is all said and done I still expect us to be in first place."

And Tavarez, who gave up a two run, game winning homer to J.T. Snow, said equally bravely, "We've got a better team than the White Sox. We've got a better team than anybody," though the Indians were not playing like it.

The winning pitcher was rookie Ryan Hancock, who probably became the answer to a trivia question with an outstanding display of hitting, pitching and fielding in just his second major league game.

Hancock became the first California pitcher to get a hit since the inception of the designated hitter in 1973.

Forced to bat because of a lineup switch, Hancock singled off Tavarez with one out. It was the first hit by an Angels pitcher since Nolan Ryan got one on September 30, 1972.

Tavarez struck out the next batter, Garret Anderson, but Snow homered and the Indians were unable to retaliate in their half of the 13th after pinch hitter Wayne Kirby led with a single.

Vizquel walked, but Lofton, in the throes of a 13-for-65 slump, popped up trying to bunt. Hancock made a diving catch and threw to second where Kirby was doubled off. It was one of five double plays by the Angels.

Then Hancock walked Franco, but Baerga bounced back to the mound to end the game.

"Kenny (Lofton) is a good bunter, but we just didn't execute," said Hargrove. "The thing that concerns me the most is that we haven't been swinging the bats well over the last week or so."

The Indians stranded 12 runners and Anderson, who started on the mound, couldn't hold leads of 3-0 and 4-1.

After they fell behind, 6-5, the Indians tied it in the ninth against Troy Percival on singles by Lofton and Franco, and Baerga's sacrifice fly.

But they couldn't deliver a knockout punch and, just like that were in an unfamiliar position.

The Indians were tied for first place and facing their first serious challenge, the likes of which they had not experienced through the entire 1995 season.

Charles Nagy

7

THE ALBERT BELLE SAGA CONTINUES

June 10-27

Though Chicago continued its hot streak, the Indians were equal to the challenge and their situation brightened considerably in the next 10 days, although another chapter in the ongoing saga involving Albert Belle soon surfaced.

Following their distressing, overtime, 8-6 loss to California, the Indians welcomed Oakland to Jacobs Field and promptly got two more good performances out of Charles Nagy and Chad Ogea on June 10 and 11.

First, they beat the Athletics, 5-4, for Nagy's seventh straight victory, 10th in 11 decisions and 13th in a row at Jacobs Field, keeping the Indians tied with the White Sox, who defeated Boston, 8-2.

Then the Tribe rallied behind Ogea to win, 6-5, in 13 innings, and regained sole possession of first place as Chicago lost to the Red Sox, 9-2, for only their fourth setback in 22 games.

From that point on - for 110 consecutive days from June 11 through the final game of the season on September 29 - Cleveland was the undisputed leader in the American League Central Division.

The Indians lost to Oakland, 9-6, in the finale of the June 10-12 series with the A's, then visited New York where they went 2-2 against the Yankees, and A.L. President Dr. Gene Budig heard Belle's and Julian Tavarez's appeals of their five game suspensions.

Budig later reduced the penalties to, first, three game suspensions for each of the players, and subsequently further lessened Belle's to two games and a $25,000 fine.

While General Manager John Hart did not celebrate the shorter sentences, he was satisfied the Indians had "our day in court."

"We didn't agree with the original ruling, but three games (suspension) is better than five," he said. "Under the circumstances, we were able to have our day in court, and that in itself is a positive, and the fact that there was a reduction in the suspensions also is a positive."

Belle would not comment, but his agent, Arn Tellem, expressed anger and, initially, even hinted legal action.

"We have been in contact with the players union to determine how, and under what circumstances Budig's decision can be challenged," he said.

"We do not believe that the American League president has the authority or jurisdiction to impose discipline on a player when all the umpires on the scene agree that the player's conduct was completely legal.

"The league has no authority to second guess the umpire's judgment call in this or any other circumstance."

Tavarez was satisfied with Budig's decision. "Three games, that's not too bad," he said. "I was ready for five games. It's not fair ... everybody knows I didn't try to hurt that guy (Brinkman), but that's baseball."

NAGY IS FIRST IN A.L. TO WIN 10

The Indians continued their distressing habit of squandering scoring opportunities, this time leaving 10 runners stranded. But Nagy refused to give in to the Athletics and prevailed with relief help from Paul Shuey and Jose Mesa.

The victory made Nagy the A.L.'s first 10 game winner.

Shuey, who pitched a one-two-three eighth inning, was recalled from Class AAA Buffalo earlier in the day, in exchange for Brian Anderson. Mesa also pitched a perfect ninth for his 22nd save.

It was another case of Nagy prevailing because of perseverance as the Athletics almost broke the game open in the second inning. They sent seven batters to the plate and took a 3-0 lead on four hits, three of them doubles.

"I threw some breaking balls I wasn't aggressive with, and they made me pay," said Nagy. "I made some adjustments after that. I had to be more aggressive. I knew I had to throw a harder breaking ball."

Which he obviously did. His only mistake in the next four innings came with two out in the seventh when Mark McGwire hit a 415 foot homer.

By then the Indians had rallied for five runs - one in the second and two in each the third and fourth innings off Doug Johns - and Shuey and Mesa preserved the victory.

Oakland manager Art Howe was lavish in his praise of Nagy. "He has four pitches he can throw for strikes at any time," said Howe. "He's as good as anyone we've faced all year."

It was the 14th time this season the Tribe had come from behind to win, as Manny Ramirez solo homered in the second, and Kenny Lofton did the same in the fourth, for a 4-3 lead.

Manager Mike Hargrove, who was ejected for the second time this season for arguing a strike call by umpire Larry McCoy, said the problem of squandering scoring opportunities had been discussed.

"It has been going on for three weeks to a month, and we are trying to do something about it," he said. "We've got to relax, but that's easier said than done."

Whatever, in their previous 18 games the Indians stranded a total of 165 runners.

Omar Vizquel offered another theory. "We are not being selective at the plate," he said. "We're swinging at bad pitches early in the count. The pressure is on the pitcher, not us. He's the one in trouble in those situations, not us."

RAMIREZ: FROM GOAT TO HERO

Ramirez, who incurred Hargrove's wrath with some weird base running the next night, June 11, at least partially atoned for his misdeeds by driving in the winning run in the 13th inning. It made a winner of Ogea, the Tribe's sixth pitcher working in relief of Dennis Martinez.

Still, the Indians would have won in regulation time if Ramirez had hustled in from third base in the eighth inning on what should have been a sacrifice fly by Lofton.

Instead, Ramirez tagged up and jogged home, but his run didn't count because he didn't cross the plate before Vizquel, who had been on first, was thrown out at second for what became an inning ending double play.

Hargrove screamed at Ramirez, and later kept the door to the clubhouse closed longer than usual.

When asked, he would only say, "Manny got my message. That's the end of it. I don't have a doghouse. I wish I could stay mad at some people, but that doesn't do anybody any good.

"Manny's a very good player, an important part of this ball club. He could have quit (after being scolded in the eighth). but he didn't. He made some good plays in right field, and came through with the sacrifice fly when we needed it."

Eddie Murray finally got his sixth homer and 485th of his career, a two run shot, and Julio Franco singled for his 2,000th career hit and scored on Carlos Baerga's sixth homer in the Tribe's four run first inning.

Murray's homer was his first since May 17, and his three runs batted in gave him 1,846, passing Carl Yastrzemski for ninth place on the all-time list..

Prior to the game Franco was asked how he felt with 1,999 hits. "I've got 1,001 to go (to 3,000)," he said. "It's not like I'm going to stop (at 2,000)." Obviously he didn't, and doubled for No. 2,001 in the seventh.

"And even if I do reach 3,000, I am not going to quit just because of that. If I don't reach 3,000, that's fine. I play for the glory of God.

"My goals are to reach the kingdom of heaven. I don't think I will be playing ball there."

Martinez couldn't protect the 4-1 lead he was given in the first inning. The A's scored twice in the fourth and single runs in the fifth and sixth, taking a 5-4 lead.

After the base running lapses by Ramirez and Vizquel in the eighth, the Indians were handed a run in the ninth, sending the game into overtime, when Jim Corsi issued three walks (one intentional), and Murray delivered a sacrifice fly.

The A's generosity was literally duplicated in the 13th when the Indians scored the winning run against Carlos Reyes, again without a hit. With one out, Belle reached on an error, Alvaro Espinoza and Murray walked, and Ramirez lofted his sacrifice fly.

McGWIRE HAMMERS TWO HOMERS

It was the Tribe's turn to reciprocate the next night, June 12, as Jim Poole, the usually reliable reliever, took over for Jack McDowell in the sixth, with two on, two out and the game tied, 5-5.

Poole walked Jose Herrera on four pitches, then served a three run double to Brent Gates that all but settled the issue.

Afterwards, McDowell, was a very unhappy camper. The Indians had fought back from a 5-1 deficit to even the score.

When asked if he was upset by his banishment, McDowell snapped, "That's a trick question because the move didn't work out. If it did work out, the question wouldn't even be asked."

That was the end of the interrogation, trick questions or not.

There were other reasons for McDowell to be upset - as there also were for Hargrove.

McGwire delivered a three run homer in the first inning, a walk and Phil Plantier's double added another run in the second, and Oakland's fourth run scored in the third on two walks, a single and fielder's choice.

It was McDowell's fourth loss in his last five starts.

The Indians fought back with runs in the first, third (on Belle's 25th homer), fourth, two in the fifth and another in the sixth (on Franco's ninth homer), but to no avail.

Belle's homer gave him 64 RBI in the Tribe's 63 games.

"It takes a lot out of an offense when you have to come from behind all the time," said Sandy Alomar. "Every night can't be an offensive night. The pitching has to show up sometimes."

Then, "The way we're playing, we're lucky to be in first place."

True - and with thanks to Boston, which beat Chicago again, 3-2, keeping the White Sox a game behind the Tribe.

After the A's broke the tie, Franco hammered a solo homer in the bottom of the sixth, but it was nullified in the seventh on McGwire's homer off Tavarez. It was McGwire's second of the game and 18th of the season.

HOME RUN No. 486 FOR MURRAY

Orel Hershiser, previously dubbed "Mr. Inconsistent" because of his bothersome early season habit of pitching a bad game after a good one, and vice versa, got the Tribe started on the right foot in the June 13 opener of a four game series in New York.

After Belle and an entourage of 10 supporters - including Indians owner Dick Jacobs - opened a two day hearing to appeal Belle's suspension, Hershiser pitched seven strong innings in a 6-2 victory over the Yankees.

It hiked the Tribe's lead over Chicago, which was idle, to 1 1/2 games.

It also was the first time since April 26 and May 2 that Hershiser won a second consecutive start, and he did so primarily on the strength of Murray's seventh homer.

The homer, Murray's second in three games since missing four games with a sore right hamstring, propelled Murray to within 14 of joining Hall of Famers Hank Aaron and Willie Mays.

Aaron and Mays were the only players in baseball history to have 500 homers and 3,000 hits. Murray got his 3,000th hit on June 30, 1995.

Otherwise, the Indians' offense - as it had been doing - sputtered often, especially in the third, fourth, fifth, sixth and eighth innings when they hit into five double plays, two of them by Baerga.

Hershiser said, "I felt I found a few things in my last start that I could repeat. I went into this outing thinking about those things. I kept the ball moving and threw strikes to both sides of the plate."

Hershiser, with a 6-4 record, allowed both of New York's runs on four hits. He walked one and struck out five.

"I never really questioned myself because I'm healthy," said Hershiser. "I just wanted to fix what was wrong. I had to figure out what was the thing I needed to do to throw one good pitch after another.

"I'd throw two or three good pitches and then two or three bad ones. To be successful in this game, you've got to throw eight out of 10 pitches where you want them."

This time he did.

"That was the best Orel has thrown all year," said Hargrove. "He was dominating with his sinker, and shut down a very good hitting ball club."

When Hershiser tired in the eighth, Assenmacher took over and continued the shutout, and Shuey - not Mesa - pitched the ninth and earned his first save of the season.

PLENTY OF SUPPORT FOR BELLE

It was a show of force that the Indians mounted as they accompanied Belle and Tavarez to their hearing with Budig prior to the game on June 13.

In addition to Jacobs, the Tribe players were accompanied by Hart, Hargrove, lawyer Ed Ptaszek, first base coach Dave Nelson, Tellem, Belle's agent, and four officials of the Major League Players Association, including Executive Director Don Fehr, associate general counsel Gene Orza, and former players Tony Bernazard and Mark Belanger.

"I'm here to show support for my players," was the only comment Jacobs would make after the 5 1/2 hour meeting. All involved had been ordered by Budig to not speak to the media about what had transpired.

The hearing also included testimony via a conference call with three of the four umpires who worked the game that night, none of whom accused Belle of breaking the rules.

When asked why such a large contingent of supporters accompanied Belle and Tavarez, it was explained by Hart, "We didn't take a real forceful stand right away (because) we knew there would be a process and we'd show support for our players at the proper time."

The union presented Budig with a frame-by-frame breakdown of Belle's collision with Vina, and stressed that Belle had been hit twice by pitches earlier.

Vina was quoted in the New York *Daily News* that, "Anybody who knows the game knows it was a cheap shot (by Belle). But he's the big money player, and so they (the players union) are trying to back him now. That's horrible."

Then, "Orza is supposed to be representing me, too, isn't he?"

Budig met with Belle and Tavarez again the next day, June 14, and five days later he announced the reduction of Belle's and Tavarez's suspensions to three games each. Then, on June 20, Budig further lightened Belle's penalty to a two days suspension, and a $25,000 fine.

Tavarez served his suspension June 18-20, and Belle sat out a double header against the Yankees on June 21. His fine was donated to the RBI (Reviving Baseball in the Inner City) youth baseball program in Cleveland.

Tellem was still angry that any penalty was imposed against his client, but dropped whatever plans he might have had to take legal action against the league.

However, one Cleveland fan, Lou DiNovi, filed a lawsuit in Cuyahoga County Common Pleas Court to prevent Belle from having to serve the suspension. It was assigned to Judge Judith Kilbane Koch, but before the suit could be heard, DiNovi dropped it for lack of support by the Indians.

And then, this last comment by Hart.

Referring to the great attention the incident had stirred up among fans and the media, Hart chuckled and said, "Being with the Indians this year is like traveling with the Beatles."

Again, he was right.

SECOND GUESSING HART ON CLARK

Ironically, it was while the Indians were in New York to play the Yankees that former teammate Mark Clark, the pitcher who was traded at the end of spring training, was getting rave reviews for the success he was having with the Mets.

Clark, who would have looked great as the Indians' fifth starter, was 6-6 with a 3.01 ERA for the Mets.

The three pitchers who had been tried as the Tribe's fifth starter - Ogea, Albie Lopez and Anderson - had a combined won-lost record of 1-1 with a 6.24 ERA.

Though all, on one occasion or another, pitched well, none did so consistently well through the first half of the season to hold the job on a regular basis.

That inconsistency on the part of Ogea, Lopez and Anderson led to much second-guessing of Hart and Hargrove by talk show hosts and their callers, especially when Clark pitched well for the Mets.

As Jim Ingraham wrote in the Lake County *News Herald* on June 15: "Clark (traded) for Ryan Thompson and Reid Cornelius had a bad odor to it the day it was made, and today it smells worse than ever," and that the deal "smelled of panic ... and it's looking worse with each passing week.".

Ogea, inadvertently, of course, lent credence to Ingraham's remarks on June 14 when he was the losing pitcher as the Indians were defeated, 4-3, by Doc Gooden and the Yankees in a game that turned ugly in the seventh inning.

Many of the 32,580 fans in the left field stands of Yankee Stadium were taunting and harassing Belle most of the game.

"You jerk! You belong in a zoo," one spectator was heard to shout at Belle according to a story in *USA TODAY.*

"'Betty Ford! Betty Ford!' a few shouted, calling out the name of another treatment center. 'Corkhead!' a kid yells, reminding Belle of his 1994 suspension for using a corked bat.'

"'Where's Vina?' rags another. 'He should've killed you, you piece of trash!'"

It got so bad that Hargrove pulled the Indians off the field in the seventh, protesting to umpire Drew Coble that he feared for Belle's safety.

When asked if he had brought up the possibility of a forfeit to Coble, Hargrove replied, "No comment" - which probably meant that he did.

After the fans complied with public address announcer Bob Sheppard's plea that they not throw objects on the field, the Indians returned to their positions and the game continued.

They trailed, 4-2, at the time, and their ninth inning rally was aborted after Jeromy Burnitz homered with two outs, and Baerga singled against reliever John Wetteland, who then retired Wayne Kirby to end it.

It also was in that game that the beginning of the end for Baerga in a Tribe uniform might have been signaled when he was dropped from his familiar third spot in the batting order to seventh.

It was the first time Baerga had batted anywhere but third - the position usually reserved for a team's best hitter for average - since June 3, 1991, a clear indication that management was growing increasingly concerned about the second baseman's performance.

Baerga's average at the time was a very uncharacteristic .271.

INDIANS ARE ANGERED BY FANS

Though Belle refused to comment on the hatred shown toward him by the fans, others in the Tribe clubhouse were outspoken in expressing their anger.

"What has Albert ever done to (the fans)?" Franco asked rhetorically. "He doesn't deserve this. These fans are miserable."

Hargrove said, "There isn't a person in the game who's subject to the volume of abuse Albert hears. It's not right. He might not be the most personable personality with the fans, but he doesn't cheat them with his performance.

"You boo, you call someone a bum, OK. But what they say to him every night, it's over the line."

It was a continuation of the harassment to which Belle was subjected since his controversial incidents in Texas on May 27, when he was angered by a fan's unwillingness to return a home run ball to him, and the collision with Vina in Milwaukee on May 31.

"I've never seen the amount of viciousness directed at one player as I've seen directed at Albert the last few weeks," Hargrove said.

It's possible that the negative publicity and response of the fans had an effect on Belle, who had been hitting .356 on May 27, but in the next 20 games batted only .243 on 19-for-78 with five homers and 14 RBI.

"If Albert goes to the bathroom, everybody has to know about it," said Espinoza. "He's getting tired of it. He's not the only player on this team. People should pick on somebody else."

Ogea, who'd been recalled from Class AAA Buffalo six days earlier and was making his first start since April 14, took a 2-2 tie into the sixth. Jim Thome had doubled and scored the Indians' first run in the second, and solo homered in the fourth.

But Tino Martinez's single and a walk to Ruben Sierra finished Ogea with two outs in the sixth.

Eric Plunk took over and promptly also walked Joe Girardi, then was tagged for a two run single by Derek Jeter before the inning ended.

Gooden, back from a drug abuse imposed suspension, won his sixth game in 10 decisions with Wetteland's 17th save. It cut the Tribe's lead to one half game over the White Sox, who beat Seattle, 4-1, for their 19th victory in 22 games.

NAGY IS THE 'STOPPER' AGAIN

Nagy, as he'd done so often previously - and would in the future - was the Indians' "stopper" the next day, June 15, scattering seven hits through seven innings, and won his eighth straight game. He also was 7-0 following Tribe losses.

With relief help from Assenmacher in the eighth and Tavarez in the ninth, Nagy and the Indians defeated the Yankees. 10-3, on the wings of Ramirez's 15th homer, Thome's 13th, and Baerga's seventh.

It enabled the Indians to pick up a full game in the standings, increasing their lead to 1 1/2 lengths over the White Sox, who lost to Seattle, 8-6, in 12 innings.

Hargrove praised Nagy again, and also was pleased by the Indians' 14 hits. "Our offense has been struggling for about three weeks," he said, partially explaining the revamped batting order he put on the field for the second straight day.

It had Belle batting third, Murray fourth, Thome fifth, Baerga sixth and Ramirez seventh. (However, it would remain that way for only three games, after which Thome went back to the third spot in the order, with Belle fourth, Ramirez fifth, Murray sixth, and Baerga seventh.)

Before the game there was another fan related incident that became a mini controversy involving Belle and Lofton.

A boy standing near the dugout with his father asked the two players to autograph a ball, but neither obliged. A New York columnist, Wally Matthews, standing with a group of reporters, told the boy, "Why don't you throw the ball at (Belle)? Maybe he'll sign it for you then."

Belle did not respond, but Lofton did. "I got hot after (Matthews) said that, especially after what happened (during the game the night before)," Lofton said.

"It was probably a stupid thing to say, but it was just a joke," said Matthews.

The Yankees beefed up their security forces for the game, which satisfied Lofton.

"People have to realize that we're professional players just trying to do a job," said Lofton, referring to the lack of crowd control the night before. "When you're in the outfield you have no control over what's happening behind you.

"I was very appreciative of what the Yankees did."

Later, Claire Smith of the New York *Times* and chairperson of the New York Chapter of the Baseball Writers Association sent a letter of apology to Belle and Lofton for the actions of Matthews.

After the game the Indians made another roster change, their 11th since Opening Day, by officially signing Greg Swindell to a contract and designating Kirby for assignment.

Boston and Los Angeles had shown interest in dealing for Kirby, and the roster move by the Indians gave them 10 days to trade or release the veteran outfielder who'd been a regular until Ramirez took his job in 1994.

He later was claimed on waivers by the Dodgers.

MARTINEZ IS 2-16 vs. YANKEES

The first solid sign that Martinez's 41 year old arm was wearing out occurred on June 16, in the finale of the four game series in New York, won by the Yankees and rising Cy Young Award candidate Andy Pettitte, 5-4.

It was Martinez's 10th consecutive loss to the Yankees, whom he hadn't beaten since June 11, 1982, reducing his lifetime record against them to 2-16.

"I have no answer for this," he said then. "If I did, I would put it in play."

Hargrove scoffed at the suggestion that Martinez is jinxed against the Yankees, especially in Yankee Stadium where his winless streak dates back to May 20, 1977.

"I don't believe in jinxes," said Hargrove. "Not with a guy who has pitched as long and as well as Martinez. Given the right circumstances, he can beat (the Yankees)."

While Martinez was hit hard, the game was something of a success for Swindell, who made his first game appearance in a Tribe uniform since October 3, 1991. Swindell replaced Martinez in the fourth with the Indians trailing, 5-0, and blanked the Yankees on three hits through the eighth.

"Greg was outstanding," said Hargrove. "There are still a couple of things we'd like to do with his mechanics, but he threw well."

Pettitte, who tied Nagy as the A.L.'s winningest pitchers - each with 11 victories - left after five following a three run homer by Ramirez, his second in two games, 16th of the season, and seventh in two-plus seasons in Yankee Stadium, which is close to the neighborhood in which he was raised.

In fairness to Martinez, part of his trouble was caused by Baerga's inability to field a grounder that led to two runs in the first inning, and errors charged to Ramirez and Vizquel that resulted in a run in the third and two in the fourth.

They were the Tribe's 49th and 50th errors in 67 games.

The loss was the Indians' 10th in 20 games since May 26, though it wasn't costly as the White Sox also were beaten again by Seattle, 7-6.

When asked if the anti-Belle harassment in the past three weeks was a distraction to the entire team, Hargrove said, "It's bothersome, but I don't think it's taken away a lot of our focus. I think being in New York is 90 percent of this (trouble). There is a lot of attention here."

BELLE'S SUSPENSION REDUCED

The Indians happily departed Yankee Stadium and went home for a three game series against Boston, June 18-20, at Jacobs Field where the fans always were overwhelming in their support of Belle.

It also was where their record was 21-9, and they'd go on to reverse their losing ways - if only temporarily.

The return also came on the heels of Budig's announced reduction of Belle's and Tavarez's suspensions, which further pleased the Indians, though many thought there should not have been any penalties imposed.

As they did in generating a head of steam in beating the Red Sox three straight early in the 1995 season - and had built up a 10 game winning streak against them - the Indians swept Boston.

They won the first game, 9-7, with Swindell picking up the victory (which would be his only one for the Tribe in 1996), 11-4, behind Hershiser, and 5-4, with Shuey shining in relief.

Vizquel, better known for his golden glove, hammered a grand slam, the second of his seven year major league career, in the second inning of the first game when the Indians trimmed their six run deficit to 6-5.

But that was only the beginning - and, almost immediately. Hart said he detected a turnaround.

"We all know (and) the players all know that we haven't hit our stride," said the general manager.

This time Hart proved to be only partly right.

Vizquel's slam gave McDowell new life, though he couldn't capitalize and was chased in the third when Swindell came on to put down a rally.

Then Swindell gave up another run on Jose Canseco's homer in the fourth before the Indians fought back again in the bottom of the inning. Again Vizquel played a key role, and he also did in the seventh.

In the sixth, Vizquel delivered a double, following singles by Baerga and Alomar, driving in one run. Another, tying the score, came home on an error, and Franco singled with one out for a go ahead run.

Vizquel singled again in the seventh, after Murray led with a double, for an insurance run.

Actually, the Indians should have scored at least two insurance runs on Vizquel's hit, but Ramirez, in another base running blunder, was thrown out at the plate because he failed to slide.

But one run was still enough for Swindell and four more relievers - Plunk in the fifth, sixth and seventh, Assenmacher and Shuey in the eighth, and Mesa, who needed only eight pitches in the ninth in shrugging off a hit to record his 23rd save.

GROWING CONCERN ABOUT McDOWELL

It turned out to be a particularly productive night for the Indians as their Central Division lead climbed to three games as the White Sox. after winning 19 of 22 games, lost their fourth in a row and sixth in seven, 5-4, to California.

Despite Vizquel's offensive prowess, all the news about him was not good. It was revealed before the game that his ailing right shoulder had grown worse.

"I don't know if I'm going to be able to make it through the entire season," he said. "It hurts on and off ... it really depends on how much working out I do. I know I can't throw like I normally do. Sometimes I almost have to push the ball over (to first base)."

There also was growing concern about McDowell, in the wake of his second consecutive failure - and before Hershiser and the Indians overwhelmed the Red Sox in the second game of the series, June 19.

The company line on McDowell was, "Jack's back has been bothering him a little, but that's not an excuse," according to pitching coach Mark Wiley. "Like a lot of pitchers, Jack is just going through a period where he is out of his rhythm."

Wiley attributed McDowell's poor performance against the Red Sox to the fact that he had not been able to work out between starts, because of the sore back.

"The big thing is simply that, most of the time, Jack is trying to make too good a pitch. He's trying to make the hitter miss the ball instead of just going out and pitching the way he can. He's not attacking hitters the way he used to. He's too tentative."

The same certainly could not be said for Hershiser who apparently was over his slump, pitching six scoreless innings to beat the Red Sox, 11-4, on June 19. It boosted his record to 7-4, and the Indians' lead to four games over the White Sox, who lost again to California, 14-2.

Boston scored its runs off Poole, with two in the seventh and eighth, and Assenmacher, with one in the ninth - though the issue was all but settled by the time Hershiser left.

"I'm in a groove right now, and the good thing about it is that now I can go back to certain mechanical checkpoints if I go bad again," said Hershiser.

Franco solo homered in the first inning, and Murray hit a two run homer in the second when the Indians went ahead, 5-0. It was Murray's eighth of the season and 487th of his career.

A NEW CLUB RECORD FOR HOMERS

In the finale of the Red Sox series, June 20, Thome and Ramirez homered - it was the 17th consecutive game the Indians had hit at least one homer, setting a new club record - but it took a ninth inning rally ignited by Tony Pena, that was climaxed by another clutch hit by Lofton to win it.

Pena started the ninth with a bloop double to right. "I knew I had to be on second base if the ball dropped," said Pena. Burnitz pinch ran for Pena, Vizquel bunted him to third, and Lofton looped a single to center off Mike Stanton.

"That's what you call good team hitting," said coach Charlie Manuel.

The team pitching also could have been called good, after Ogea got past the third inning in which he gave up three hits with one out, and two more with two outs as the Red Sox scored all their runs. "After the fourth, Chad was fine, and so was Shuey (in the eighth and ninth)," said Hargrove.

The Indians scored single runs in each the first, fourth, fifth and eighth, before Pena and Lofton won it with their hits in the ninth

Shuey shut out the Red Sox in the final two innings, providing the Indians their 13th straight victory over Boston.

It was the fifth game the Indians won in their last at-bat, compared to 29 in 1995, although when that statistic was mentioned, Hargrove grumbled,

"I'm tired of talking about last year."

The victory added another game to the Tribe's lead, boosting it to five as the White Sox lost for the sixth time in a row, 8-5, to Seattle.

YANKEES SWEEP THE TRIBE

But just as suddenly as the Tribe's fortunes had switched from bad to good - and Chicago's went from good to bad - the Indians faltered again.

It coincided with the Yankees' return visit to Jacobs Field and continued, albeit not immediately, in Boston

With Belle serving his two game suspension in the day-night double header on June 21 that opened the four game series against New York - and, perhaps, *because* of his absence - the Yankees beat the Indians, 8-7 in 10 innings, and 9-3.

Then, despite Belle's return the next day, New York also won the next two games, 11-9, and 6-5.

Mesa, who seemed to have regained the skill that had made him the most dominant closer in the major leagues in 1995 and the first three months of 1996, converted a total of 69 saves in 72 opportunities. But this time he was the culprit - though not the only one - in the first loss.

Mesa surrendered four runs in 1 2/3 innings after entering the game in the ninth with the Indians holding a 6-4 lead. Nagy, who figured to be the winner of his ninth consecutive game for a 12-1 record, pitched into the eighth on a yield of three runs on five hits.

Assenmacher was charged with another run before getting through the eighth, and then the Yankees blew off the lid against Mesa. It was only his second blown save of the season, and fourth in 73 opportunities over two seasons.

It also was the sixth time the bull pen had blown a save in 31 chances in 1996, and the first time in Nagy's 15 starts that he'd left a game with a lead that the relief corps didn't protect.

Even before Nagy went to the showers he was preceded by Alomar. The catcher was ejected by plate umpire Tim Tschida in the fifth inning for arguing a fourth ball call on Wade Boggs.

"Sandy never says a word back there unless he feels strongly about it," said Hargrove, obviously supporting his catcher's complaints.

Gerald Williams started Mesa's downfall with a single leading off the ninth. Mike Aldrete did the same and Boggs walked again, loading the bases. Mesa fanned Jeter, but Paul O'Neill followed with another single cutting the Indians' lead to 6-5, but the tying run scored as Tino Martinez grounded out.

Mesa struck out Bernie Williams to end the inning. But the damage was done, the game was tied, and more trouble developed in the 10th for Mesa and Poole - and the Tribe.

It began with one out as Mesa walked Girardi. He struck out Gerald Williams, but pinch hitter Mariano Duncan singled. The hit finished Mesa but Poole was no improvement. He immediately walked Boggs and Jeter singled for two runs before the inning ended.

'NOBODY CAN BE PERFECT' - HARGROVE

The Indians got one run back in their half of the 10th as Burnitz, playing in place of Belle, solo homered, but the magic that had helped them go 13-0 in extra inning games in 1995 was missing.

The blow by Burnitz extended the Indians' homer streak to a club record 18 consecutive games.

And a seventh inning single by Murray was his 3,141st hit, one away from tying him with Robin Yount in 13th place on baseball's all-time list. The late Paul Waner was 12th with 3,152.

Of Mesa's performance, Hargrove said, "Nobody can be perfect. It always comes as a shock when it happens. He just looked a little tentative."

Mesa wouldn't talk.

Joe Torre, the Yankees manager, called it "a huge win," which it was. "To come back and score seven runs in the last three innings is more than we could have expected, especially when we haven't been hitting the last week," he said.

Not only did it give Torre's team a boost in morale, it obviously also provided the Yankees with momentum. They scored seven runs in the first three innings of the second game, bombing Tavarez, who was making his first major league start since May 26, 1994.

Four hits produced two runs in the first, another run scored in the second, and Andy Fox's two run homer, that kayoed Tavarez, was the big blow of the four run third.

Most of the fans among the 87th consecutive sellout crowd of 42,454 in Jacobs Field cheered derisively when Tavarez was removed.

"There was nothing wrong with (Tavarez's) velocity ... his sinker was flat and, in his last two or three outings he's lost command of his pitches," Hargrove said of Tavarez.

Ramirez was another Tribesman whose efforts were not appreciated by the fans in the second game debacle. Ramirez was soundly booed when he did not run as hard as expected in an unsuccessful attempt to catch a fly ball off the bat of Tino Martinez in the fourth inning.

Hargrove also expressed his displeasure. "I told Manny that's not the way we play here. I put him on notice not to play that way again."

Swindell came on to pitch 5 1/3 strong innings, but by then the damage was done and the Indians were unable to catch up.

MARTINEZ LOSES TO YANKEES AGAIN

It got worse for the Indians in their next two games. In their loss to the Yankees in Game 3 of the series on June 22 - despite Belle's return from a two game suspension - Martinez blew a 5-0, five inning lead, and Ramirez didn't help with some more weird base running.

Martinez's lifetime record against New York fell to 2-17, and 0-8 since he joined the Indians in 1994. The Yankees erupted for nine runs in the sixth inning, highlighted by a three run homer by Sierra that tied the score.

After Sierra's homer, Martinez pitched to one more batter, Aldrete, who singled with one out, and was replaced on the mound only to have the bull pen fail again.

This time it was Plunk, and then Alan Embree and Shuey who were the culprits, before Poole pitched a scoreless ninth.

By then, however, it was too late for the Indians.

The Indians rallied for two runs in their half of the sixth, cutting their deficit to 9-8, but never got any closer. The Yankees added single runs in the seventh and eighth, enabling them to withstand the Tribe's last gasp, one run rally in the ninth. Ramirez's base running *faux pas* occurred in the sixth with him on second and the bases loaded, nobody out and two runs in, cutting the Tribe's deficit to 9-7.

Baerga lined what appeared to Ramirez would be a hit to center. He took off with the crack of the bat, but Jeter, racing to his left, snared the ball and Ramirez was easily doubled.

"Manny's base running error cut the inning a little short," said an obviously frustrated Hargrove. "You're taught to freeze on line drives and wait to see if they get through the infield. There was nobody out. He should have frozen, and he didn't.

"Manny Ramirez is a great talent who is having trouble with the finer points of the game." Indeed he was. The entire season.

The third run of the Indians' early lead was Murray's fourth inning leadoff homer against Kenny Rogers. It was Murray's 10th of the season, drawing him to within 11 of his goal to hit 500. He also singled giving him 3,143 career hits for sole possession of 13th place all-time.

THOME: 'I SCREWED UP'

Thome also suffered a case of brain-lock on the bases in the ninth inning when the Indians were trying to mount another comeback.

After Baerga opened the inning with a single, Thome tripled for the run that cut the Yankees' lead to 11-9.

One out later Lofton lofted what should have been a sacrifice fly to center. But it wasn't because Thome also failed to tag, instead breaking for home when the ball was hit and was halfway to the plate when the catch was made.

Thus, he had to scramble back to third and died there when Vizquel flied out.

"I screwed up," was Thome's only explanation. "I wasn't thinking."

Embree's appearance marked his third tour with the Indians after being recalled from Buffalo earlier in the day in exchange for Herbert Perry.

It was the team's 12th roster move of the season, and gave the Indians a 13 man relief corps that Hart and Hargrove felt was necessary, in view of the recent circumstances.

"We felt the bull pen was stretched thin because of the day-night double header and the rain delays we had earlier in the week, but we won't stay at 13 for long," said Hart.

It also was during the 11-9 loss to the Yankees on June 22 that Franco suffered a pulled right hamstring running from first to third base in the sixth inning and had to be replaced.

"If the injury to Julio is serious, the timing is bad," said Hargrove.

"When you send a guy out, he has to stay in the minors for 10 days unless there is an injury."

In this case the "timing" to which Hargrove referred was the decision to demote Perry, a first baseman, to make room for the return of Embree.

It was bad because, as it turned out, Franco's hamstring injury would plague him for more than two months and the situation would be further complicated by Murray's inability - or *unwillingness* - to play first base.

INDIANS LOSE 14th OF 27

It was more of the same the next day as the Yankees won 6-5, completing their sweep and giving the Indians 14 losses in 27 games dating back to May 26 when they had a four game lead over Chicago.

The only saving grace was that the White Sox, who had won 19 of 22 games to climb within a half game of the Indians on June 14, then went on to lose eight straight through June 22, falling back once again to 4 1/2 behind.

Still, the Tribe was in near disarray after the Yankees left town and there were rumors - despite the Indians' early season success on the heels of their remarkably easy march to the pennant in 1995 - that Hargrove's job was in jeopardy.

Hart denied the speculation and Hargrove wouldn't comment, saying only, "I have no control over what people think."

McDowell didn't help matters by failing again in the finale against the Yankees, giving up all six of New York's runs, including solo homers by O'Neill, Tino Martinez and Bernie Williams in 6 1/3 innings.

Williams' homer broke a 2-2 tie in the sixth, and New York went ahead, 6-2 in the seventh on a two run triple by Boggs that kayoed McDowell.

The Indians rallied on Baerga's two run homer off Gooden in their half of the seventh, but fell a run short in the eighth when Burnitz walked, Alomar singled and Lofton lofted a sacrifice fly. Wetteland earned his 22nd save in the ninth.

Now, in seven starts since May 16, McDowell's record was only 1-5 with a 6.59 ERA, though he denied having any physical problems.

"It seemed that every mistake Jack made went over the fence," Alomar said of the home runs allowed by McDowell.

"Jack doesn't like to talk about mechanics," said Hargrove. "He says he goes through something like this every season and then, once he finds (his split-finger fast ball) he locks in and he's OK the rest of the year."

It was the first time the Indians were swept in a four game series at home since 1994, and raised the Yankees' 2 1/2 season record to 12-2 (and 6-0 in 1996) at Jacobs Field, where the Indians are 111-35 against the rest of the A.L.

Will the Yankees' success against the Indians be a factor in the postseason? "No, not necessarily, because everything goes out the window in the playoffs," said Boggs.

"Baseball is a fickle game," said Wetteland. "Because we swept them doesn't mean the Indians are not a great team. They are. They have an extremely dangerous lineup."

"The Yankees definitely are the best team we've played this year," said

Baerga. "If they didn't play great defense in this series, we would have won three games," although Hargrove's analysis was a little different.

"Our pitching, with a few exceptions, didn't show up," said Hargrove.

In the four losses to the Yankees the Indians' bull pen - which previously had been a strength - compiled a cumulative 7.04 ERA, allowing 12 earned runs on 13 walks and 21 hits in 21 2/3 innings.

The fourth loss to New York cut the Indians' lead to 3 1/2 games as Chicago halted its losing streak, beating Seattle, 7-6, in 10 innings. It set the stage for eight games between the White Sox and Indians in the next 13 days.

KENNEDY: 'WE'LL HAVE OUR DAY'

But first the Indians had a two game date in Boston, against the usually cooperative Red Sox, whom they'd beaten 10 straight in 1996, and 13 in a row going back to the 1995 division playoffs.

"It's awful, it's thoroughly embarrassing," Red Sox manager Kevin Kennedy said of his team's inability - to date - to beat the Tribe. "I know people are laughing at us, but we'll have our day. We have too many fighters on this team and we'll pay 'em back."

The payback didn't begin immediately, thanks to Hershiser, who combined with Shuey to hurl a seven hit, 4-0 victory on June 25. It was Hershiser's fourth straight triumph. In those four games Hershiser allowed two earned runs in 27 1/3 innings with 16 strikeouts, six walks and an 0.66 ERA.

Those four games came in the wake of a six game slump, from May 7 to June 2, in which Hershiser failed to pitch more than five innings in four of those starts.

"I can't tell you what I found," Hershiser said, "because if I go into a slump again you can say, 'Swell, why don't you just do this.' But I wasn't over thinking (during the losing streak), it was something physical."

In his seven innings against the Red Sox, Hershiser yielded five hits, struck out two and walked one.

He was supported by Murray, Ramirez and Thome, all of whom hit homers - Murray's and Ramirez's back-to-back off Tom Gordon in the sixth. Murray's was the 489th of his career, and 10th of the season.

For Ramirez, coming off a homestand in which he hit .160 (4-for-25) and was booed for his lack of hustle in right field and his mistakes on the base paths, it was homer No. 18. Thome's homer was his 15th.

BAERGA TRADE RUMORS BEGIN

It was June 24, the day before the Indians-Red Sox series began, an open-date in the schedule, that a rumor surfaced for the first time that Baerga, a favorite of Cleveland fans since 1990, might be traded.

The story first appeared in the Lake County *News Herald* and Lorain *Morning Journal* under the byline of Jim Ingraham, saying that trade talks involving Baerga were going on between Hart and the Florida Marlins.

Coming to the Indians, it was speculated by Ingraham, were outfielder Jeff Conine and infielder Kurt Abbott, though Hart immediately denied the report.

"This is totally and officially unfounded," said Hart. "It's not accurate (and) there's no point in discussing it further."

Then he did, saying, "This is a joke, a joke. It's not happening. Carlos Baerga is going nowhere. The whole thing is bizarre. Just bizarre."

Still, there was no doubt that the Indians were disappointed in Baerga's performances to date. A career .305 hitter who had averaged nearly 18 homers in each of his five full seasons with the Tribe, Baerga was batting .273 with eight homers and 46 RBI.

Perhaps even more important, Baerga's range at second base had fallen off noticeably. Some in the Tribe hierarchy blamed it on the fact that he came to training camp overweight and out of shape, and also that he did not work as hard in pre-game practice as previously.

In Ingraham's report it was further speculated that the Indians wanted Conine to play first base so that they would be free to unload Murray and have Franco be a full time designated hitter.

"We haven't even considered that," said Hart. "It's so far-fetched it's not worth a comment."

Also, during the open date prior to the Boston series, Hargrove announced that, henceforth, Jeff Newman would return to his duties as third base coach. He replaced Toby Harrah, who would become bench coach.

"For five years I've thought Jeff was one of the best third base coaches in the league," said Hargrove. "Toby did a good job, but I think our players are more familiar with Jeff's style."

Harrah called it a "great move." He said, "I'll do anything I can to help this club win."

Newman said, "I told Mike I'd do whatever he wanted me to do."

Hargrove denied that the switch was made because the Indians have suffered several base running mistakes at third base. "That's not the reason we made the move," he said.

MESA BLOWS ANOTHER SAVE

The Indians' success against the Red Sox - call it skill, luck, or whatever - ended the next night, June 26, as Kennedy's promised "payback" resulted in a 6-4, 15 inning victory over the Indians as Mesa failed again.

This time the ace reliever was unable to protect a 4-1 Tribe lead in the ninth, and the Red Sox prevailed in the sixth extra inning on a two run homer by Tim Naehring off Embree.

It was the ninth homer Embree had allowed in 21 2/3 innings in 1996.

But the game never should have gone into overtime - at least not considering how well Nagy had pitched through the first eight innings.

It was the second consecutive save opportunity that Mesa was unable to convert, both of them wiping out victories for Nagy, who was 8-0 in his previous 10 starts.

It also gave Mesa three blown saves in his previous eight appearances in which he allowed more earned runs (12) than he did in 62 games in 1995 (when he gave up only eight). Overall his ERA climbed to 4.64. Last year it was 1.13.

In this one, Nagy had allowed only four hits and one run before Hargrove called for Mesa to close out the game in the ninth.

John Valentin greeted Mesa with a homer and, after Mo Vaughn was retired, Canseco and Mike Stanley singled. Canseco scored on a soft single to center by Reggie Jefferson, and Naehring brought in the tying run with another single.

Assenmacher came on to get the second out, then Plunk got the third and the game went into overtime, during which the Indians loaded the bases in each the 10th and 11th innings, but failed to score.

A major factor in the loss, the Indians' sixth in seven games, was the fact that Lofton got himself ejected by umpire Larry Young in the very first inning for arguing a called third strike.

With Franco on the bench for a third straight game nursing a pulled right hamstring, Hargrove's hands were tied as he had only backup catcher Tony Pena in reserve (because the team was carrying 13 pitchers).

After the game the Indians returned Embree to Buffalo and activated utility infielder Scott Leius from the disabled list.

The Indians' penchant for arguing with umpires - and often getting themselves ejected - had suddenly become a problem, one that Hargrove addressed with Lofton afterwards.

Getting a reputation as a whiner "is something all players have to guard against," said Hargrove.

"Kenny said he didn't say anything bad (to Young), but I guess he said it to the wrong guy, which is what I talked to him about."

READY FOR THE WHITE SOX

With that, and their lead over the idle White Sox down to three games, the Indians flew into the Windy City for another head-to-head confrontation with Chicago with first place at stake.

The two teams would play eight games - four in Chicago and four in Cleveland - in the next 11 days to conclude the first half of the season and set the stage for the All-Star Game.

8

FIRST HALF WAS
NO CAKE WALK

June 27-July 7

The principals insisted there was nothing "crucial" about the four game series between the Indians and White Sox in Chicago, June 27-30.

"Seriously? The Indians are here? Heck, I thought we played them next week," dead panned White Sox shortstop Ozzie Guillen.

Then, "The Indians, huh? OK. Let's play the Indians. That's fine with me."

On the other side of the field, Orel Hershiser was equally low key.

"I haven't heard any of our guys talking about it," he said of the head-to-head confrontation that could wipe out the Tribe's three game lead over the White Sox.

"It's great for the fans, but after this series there's still so much time left that even if one team or the other sweeps the series, there's still time to make up the ground. Maybe all that's at stake is a psychological edge."

Of the Indians' fortunes to date, Hershiser said, "We feel we're playing just as well as last year. Our record is a little behind last year's, but the key is that Chicago has been playing so much better."

The White Sox went 19-3 in a hot streak that ended June 10, vaulting them into a tie with the Tribe for first place.

But then they lost nine of their next 13, including eight straight, before starting the four game series against the Indians in Chicago that some considered "crucial."

Immediate history favored the Indians. They had won the only two meetings of the teams in 1996, 5-3 and 9-5, on April 30 and May 1, and were 8-5 against Chicago in 1995.

But in 30 games in new Comiskey Park since it was opened in 1991, the Indians' record there was only 9-21.

"This is a pretty important series for both of us because we haven't played each other in almost a month," said Mike Hargrove. "But it's not what I'd call a huge series."

BEVINGTON: 'WE'RE CHASING OURSELVES'

And Chicago Manager Terry Bevington practically sneered at those who suggested that it was necessary for the White Sox to win at least three of the four games to prevent another runaway by the Indians.

"We're not trying to catch anyone," he said. "We're not chasing anyone. Most of the time the only team we are chasing is ourselves. All we are trying to do is perform up to our capabilities."

When asked if he thought the Indians were as good as they were in 1995 when they finished 32 games ahead of the White Sox, Bevington said, "I wouldn't comment on something like that."

But then, "It's safe to say, though, that most of (the Indians) had career years last season. It is not to say that it can't happen again, but it will be tough."

Ron Schueler, the White Sox general manager who said in spring training that the Indians' pitching was "a little suspect" because of the advanced ages of Dennis Martinez, Hershiser and Jack McDowell, declined to react to what the fans considered to be a pressure-packed series.

"So far, we're not too far off," said Schueler, "but I'm not going to get into a war of words. These are two good teams. Let's let them settle it themselves."

Which they did - and, initially, it seemed like an impending disaster for the Indians.

Greg Swindell was routed by the White Sox in the opener as he was making his first start for the Tribe since rejoining the team on June 15, following his release by Houston.

"I'm not trying to prove anything to anybody right now," he said before the game. "I've been trying to do that for the last three years and it hurt me. The only person I'm trying to prove something to is myself."

All that Swindell proved - to anybody - was that he didn't have much of anything in that game. After the Indians took a 2-0 lead in the first inning, Swindell was kayoed in the second, charged with six hits and seven runs, and the Indians lost, 15-10.

TRIBE LEAD SHRINKS TO TWO

It was their sixth setback in seven games, 16th in their last 30, and cut their lead to two over Chicago. It was a deficit the White Sox could make up the next two nights, and overcome in the finale of the series.

To make matters worse, Chad Ogea was no improvement over Swindell as he was charged with three more runs before getting out of the second inning with the White Sox ahead, 10-2.

After falling behind, 14-3, the Indians tried to fight back in the sixth inning. Carlos Baerga solo homered and Manny Ramirez hit his second homer of the game, cutting their deficit to 14-5.

After Robin Ventura homered off Jim Poole in the bottom of the sixth, Scott Leius whacked a three run homer in the seventh, making it 15-8. But the Indians were held to single runs in each the eighth and ninth.

And, during the loss, Albert Belle became embroiled in another incident that further tarnished his image.

This time he was accused of intentionally throwing a cup of Gatorade on WGN television cameraman Wyn Griffiths and his camera during the seventh inning

Belle, as has been his custom, refused to comment, but Kenny Lofton and coach Dave Nelson both called it an accident. They insisted that Belle only tried to kick the cup of Gatorade out of the dugout and the contents splashed the cameraman.

However, Griffiths claimed, "I was shooting something completely away from the dugout at the time. Belle came over and got a drink. He took a cup of pink Gatorade, that sticky stuff, and threw it on me and the camera.

"As soon as Belle threw it, he walked into the dugout (tunnel) and didn't say a word."

Hargrove said he didn't see what happened and couldn't comment.

In yet another alleged incident, which was reported by the Chicago *Tribune,* Belle and a reporter argued behind the batting cage prior to game.

According to the *Tribune,* Belle said to the unidentified reporter, "Get out of the way."

The reporter replied, "Look Albert, you tried your intimidation thing on me last year ... I'm not putting up with any more of your (abuse)."

Then Belle was supposed to have responded, "I'm going to take my right foot and place it so far ... they'll never be able to find it."

The reporter said, "Go ahead, I wish you'd try."

The incident ended with that.

Hargrove said, "We've talked to (Belle) 100 times, telling him that he's got to realize that when he blinks, it's taken negatively.

"Do I think it's fair? No. But then again, a lot of what's happening he's brought on to himself."

OGEA IS NO IMPROVEMENT

Of Swindell's pitching problems, Hargrove said, "Greg had a lot of trouble getting his change-up over. He had to come in with his fast ball and he put it in the wrong spots."

As for Ogea, who was victimized by an error by Jim Thome in the second inning, the manager said, "Chad couldn't make a pitch after that error."

Jose Mesa pitched the ninth and was only so-so, leaving some doubt in the minds of Hargrove and pitching coach Mark Wiley. Mesa had failed to convert his last two save opportunities, which contributed greatly to the Indians' skid going into the Chicago series.

Regarding Mesa, who was 23-for-26 in save situations, Hargrove said, "It's more of a problem than it was a week ago (and) there are some things we have to talk to him about.

"To me, in the loss to Boston (the previous day) Jose wasn't throwing as hard as he is capable of doing, and I don't know why."

But the poor pitching that cost the loss to the White Sox wasn't the extent of the bad news.

First, Julio Franco returned to the lineup after sitting out three games because of a pulled right hamstring, but reinjured his leg in the eighth inning. He had to be replaced at first base by Sandy Alomar.

The Indians also received word that Herbert Perry, the Tribe's first baseman of the future - and who would have been recalled to fill in for Franco - had undergone surgery a few days earlier to repair a torn cartilage in his left knee.

Perry suffered the injury at Class AAA Buffalo and was not expected to play the rest of the season.

HARGROVE GROWS IMPATIENT

Hargrove's growing impatience began to show more distinctly the next night, June 28, before the White Sox won again, 4-2, cutting the Indians' lead to one game.

Hargrove held a 40 minute clubhouse meeting, during which he reportedly came down hard on Ramirez, for his base running blunders and often lack of hustle.

He also was critical of Lofton's complaints to umpires that, most recently in Boston on June 26, resulted in his first inning ejection, leaving the Indians short handed.

All Hargrove would say of the meeting was, "It's been the way we've played the last three weeks. We needed to talk about some things. I think we may have lost some of our focus."

Lofton's ejection was the sixth for the Indians in 77 games. Chased earlier were Martinez on April 24, Eddie Murray on May 11, Lofton on May 22, Hargrove on June 10, and Alomar on June 21.

"Getting a reputation for being whiners is something we have to guard against," said Hargrove.

The meeting did not produce an immediate improvement as Martinez was forced out of the game in the fourth inning with a strained flexor muscle in his right forearm that would prematurely end his season.

The Indians had staked Martinez to a 2-0 lead with a run in the first on singles by Omar Vizquel and Baerga around a Chicago error. Murray delivered his 11th and 290th career homer in the fourth.

But Poole, who replaced Martinez, permitted the White Sox to tie the game in the fifth. The rally was stomped out by Julian Tavarez, but he became the loser by yielding two more runs in the sixth.

Despite the loss, Poole was upbeat. "First of all," he said, "when I open the sports page tomorrow, we'll still be in first place. Second, it's only June. And third, we have a damn good club. We'll be all right."

CAN HE, OR WON'T HE PLAY FIRST BASE?

Something else that came out of the game - with Leius forced to play first base because of Franco's injury - was a column by Bud Shaw in the Cleveland *Plain Dealer*. In it Murray was criticized for his apparent unwillingness to play in the field.

Significantly, neither General Manager John Hart, nor Hargrove, Murray or anybody else challenged the accuracy of Shaw's report.

Murray had said he was unable to play first base because of a sore left shoulder, although, as Shaw pointed out, it didn't prevent him from swinging a bat.

Earlier in the season he had been accused of being resentful because Hart had, first, tried to replace him with Paul Molitor or Mark Grace during the off-season, then of cutting his salary by $1 million to $2 million.

Hart's only comment on the situation: "When I heard Eddie couldn't play (first base), I was a little taken aback."

And this: "Knowing Eddie as the professional that he is, I think he can divorce himself from whatever perceived problem there might be in relation to his contract."

INDIANS REGAIN TWO GAME LEAD

The Indians finally regained their winning ways, and their three game lead, with victories the next two days.

They beat the White Sox, 3-2 in 10 innings, as McDowell pitched his best game (but didn't get the victory) on June 29, and 4-2 the next night, as Hershiser won his fifth straight for a 9-4 record.

It helped Hershiser win the A.L. "Pitcher of the Month" award for June.

McDowell pitched eight strong innings, allowing his former teammates one run on six hits. The Indians prevailed on Thome's two run, two out single in the 10th after three walks (two intentional) had loaded the bases.

The White Sox retaliated for a run on Frank Thomas's 22nd homer off Paul Shuey in the bottom of the 10th, but the next two batters were retired.

"We all knew we needed to kick ourselves in the butts and get going," said McDowell, whose record held at 6-6, but was only 1-5 in his previous seven starts. "We did not want to leave here in a hole and then ask ourselves, 'How did we get here?'"

Thome echoed McDowell. "Everybody was getting a little tight around here," he said. "This should loosen us up. If we come out of it with a split, it's going to make for a fun time when (the White Sox) come to our place next week."

It was interesting that Hargrove turned to Shuey in the 10th inning save situation, though the manager was unwilling to say that Mesa no longer was in that role.

"Shuey was hot and he was in the strike zone," was the only explanation Hargrove offered for not going to Mesa.

Before the game the Indians placed Martinez on the 15 day disabled list and recalled relief pitcher Danny Graves from Buffalo. In 33 games with the Bisons, Graves was 3-1 with a 1.34 ERA and 17 saves.

Hargrove said Graves would take Tavarez's place in middle relief, that Tavarez would fill in for Martinez in the starting rotation, and that Ogea would be the fifth starter, replacing Swindell.

Tavarez started once previously in 1996 (and was ripped by the Yankees), and Ogea had three starts among his 11 appearances.

INDIANS GO 14-14 IN JUNE

Hershiser's performance on June 30 was impressive, despite his inability to go all the way , and though Mesa was shaky in the ninth, giving up a run on two hits and a walk, he protected the victory.

"Orel has found his sinker," Hargrove said of Hershiser, who scattered five singles and struck out three. The only run charged to Hershiser was unearned because of an error by Leius, following a walk and a hit by Guillen.

But the Indians retaliated with three runs in the fifth on back-to-back doubles by Murray and Ramirez, and Alomar's sixth homer. Singles by Alomar and Lofton, made it 4-1 in the seventh.

"I just got tired," Hershiser said of his departure after eight innings, "and in that situation Jose (Mesa) is a lot better than I am."

The choice of Mesa to close the game came as a surprise to some. Hargrove had indicated that Shuey had been promoted to that role in view of Mesa's slump in blowing his previous two save opportunities.

"We've got to start rebuilding Jose's confidence," is the way Hargrove explained the move - which provided a few anxious moments before the issue was settled.

Mesa gave up a leadoff single to Thomas. Then, after retiring the next two batters, walked Ray Durham. Norberto Martin followed by lofting a pop fly in short right field that Baerga couldn't hold and was ruled a single, scoring Thomas.

At that point, "My spine started to tingle," said Hargrove. "I don't know whose palms were sweating more, mine or (pitching coach) Mark Wiley's."

He could have added that Hershiser undoubtedly was worried, too.

But Mesa ended the uprising by getting Ron Karkovice to fly out.

It gave the Indians a .500 record in June, but enabled them to leave Chicago in as good a position - with a three game lead - as when they'd arrived four days earlier.

Bevington claimed to be undaunted by his team's inability to gain ground on the Tribe in the series that he'd earlier insisted was not crucial.

"It's who's in first (place) on the last day of the year, not who's in first on June 30," he said. "Every game is a big game."

Hargrove was low-key, too. "I don't think (that winning the last two games of the series) proves anything except that we're two evenly matched teams and I think it's going to be a race all year," he said.

ANOTHER CHALLENGE IN FOUR DAYS

There certainly would be more to prove soon.

In just four more days, following a three game series against the hapless Kansas City Royals who were lodged in the basement of the A.L. Central with a 34-47 record, 15 1/2 games off the pace, the White Sox would challenge the Indians again, this time in Cleveland, July 4-7.

And it wouldn't be coming at a particularly good time for the Tribe.

In addition to the ongoing uneasiness regarding Mesa, there also was some concern about Belle, who hit only four homers in June (compared to 12 in May), and was in the throes of a slump for more than a month.

In the wake of all the negative publicity he'd been receiving since that May 28 squabble with a fan in Arlington, Texas who refused to give up the ball he'd hit for his 21st homer, Belle had batted just .226.

It was even worse during the month of June. Belle hit only .200 since May 31, when he collided with Brewers second baseman Fernando Vina and became the focal point of criticism by fans outside of Cleveland.

Though Belle's average was a still-respectable .306 on July 1, it was .043 less than it had been a month earlier. It led to speculation that Belle was beginning to hear - and be affected by - the vocal abuse heaped upon him everywhere the Indians played away from Jacobs Field.

A RECORD FIFTH STRAIGHT LOSS AT HOME

Despite the slump, and Belle's apparent unpopularity around the league, he and Lofton were among the leading vote-getters for starting positions on the A.L. all-star team.

After it was announced on July 1 that Belle had received 1.7 million votes, second only to Seattle's Ken Griffey Jr. among A.L outfielders, he ended his 15 game and 57 at-bat homerless streak against Kansas City, though the Royals beat the Tribe, 4-2.

It was a record fifth straight setback at home for the Indians in front of 40,814 fans who comprised the 90th consecutive sellout crowd in Jacobs Field, an ongoing major league record.

The loss, the Tribe's eighth in 11 games, had no effect on the standings though, as the White Sox also were beaten, 10-7, by Minnesota, and remained in second place, three lengths behind.

Charles Nagy, who hadn't lost since April 27 - and the next day would be named the A.L.'s starting pitcher in the All-Star Game - was hit hard by the Royals, relinquishing eight hits, four for extra bases, and all of K.C.'s runs in seven innings.

"I threw a lot of bad pitches, they hit four of them and it cost me," said Nagy, whose record fell to 11-2, second best in the A.L. to New York's Andy Pettitte (12-4). It was only Nagy's fourth loss since June 28, 1995.

One of those "bad" pitches became Mike Macfarlane's eighth homer in the first inning. Belle solo homered to tie the score in the second, and Baerga's two out single scored Alvaro Espinoza for a 2-1 Tribe lead in the third.

But Macfarlane re-tied it with his second homer in the fourth. Then the Royals went ahead on another homer by Joe Randa in the fifth, the same inning in which Keith Lockhart jumped on another of Nagy's "bad" pitches for a run scoring double after Johnny Damon singled.

Hargrove wouldn't blame the loss on the fact that the Indians were flat in the wake of the big series in Chicago.

"There was so much emotion and tension in the series against the White Sox that, frankly, there was some concern about a letdown," he admitted. "We talked about it before the game, but I didn't sense a problem. Their guy (Chris Haney) just threw a very good game."

It was the Indians' 81st game - the exact halfway point in the season - and left them with a 49-32 won-lost record, compared to 57-24 in 1995 when they led the Central Division by 15 1/2 games. (They also were in first place in the A.L. Central by one length in 1994 with an identical 49-32 mark.)

THREE MORE TRIBE ALL-STARS

The next day, July 2, after it was announced that Hargrove had selected Nagy, Alomar and Mesa to join Belle and Lofton on the A.L. all-star team, the Indians bounced back to beat Kansas City, 3-2.

The victory was achieved in the bottom of the ninth as Franco, who'd missed the previous seven games because of a strained right hamstring, singled with two outs against Hipolito Pichardo. It broke a 2-2 tie and handed Tim Belcher his fourth loss in 10 decisions.

The Tribe's rally saved Mesa from more embarrassment as he failed for the third time in four save opportunities - and fourth in eight - yielding a run to the Royals in the top of the ninth.

Until then the Indians were clinging to a 2-1 lead in behalf of Ogea. The Royals broke on top, 1-0, in the fourth, Lofton smashed a solo homer in the sixth, and the Tribe went ahead in the eighth as Jeromy Burnitz was hit by a pitch, Lofton singled and Vizquel delivered a sacrifice fly.

Assenmacher and then Paul Shuey held the Royals at bay in the seventh and eighth, but Mesa asked for trouble upon taking over in the ninth.

He was greeted by Jose Offerman's double and, with one out, scampered to third on the first of two wild pitches by Mesa.

Quickly, however, the fans' dismay turned to cheers as Offerman was retired trying to score on Mesa's second wild pitch, but again the emotions of the fans - as well as the Indians - changed almost immediately.

Mesa walked David Howard who scored on successive singles by Damon and Tom Goodwin.

Poole was summoned and quickly complicated matters by walking Joe Vitiello, before finally ending the uprising by retiring Macfarlane - but only because Espinoza, playing first base, dug a bad throw from Thome out of the dirt for the third out.

But the Indians wouldn't give up, even after the first two batters in the bottom of the ninth went out, and despite a 50 minute rain delay before Ramirez launched the rally with a single.

Alomar followed with another hit, and Franco smacked a 2-and-0 pitch to right field to bring Ramirez home with the game winning run.

"The only thing on my mind during the rain delay was that I had to get a hit," said Franco.

The only thing on the reporters' minds after the game was Mesa, whose slump was getting serious.

"Jose is still our closer," Hargrove answered the obvious question. "We're just barely halfway through the season. At the first sign of trouble you can't go and take someone's job away."

However, then Hargrove added, "But we may have reached the point where we need to re-examine things."

In his last five games Mesa was 0-1 with 17.34 ERA after giving up nine runs on 15 hits in 4 2/3 innings, and was 24-for-28 in save opportunities for the season.

NO ALL-STAR RECOGNITION FOR FRANCO

Franco, incidentally, was conspicuously absent from the list of reserves chosen for the A.L. all-star team by Hargrove. He also was not among the leading vote-getters in the balloting by the fans despite his mid-season batting average of .326 with 10 homers and 55 RBI.

All of which could have created a problem for the Indians.

Included in Franco's two year, $4.5 million contract he signed on Dec. 7, 1995 was a $50,000 bonus he'd receive if selected to the all-star team.

However, the Indians did not nominate Franco as their first baseman on the ballot distributed to the fans, instead naming Murray at that position.

Franco, a three-time all-star and the A.L.'s Most Valuable Player in the 1990 game, acknowledged that it bothered him. "It would bother anyone, but there is nothing I can do about it," he said.

The next day Wiley embarked upon what was called "a rehabilitation program" for Mesa.

"(Mesa and Wiley) will work on things we feel will get Jose back to where he needs to be," said Hargrove. "He's doing things mechanically that don't allow him to put the ball where he wants it. He was overthrowing and couldn't control where the ball was going."

RECORD CROWD AT JACOBS FIELD

And then, despite Hargrove's vote of confidence for Mesa - "Jose is still our closer," he'd said - Shuey was called upon the next night, July 3, and blanked the Royals in the ninth inning to preserve a 6-4 victory for Tavarez.

It wasn't a perfect save for Shuey as he gave up a hit and walked a batter, and needed 22 pitches to close out the game, but Hargrove was satisfied.

So were the 42,470 fans who comprised the largest regular season crowd in Jacobs Field's two-plus year history.

"(Shuey) did what we wanted him to do," was the way Hargrove commended the performance, stopping short of saying the closer's job had been given to Shuey.

"It belongs to both Shuey and Mesa right now," he said.

With runners on first and second and one out, and pinch hitter Rod Myers at the plate, Wiley paid a visit to Shuey, while Mesa remained seated in the bull pen.

"I did exactly what Wiley told me," said Shuey. "He told me to keep the ball down and get a double play." He did.

"When the Indians called me up (for his fifth stint in the major leagues since being drafted No. 2 overall in 1992), I didn't expect anything like this, and I didn't know what to expect tonight. There's been absolutely no communication.

"I've heard a lot of stuff from reporters, but nothing from any coaches. I'll just keep pitching when they give me the ball. The way I look at it, if I'm still here after the All-Star break, it's a bonus."

Though Tavarez got the victory, his first as a starter since Aug. 19, 1993, it wasn't a particularly masterful performance. He gave up nine hits and four runs, including Craig Paquette's two run homer when the Royals took a 3-0 lead in the third inning.

Belle homered leading off the fourth. It was his 27th of the season, but only his second since June 12.

After K.C. went ahead, 4-1 in the fifth, the Indians rallied for five runs in the bottom of the inning on three consecutive walks, Thome's double, two more walks and Alomar's double. Swindell blanked the Royals from the sixth through the eighth.

The victory, coupled with the White Sox's 6-5 loss to Minnesota - it was their eighth defeat in 13 games - boosted the Tribe's lead over Chicago to four lengths.

And then it was time for the two teams to meet again, this time in Cleveland.

MESA FAILS AGAIN, AND TRIBE LOSES

This time it was not a save opportunity, but that didn't make losing to the White Sox any easier to take as Mesa failed again on July 4 in the opener of another "crucial" series that everybody said wasn't crucial.

The White Sox prevailed, 6-5, cutting the Indians' first place margin to three games, as Mesa took over a tie game in the 10th inning and, with one out, was tagged for a couple of soft singles by Durham and Guillen. Tony Phillips followed with a sacrifice fly that broke the deadlock.

Then Roberto Hernandez, Chicago's ace reliever who hag displaced Mesa as the A.L.'s premier closer, stopped the Tribe in the bottom of the 10th.

"Jose caught some bad luck today," Hargrove said of Mesa's performance. "This (getting Mesa back on track) is not going to be an overnight process. He didn't lose his confidence overnight, and he's not going to regain it overnight."

Equally discouraging as Mesa's inability to shut down the White Sox was McDowell's performance against his former teammates.

Staked to a 2-1 lead in the fifth, McDowell, winless since June 7 and the loser in two of his five starts since then, pitched out of a bases loaded jam by striking out two batters in the sixth.

But the White Sox got to McDowell with four straight hits that resulted in four runs in the seventh, and he was banished.

"This game has been the story of my year so far," said a crestfallen McDowell. "Things are just not working out." They surely were not.

The Indians took McDowell off the hook, tying the score with three runs in their half of the seventh, and Poole, Eric Plunk, Assenmacher and Shuey blanked Chicago through the ninth.

But the Indians couldn't score either, and - bad luck or whatever - Mesa let the game get away again.

"Everybody talks about Cleveland's lineup, but if you look at ours, one through nine, I think it's as good as anybody's in the game, and so is our pitching staff," said Durham.

"This thing isn't over yet," added Durham.

Under the circumstances - with Mesa and McDowell struggling, Martinez ailing, and the fifth spot in the starting rotation still unsettled - there was no dissenting opinion.

INDIANS ARE BOOED AFTER LOSING

It got even worse the next day, July 5 - so bad, in fact, that the 100th consecutive sellout crowd of 42,536 fans, who comprised another new regular season record at Jacobs Field, booed the Indians at the end.

Chicago won, 7-0, on a six hitter by Wilson Alvarez and Hernandez, cutting the Indians' lead to two games, and provided the White Sox with hope for a series sweep that would leave the teams tied at the All-Star break.

It was the first time the Tribe was shutout since Sept. 11, 1995.

"The last month has been frustrating for everybody," said Hargrove. "We can't seem to get anything sustained going."

It was, among other things, a pointed reference to the fact that the Indians' record since May 26 was 18-20, and that they'd lost 10 of their previous 15 games.

The loss was Hershiser's first after five consecutive victories in June, and his streak of scoreless innings was halted at 26, although he pitched much better than the score indicated.

Once again the bull pen failed, this time by Poole, who couldn't keep the Tribe close. He took over in the ninth, with the Tribe trailing, 2-0, and quickly let the game get out of hand.

Guillen's leadoff double, a walk, Alomar's error, two intentional walks around a double play, Ventura's double, and Karkovice's single produced five more runs before Poole got the third out.

"It was not very pleasant," Hargrove said. It was a massive understatement.

As for Hershiser, Hargrove said, "Orel pitched well enough ... we just didn't help him, either in the field or at the plate."

Or, for that matter, in the strategy department, though the White Sox rendered Hargrove's error in judgment a moot point.

With the Indians trailing by only 1-0 in the seventh inning, Guillen, leading off, reached second on an error by Franco, playing only his first game at first base in 12 games, since June 22 when he pulled a hamstring muscle in his right leg.

Hershiser retired the next two batters and, with Thomas at the plate, Hargrove elected to pitch to the White Sox slugger.

After fouling off four pitches, Thomas singled for a 2-0 lead, and everything that followed was downhill for the Tribe.

"It was a good battle and he got a hit," said Hershiser. "The key to the game was that they scored and we didn't ... not that Thomas got a hit in that situation."

Hargrove's explanation to the second guessers: "With (Harold) Baines up next, we tried to get Thomas out."

As for the Indians' dwindling lead, Hershiser said, "It's going to be a good, long second half to see who wins this thing. We have to take inventory of ourselves and see where we can improve - and we will."

Alvarez, the hard-throwing left hander whose record climbed to 10-4 with the victory, spoke of the renewed confidence it generated among the White Sox.

"By winning the first two games of this series," he said, "it means we have a chance to go home and start the second half in a first place tie. That would be nice."

VIZQUEL: 'THE BIG HORSES TALKED'

The Indians called a players-only meeting the next day, July 6, and a lot of things reportedly were said, some very forcefully during the 45 minute session.

"The big horses talked," said Vizquel. "Orel Hershiser jumped on some guys. He's trying to get them to play better. Eddie Murray and Tony Pena also talked. It was a pleasure to listen to them. They are guys who have been through everything there is in baseball. It was a good meeting."

But it made no immediate improvement.

The Indians lost again, 3-2, for the 21st time in 39 games, and their lead in the A.L. Central was cut to one measly game over the onrushing White Sox.

"It seemed like we would play with intensity for two innings, and then lose it," said Vizquel, although Franco said that wasn't the problem in this loss.

"We were alive out there," said the first baseman.

But, except for Thome, they didn't hit, and the White Sox did. Especially Baines, the same Harold Baines who went 1-for-12 in four games against the Indians earlier in the week, in a four game series in Chicago..

Thome solo homered in the fourth, but was upstaged by Baines, who smashed a two run homer in the seventh.

"I threw a split (finger fast ball) down and away and he went out and got it," said Nagy, who was deprived again of a victory that would have raised his record to 12-2. "It makes you second guess yourself. Maybe I should have busted him in."

The Indians tied it in the bottom of the seventh on doubles by Ramirez and Vizquel, and then it was time for Shuey to second guess himself.

After replacing Nagy in the ninth, Shuey retired Thomas, but Baines homered again. Then Hernandez registered his 26th save, shutting the Tribe down in the ninth.

"We wanted to take three of the four games here because you always want to win a series," said Baines.

"Now, we want to make it four-for-four and go into the break tied with the Indians."

OGEA FINALLY TAKES CHARGE

The slide finally ended on July 7, and none too soon. The Indians went into the All-Star break clinging precariously to a one game lead over the suddenly hot again White Sox, who'd won three straight and four of their last six.

The Tribe beat the White Sox, 6-1, as Ogea, finally established as the Indians' No. 5 starter by decree of Hargrove, pitched six strong innings, yielding only one run on Ventura's homer in the second.

That only tied the game, and the Indians got two runs in the third and another in the fifth, and knocked out Alex Fernandez in the seventh with two more runs.

Unlike the first three games of this important - "Don't call it crucial," the principals kept telling us - series that ended the first half of the season, the Indians delivered in the clutch and the pitchers kept the White Sox at bay.

Murray, still the subject of rumors that he'd be traded, reached another milestone in the seventh inning of the game. He singled for his 3,155th hit, moving him ahead of George Brett into 11th place on the all-time list.

With 11 homers, Murray still needed 10 that would vault him into the exalted and exclusive company of Hank Aaron and Willie Mays as the only players in baseball history with 3,000 hits and 500 homers.

"Our players really need this break," said Hargrove. "I think this club is tired mentally."

Though Hargrove didn't name anybody, there was no doubt he believed Mesa was among those who were tired - probably physically as well as mentally.

When Ogea needed relief in the seventh, it was Assenmacher who replaced him, and remained on the mound through the ninth, allowing only a harmless single and striking out four in 2 1/3 innings for his first save.

And while the victory ended the three game losing streak, it was only the Indians' sixth in 17 games dating back to June 20, when they beat Boston, 5-4.

"We were a completely different team today," said Vizquel. "Now we need to relax and think about jet skis and movies for a few days."

HARGROVE: 'INCONSISTENT IS THE WORD'

"Inconsistent is the word I'd choose to describe our first half," said Hargrove. "The last month we've been getting inconsistent pitching and hitting. Those things happen in the course of a season" - except that they didn't in 1995.

"But I'm tired of everybody comparing us this season with what we did last season," Hargrove countered.

Inconsistency also best described the individual performances to date by Murray, who had become mostly a singles hitter; Baerga, suffering through the worst season of his career; Belle, who hit only .215 the last six weeks of the first half, a slump that cost him nearly 50 points in his average, which was down to .293; McDowell, who was only 6-6 in 17 starts; Mesa, who had lost his confidence (and, some feared, his overpowering fast ball as well); it wasn't until the final game prior to the All-Star break that Ogea beat out Albie Lopez and Brian Anderson and took charge as the No. 5 starter; and middle-long relievers Alan Embree and Tavarer" and already had committed eight errors (five of them on throws) compared to only nine in all of 1995.

Obviously, all was not well ... and the Indians' quest for another A.L. pennant - and even more - in 1996 was not the cake walk some had thought it would be.

At least, not in the first half.

Kenny Lofton makes it look easy in a game against the Detroit Tigers.

9

THE MIDSUMMER CLASSIC

July 8-10

It was an Indians-dominated All-Star Game at Veterans Stadium in Philadelphia on July 9, as Mike Hargrove managed the American League team that included five of his players and two coaches.

Hargrove was the first Tribe manager to call the shots in the Midsummer Classic since Al Lopez in 1955.

Elected by the fans to start for the A.L. were outfielders Albert Belle (whose 1.7 million votes were second only to Seattle's Ken Griffey Jr. among outfielders in the balloting) and Kenny Lofton, while Hargrove picked pitchers Charles Nagy and Jose Mesa, and catcher Sandy Alomar.

Making the team was financially lucrative for all but Mesa.

By being voted to the starting lineup, Lofton earned a $25,000 bonus, plus an automatic increase of $500,000 in his 1997 contract, boosting his salary to $4.75 million; Nagy and Belle each gained $50,000 incentive bonuses, and Alomar got a $25,000 grant. Mesa's bonus was tied to the Rolaids Relief points.

Also added to the squad by Hargrove were Tribe coaches Jeff Newman, Mark Wiley, Toby Harrah and bull pen catcher/coach Dan Williams.

The National League won for the third straight year, 6-0, with the loss charged to Nagy, who started for the A.L. Lofton went 2-for-3, but Belle and Alomar were hitless, Belle in four at-bats and Alomar in two. Mesa didn't pitch.

In addition to the game, the three-day break was dominated by trade talk and rumors, much of it involving the Indians whose anticipated runaway to another pennant had been slowed by a sub-.500 won-lost record - 19-21 - in the preceding six weeks.

Hottest among the speculation was that Eddie Murray would soon be traded away, or even released, and that the baseball career of Carlos Baerga, often called the "heart and soul" of the Indians, would continue somewhere other than in Cleveland.

Though General Manager John Hart had little to say about the rumors, he was obviously concerned about the Tribe's slide toward mediocrity.

There also was no doubt, based on Hart's well-known *modus operandi,* that, with the July 31 trading deadline nearing, he would take action before the problem intensified.

INDIANS TRADE POOLE FOR CARREON

As it turned out, the only deal Hart made during the break was to send relief pitcher Jim Poole to San Francisco for outfielder-first baseman Mark Carreon.

Carreon, 33, was hitting .260 (76-for-292) with nine homers and 51 RBI in his fourth season with the Giants. He previously played for the New York Mets from 1987-91 and Detroit in 1992.

A big reason the Indians acquired Carreon, a right handed batter, was to provide protection at first base, where Murray no longer could (or would) play, and also because Herbert Perry was out for the season after undergoing knee surgery, and Julio Franco was slow in recovering from a pulled right hamstring muscle.

"I wasn't going to leave this club naked at first base," said Hart.

"We needed a professional right handed hitter. Mark Carreon is a versatile guy who can play first base and all outfield positions. He's also hit well against left handers, and that's been a concern on this club for the last couple of years."

The next day the Indians placed Franco on the 15 day disabled list, and recalled Alan Embree from Class AAA Buffalo.

And in another roster move prior to the start of the second half, Greg Swindell also was added to the disabled list with tendinitis in his shoulder, making room for the promotion of outfielder Brian Giles from Buffalo.

Otherwise, Hart admitted - without revealing any names - that he and assistant general manager Dan O'Dowd talked trade with virtually all the other 27 major league teams. He said they had narrowed to about eight those with which a deal might be made.

"We investigated what may be out there now, or what may be available to us near the trading deadline," which was three weeks away, Hart was quoted as saying.

"(But) for now we are going to let the club settle in and see how we get off the mark in the second half. We'll follow the health of Franco and Dennis (Martinez), and the progress of Jose (Mesa).

"Then as we get 10 days to two weeks into the second half, we'll see if there's something we may want to do."

Martinez was still on the disabled list, where he'd been assigned on June 29 because of a strained flexor tendon in his right elbow. Mesa, while physically sound, was struggling with his pitching mechanics.

About Mesa, Hart said, "I really do think he'll be fine, but until he starts to turn it around, there is still this uneasy feeling I have.

"For me, Jose was our MVP last year. I didn't expect him to duplicate that season this year. But we felt if he could have an 80 to 85 percent success rate in save opportunities, that would be good enough."

MURRAY-HART RELATIONSHIP STRAINED?

The speculation concerning Murray, according to published reports in Baltimore as well as Cleveland, was that the relationship between Hart and Murray was badly strained. One source claimed that Hart and Murray no longer were on speaking terms.

Their differences were said to be based on Murray's resentment concerning his contract negotiations with Hart the previous winter, and on what Hart considered was Murray's lack of production.

At the All-Star break Murray was batting .260, but only .203 with runners in scoring position (in 83 games), with a slugging percentage of .393, which was eighth among the regulars - and even .015 below Omar Vizquel's .408, and only .001 higher than Baerga's .392.

Included among Murray's stats were 84 hits, of which 11 were home runs with one triple and eight doubles, and 39 RBI. In 323 official plate appearances, Murray had struck out 45 times and drew 32 bases on balls.

One report was that Baltimore, the team with which Murray began his major league career in 1977, and for which he played through 1988, was interested in re-acquiring him.

The deal that allegedly almost happened was Murray and Jeromy Burnitz to the Orioles for outfielders Bobby Bonilla and Jeffrey Hammonds. Hart and his Baltimore counterpart, Pat Gillick, reportedly agreed to the trade, but it was shot down by Orioles owner Peter Angelos.

Later, it also was written, the proposed deal was expanded to include Albie Lopez from the Indians and pitcher Kent Mercker from Baltimore, but that also failed to materialize.

Though none of the principals would comment, speculation continued that Murray would soon be wearing another uniform - or none at all.

So did rumors persist that the Tribe was still trying to trade Baerga, as first reported on June 24 by Jim Ingraham in the Lake County *News-Herald* and Lorain *Morning Journal*.

A PLATFORM FOR BELLE AND LOFTON

The All-Star Game, in addition to being an exhibition between the best players in the A.L. and N.L., also in 1996 provided a platform for Belle, as well as Lofton, before the national media.

Belle, in a release reportedly written by his agent, Arn Tellem, and issued on July 9 by the Indians public relations department, thanked Cleveland fans for their support, to wit:

"The All-Star break gives me a chance to tell you all how much I appreciate your support over the last few years, and this one in particular. As you know, these past seasons have not been without controversy for me. The challenges I have faced have been far easier for me to deal with knowing that I have your total support.

"The positive reception I receive from you each time we play in Cleveland has been a great comfort to me. I know I can count on a warm homecoming from all of you whenever the team walks onto Jacobs Field. That knowledge has sustained me; it has been a major force in my effort to do my best for the Indians, and for all of you.

"I want you to know that I will continue to work hard in the coming weeks. My primary goal is to help the Indians get both the pennant and a World Series victory this fall. With your continued and deeply appreciated support, I know that this will be possible."

BELLE: 'I MIGHT SIT OUT THE 1997 SEASON'

The next day Belle was quoted in the July 10 edition of *USA TODAY* that he was considering "sitting out" the 1997 season. His contract with the Indians was to expire at the end of 1996, at which time he would become a free agent.

"My body is pretty beat up. It's wear and tear from a long, grinding season. Maybe I'll sit out the year and just relax," he reportedly said.

"I've been known to do unusual things, so I wouldn't rule it out. It's pretty real."

The story went on to quote Belle:

"I feel more like a politician than a baseball player. There are certain situations I'm not real happy with. There's been a smear campaign against a baseball player," obviously meaning himself.

"Why? I don't know. Maybe they want to get back at him."

Who's they? Belle didn't say, though he apparently meant the Baseball Establishment.

"Coming into this season, I knew I was definitely going to be under a microscope and that every move I made was going to be monitored," he continued in the newspaper article.

"I was prepared for it, and I've tried to keep these sort of things from happening. But it's not being prevented."

Of his collision with Vina, for which he was suspended two days and fined $25,000 by A.L. President Dr. Gene Budig, Belle was quoted as saying,

"The umpires thought it was a clean, legal play, except one man (Budig) didn't. I served my suspension on a Friday, and three days later Chad Kreuter of the White Sox runs down the line toward second base and runs over Randy Velarde of the California Angels and did the same exact thing I did.

"But nobody from the league said a word. That's what upsets me."

As for the controversy that resulted in his wanting a fan to return the baseball he hit for his 215th career homer, Belle said, "I would have given him two autographed balls, because that's what I've always done in the past. I did it earlier when I hit my 200th home run.

"But this guy comes up saying he wanted an autographed jersey or an autographed bat. I felt that was too much and I told him that."

When *USA TODAY* asked Belle about his stalled contract negotiations with the Indians, he replied, "This is probably the most leverage I'll have in my career. Once the season is over, I'll think about whether I want to play baseball in 1997 or take the year off."

There was speculation, in fact, that Belle's intention was to take a year off from baseball and then join the Arizona Diamondbacks when they begin play in 1998.

Belle did not agree to other requests for interviews.

When Hart was asked to comment on the *USA TODAY* story, he said, "If I was a betting man I'd take the odds that Albert would play next year."

NAGY IS 'AMAZED' AND 'BAFFLED'

During the workout day preceding the game, one television cameraman shot video footage of Belle's empty locker, eliciting this comment from Nagy:

"It amazes me that Albert says he doesn't want to talk to the press, and the press keeps trying to talk to him. That baffles me. It's like every reporter wants to be the next Hannah Storm. I guess people like to write articles on guys who don't talk. It just makes me shake my head."

Lofton spoke out, he said, on behalf of his teammates because he was tired of the bad image the Indians have nationally.

"The Cleveland Indians are perceived the wrong way, and it starts in one place - with the media," Lofton was quoted prior to the workout

"If the media would say the Indians are a bunch of good guys, the public would believe it. But they don't. All you hear about is what a bad group of players the Indians are. For what? What have we done?"

Lofton then mentioned virtually every player on the Indians team, pointing out that they are all good guys.

In an obvious reference to Belle, Lofton said, "Our starting players, we've got nine good guys, and one guy who has had a couple problems and was punished for it. But that is it. And all you hear is that the Indians have this terrible team.?"

Then, specifically mentioning Belle, Lofton said, "Belle is getting booed even though what he did (in his collision with Fernando Vina on May 31) wasn't wrong

"Why is he being booed? Because of the media. Nobody writes that Albert got hit by pitches twice before that play. All they write about is Albert knocking over Vina."

In the workout day festivities on July 8, Belle declined without explanation to participate in the annual All-Star Home Run Derby in which he finished second to Frank Thomas in 1995. It was won by Barry Bonds of the San Francisco Giants, who beat Oakland's Mark McGwire.

Nagy called the opportunity to start for the A.L. "a great honor." He said, "When you think of pitchers who start All-Star games, you think of guys like David Cone, Randy Johnson and Roger Clemens ... and now, here I am." It was Nagy's second All-Star Game; he previously made the team in 1992.

He was the first Tribe pitcher to start an All-Star Game since Gaylord Perry in 1974, and the fourth ever. Bob Feller got the honor in 1941 and 1946, and Luis Tiant in 1968.

LOFTON GOES 2-FOR-3, STEALS TWO BASES

Lofton, who was batting .315 for the Tribe and led the major leagues with 42 stolen bases in 54 attempts, singled as the game's first batter. He promptly stole second and went to third on Robby Alomar's fly for the second out, but died there as Belle struck out.

But the N.L. got the run back in a hurry against Nagy, who pitched the first two innings. He gave up a run in the first as Lance Johnson opened with a double and came around on two ground ball outs.

Two more runs were scored off Nagy in the second inning, the first on Mike Piazza's solo homer, and the second on singles by Chipper Jones and Henry Rodriguez.

Lofton flied out in the third, and singled and stole second again in the sixth, before giving way to Joe Carter in seventh.

Belle, the first Cleveland player to be named to four consecutive All-Star teams since Sam McDowell (1968-71), and the first position player to do so since Larry Doby made it seven straight seasons (1949-55), played the entire game but did nothing to enhance his status as one of baseball's greatest sluggers.

Belle struck out again in the fourth and sixth innings, and lined out in the eighth. The last player to strike out three times in an All-Star Game was Johnny Bench in 1970. Mickey Mantle was the last A.L. player to do it, in 1956.

On the other hand, Lofton's two stolen bases tied a record set by Willie Mays in 1963, and equaled by Kelly Gruber in 1990 and Robby Alomar in 1992.

"If I'd known I had tied a record, I would have stolen another base," said Lofton.

"This is like the World Series. It's fun to show people what you can do. With the lineup we had, anything could have happened, but their pitchers shut us down," added the Indians center fielder.

"I helped (the N.L.) out a little by letting Piazza hit the big home run," said Nagy, "but this game is all about fun and it's great being here. You like to go out and do well, but at least Mike (Hargrove) didn't have to come out and drag me off the mound."

Hargrove said, "It would have been nice to win, but it was an honor, a thrill for all of us to be here. The National League didn't miss a mistake we made all night."

Of Nagy's pitching, Hargrove said, "Charlie hung a couple of pitches and I've seen him better, but I was still proud of the way he pitched."

1996 ALL - STAR GAME

AMERICAN LEAGUE 000 000 000 - 0
NATIONAL LEAGUE 121 002 00X - 6

AMERICAN	AB	R	H	RBI	SO
Lofton cf	3	0	2	0	0
Carter cf	1	0	1	0	0
Boggs 3b	3	0	0	0	0
e-Fryman ph-3b	1	0	0	0	1
R. Alomar 2b	3	0	1	0	0
Knoblauch 2b	1	0	1	0	0
Belle lf	4	0	0	0	3
Vaughn 1b	3	0	1	0	0
Mcgwire 1b	1	0	1	0	0
Rodriguez c	2	0	0	0	1
c-S. Alomar ph-c	2	0	0	0	0
Ripken ss	3	0	0	0	0
Percival p	0	0	0	0	0
Hernandez p	0	0	0	0	0
f-Wilson ph	1	0	0	0	0
Anderson rf	2	0	0	0	0
Pavlik p	0	0	0	0	0
d-A.Rdriguez ph ss	1	0	0	0	0
Nagy p	0	0	0	0	0
a-E.Martinex ph	1	0	0	0	0
Finley p	0	0	0	0	0
b-Buhner ph-rf	2	0	0	0	0
Totals	**34**	**0**	**7**	**0**	**5**

NATIONAL	AB	R	H	RBI	SO
Johnson cf	4	1	3	0	0
Larkin ss	3	1	1	0	0
Smith ss	1	0	0	0	0
Bonds lf	3	0	1	1	0
Martinez p	0	0	0	0	0
Sheffield rf	1	0	0	0	0
McGriff 1b	2	0	0	0	2
Glavine p	0	0	0	0	0
Caminiti 3b	2	1	1	1	1
Worrell p	0	0	0	0	0
Wohlers p	0	0	0	0	0
Leiter p	0	0	0	0	0
Piazza c	3	1	2	2	1
Hundley c	1	0	0	0	0
Kendall c	0	0	0	0	0
Bichette rf	3	1	1	0	1
Trachsel p	0	0	0	0	0
Grudzielanek 3b	1	0	0	0	0
Jones 3b	2	1	1	0	0
Bottalico p	0	0	0	0	0
Burks lf	2	0	1	0	1
Biggio 2b	3	0	0	1	1
Young pr-2b	1	0	0	0	0
Smoltz p	0	0	0	0	0
a-Rodriguez ph	1	0	1	1	0
Brown p	0	0	0	0	0
Bagwell 1b	2	0	0	0	1
Totals	**35**	**6**	**12**	**6**	**8**

a-grounded out to shortstop for Nagy in the 3rd; b-lined to center for Finley in the 5th; c-flied to center for I Rodriguez in the 7th; d-fouled to right for Pavlik in the 7th; e-struck out for Boggs in the 8th; -flied out to right for Hernandez in the 9th.
BATTING - 2B: Vaughn (1, Smoltz), **Runners left in scoring position, 2 out:** Belle 2, Anderson 1, Vaughn1. **GIDP**: S. Alomar. Team **LOB**: 7
BASERUNNNG - SB: Lofton 2 (2nd base off Smoltz/Piazza, 2nd base off Martinez/Piazza
FIELDING - DP: 1 I Rodriguez - Ripken

a-singled for Smoltz in the 2nd
BATTING-2B: Johnson (1, Nagy);Piazza (1, Finley); Bichette(1,Pavlik). **3B:** Burks (1,Hern andez).**HR:**Piazza (1, 2nd inning off Nagy 0 on 0 out) **Runners left in scoring position**, 2 out: Bichette 1, Caminiti 1, Young 1. **Team LOB:**5
BASERUNNING SB: Johnson (1 2nd base off Pavlik/I.Rodriguez) **CS**: Bonds (1. 2nd base by Finley I.Rodriguez; Johnson (1, 3rd base by Pavlik I.Rodriguez)
FIELDING - E: Caminti (1, ground ball).DP: 1(Smith-Young-Bagwell)

AMERICAN	IP	H	R	ER	SO	HR
Nagy L, 0-1	2	4	3	3	1	1
Finley	2	3	1	1	4	0
Pavlik	2	3	2	2	2	1
Percival	1	1	0	0	1	0
Hernandez	1	1	0	0	0	0

NATIONAL	IP	H	R	ER	SO	HR
Smoltz W 1-0	2	2	0	0	1	0
Brown	1	0	0	0	0	0
Glavine	1	0	0	0	1	0
Bottalico	1	0	0	0	1	0
Martinez	1	2	0	0	1	0
Trachesel	1	0	0	0	0	0
Worrell	1	2	0	0	1	0
Wohlers	2/3	1	0	0	0	0
Leiter	2/3	0	0	0	0	0

WP: Pavlik 1. **Pitches-strikes**: Smoltz 26-17; Brown 18-11; Glavine 15-11; Bottalico 14-9; Martinez 18-10; Trachsel 8-5; Worrell 13-9; Wohlers 8-6; Leiter 9-6; Nagy 35-24; Finley 32-23;Pavlik 35-27; Percival 15-11; Hernandez 8-6. **Ground balls-fly balls:** Smoltz 1-4; Brown 2-1; Glavine 2-0; Bottalico 0-2; Martinez 1-1; Trachsel 1-2; Worrell 0-2; Wohlers 2-0; Leiter 0-1; Nagy 5-0; Finley 0-1;Pavlik 3-1; Percival 1-1; Hernandez 2-1. **Batters faced:** Smoltz 8; Brown 3;Glavine 3; Bottalico 4; Martinez 5; Trachsel 3; Worrell 5; Wohlers 2; Leiter 1; Nagy 10; Finley 8;Pavlik 9; Percival 4; Hernandez 4.
UMPIRES- HP: Marsh, **1B:** Mccoy, **2B:** Reliford, **3B:** Brinkman, **LF:** Poncino, **RF:** Meriwether
GAME DATA - T: 2:35. **ATTENDANCE:** 62,670

Omar Vizquel leaps over the Tiger's Bobby Higginson during a double play.

10

'IF THE BIG DOGS DON'T HUNT...'

July 11-25

General Manager John Hart's admonition rang in the Indians' ears as they embarked upon the second half of the 1996 season clinging to a two game lead over Chicago in the American League Central Division.

"If the big dogs don't hunt, we're in trouble," said Hart, as the Tribe put its 52-35 won-lost record on the line and opened a four game series in Minnesota on July 11.

When asked to identify the "big dogs," Hart's response was interesting, considering one whose name he didn't mention.

The big dogs, said Hart, were Albert Belle, in the throes of a hitting slump, during which he went 29-for-137 (.212) with six homers and 21 RBI, shrinking his .353 batting average to .293, and Jose Mesa, the once nearly-invincible closer who had blown three of his previous four save opportunities, and was 24-for-28 in the first half.

A player Hart would have been expected to include among the "big dogs" was Eddie Murray, but the designated hitter whose batting average was .260 with nine homers and 50 RBI, wasn't mentioned by the general manager.

The significance of Murray's absence in Hart's comments would come to light later.

First, Mike Hargrove announced on July 11 that, henceforth, the switch-hitting Murray would play only against left handed pitchers, and that Jeromy Burnitz, a left handed batter, would be the Tribe's DH against right handers.

Hargrove's decision angered many of the Indians, especially Dennis Martinez, Manny Ramirez and Kenny Lofton, who considered the decision was demeaning to Murray, a future Hall of Famer.

Then, on July 21, Murray was traded to Baltimore, confirming speculation that had been rampant for more than a month, though the deal was considerably different than what had been rumored - Murray and Burnitz for Bobby Bonilla and Jeffrey Hammonds.

Instead, the Indians received Kent Mercker, a left handed pitcher who, it had been said, had lost his fast ball.

That, too, further angered the Tribesmen, several of whom inked Murray's number, 33, on their caps to show their resentment toward management for making the trade.

It was prior to the Indians' first game of the second half against Minnesota that Murray was informed that "some of your at-bats" would be given to

Burnitz.

Hargrove called Murray into the manager's office at the Metrodome in Minneapolis and told him, "I'm going to be giving some of your at-bats to Jeromy."

According to Hargrove, Murray replied, "Is that it?"

Hargrove said, "That's it," and Murray left the office.

"(The meeting) lasted about 30 seconds," Hargrove said.

"I'm going to try to get Jeromy many more at-bats," the manager elaborated to the media. "He'll probably be the DH against most right handers, but he could also play in left field or right field, and we could use Albert (Belle) or Manny (Ramirez) at DH."

HART: 'BURNITZ WON'T BE TRADED'

As for speculation at the time that Burnitz might be traded with Murray to Baltimore, Hart said, "Jeromy Burnitz is not going anywhere. We like him, but we really don't know much about him as a player yet."

Hargrove said of Burnitz, "He could be the kind of guy who hits 15 homers and drives in 70 or more runs if he gets 500 at-bats."

In his first game as the Tribe's left handed DH in place of Murray on July 11, Burnitz batted sixth and went 1-for-4 in an 11-7 victory over the Twins.

The big offensive guns for the Indians were Ramirez, who hit a grand slam, and Belle and Jim Thome, who also homered. Ramirez drove in five runs, and Belle, going 3-for-4, had four RBI in support of Jack McDowell, who needed a lot of help.

McDowell, who hadn't won a game since June 7, was staked to an 11-3 lead, but was chased in the sixth inning when the Twins rallied for four runs. Relievers Julian Tavarez and Eric Plunk - not Mesa - came on to hold the Twins at bay and McDowell's record climbed to 7-6.

Part of McDowell's problem, he said, was that he was hit in the back by a ball thrown by Sandy Alomar when Minnesota's Rich Becker stole second in the second inning.

"My back started to tighten up after that," said McDowell. "I got hit on the right side, and that's where all the muscles are that you use when you pitch."

In five starts in the previous five weeks McDowell was 0-2 with an 8.58 ERA (27 runs in 28 1/3 innings).

The next day Orel Hershiser secretly placed targets on the backs of several of his pitcher-teammates, poking fun at Alomar, who took it well.

"Aw, I just had a bad grip on the ball (that hit McDowell in the back) and I wasn't even going to throw it," said the catcher. "I tried to hold the ball, but it slipped out."

Beating the Twins in the opener of the four game series was important for the Indians as they gained a game on the White Sox, who lost to Kansas City, 3-2. It was Chicago's 10th defeat in 18 games after a 19-3 hot streak in mid-June.

GILES HOMERS IN FIRST AT-BAT

The Indians also won the next two games in the Metrodome, 7-5, a victory that should have been credited to Hershiser but instead went to Mesa, and 19-11, on July 12 and 13.

In the first of those games, Hershiser took a 2-0 lead into the seventh inning, the second run coming on Belle's 29th homer and second in two nights.

After the first two batters were retired in the Twins seventh, Thome's throwing error opened the door to four unearned runs and an early shower for Hershiser.

Alvaro Espinoza solo homered in the eighth, after which the Twins retaliated in their half of the inning for another run off Mesa. But then it was Brian Giles' turn to become a Tribe hero in the ninth.

In his first trip to the plate since being recalled from Buffalo, Giles, pinch hitting for Alomar, tied the score, 5-5, with a two run homer.

On base ahead of Giles was Burnitz who had reached on a fielder's choice as a pinch hitter for Murray - probably the first time in Murray's career that anybody batted for him.

Then Thome untied it with a bases loaded single, and Paul Shuey replaced Mesa in the bottom of the ninth to blank the Twins and record his third save - which gave Mesa the victory.

Many players on the team - especially Martinez - were angered that Burntiz was sent to the plate to bat for Murray, considering it to be a slap in the face to a future Hall of Famer.

"That's not showing (Murray) any respect. It hurt him," said Martinez. When reminded that the Indians were trying to trade Murray, Martinez said, "Good. That's the best thing. He is not happy here."

The Indians' 19 runs against the Twins the next day were the most they'd scored in a game since they reached 20 against Oakland on May 4, 1991. They did it with a season high 22 hits, including 12 doubles, breaking a 75 year old club record. It also tied the A.L. mark set by Boston in 1990.

"We had so many people going around first base that I got dizzy sitting in the dugout and watching," said newcomer Mark Carreon.

"We really started swinging the bats like this in the last game before the All-Star break," said Hargrove. "We've got to keep it going because we didn't hit like this the whole first half. We can't take a deep breath. We've got to keep hitting."

The latter was a reference to the fact that the White Sox apparently also were over their slump. They'd won two straight over Kansas City, 7-6 and 3-1, to keep pace with the Tribe, three games behind.

BELLE HOMERS IN THIRD STRAIGHT GAME

In routing the Twins, Belle homered for the third straight game, giving him 30 for the season, and Ramirez and Burnitz also homered.

But so did Becker for Minnesota, twice off Chad Ogea, who was still trying - but not very impressively - to nail down the fifth starting job in the pitching rotation. Ogea left after five innings with a 12-6 lead, and his fifth victory in six decisions.

Burnitz, starting for the second time in place of Murray, also doubled and finished the game with five RBI, and Carlos Baerga, whose bat had been quiet most of the first half, went 3-for-5 with a double and four runs scored.

The big lead provided an opportunity for Mesa to get in some work in the ongoing effort to help him regain his confidence. He gave up a hit but pitched a scoreless ninth.

MOLITOR BEATS THE INDIANS

The Indians should have saved some of those runs for the July 14 finale of the Minnesota series, which they lost, 5-4, on a ninth inning home run by Paul Molitor.

Yes, the same Paul Molitor the Indians had tried so hard to sign as a free agent the previous winter, and whose rejection (along with one by Mark Grace) resulted in the decision to bring Murray back to the team.

And, once again, Charles Nagy was deprived of a victory. He pitched well enough to win, but left after seven innings with the score tied, and Molitor's homer was delivered off Plunk, with one out.

It was Nagy's seventh career start in the Metrodome where his record is 0-4.

But that's not a subject he wanted to talk about.

The loss cut the Tribe's lead over Chicago to two games as the White Sox beat Kansas City a third straight time, 3-2.

Until Molitor ended it, Carreon figured to be the Indians' star of the game. He went 3-for-4, including a two run homer in the seventh that forged the 4-4 tie. It gave Carreon nine hits in 15 at-bats since joining the Tribe in the July 9 deal that sent Jim Poole to San Francisco.

"Before the trade I was treading water for the last couple of months," said Carreon. "I had some bright spots, but now my concentration has peaked."

In addition to losing, Hargrove was "concerned," he said, by the fact that the Indians committed two more errors - by Ramirez and Baerga, his 14th - giving them 11 in the four game series, and 70 in 91 games

"That's a concern," said Hargrove. "I'm not using it as an excuse, but we haven't played on artificial turf for a long time." Not since May 5, in fact.

TAVAREZ FAILS AGAIN

Tavarez got another chance to start in place of Martinez when the Indians opened a three game series in Kansas City on July 15, but pitched poorly again. The weak hitting Royals, with the second worst record in the A.L., won, 6-3.

Fortunately for the Indians, Chicago also lost, 16-5, to Minnesota.

It was Tavarez's third unsuccessful spot start, which was puzzling considering how well he pitched in 1995 when he posted a 10-2 record with a 2.44 ERA in 57 games, all as a reliever.

In the wake of the loss, in which Tavarez was knocked out of the box in the fourth inning, charged with five runs on eight hits, speculation began anew that he would soon be shuffling off to Buffalo.

Tavarez's immediate future, it seemed, depended upon how quickly Martinez would return from the disabled list, where he'd been placed June 29.

"Dennis threw in the bull pen (July 14) and was outstanding," said Hargrove. "He had no pain and threw strikes to both sides of the plate."

Martinez, however, was not so positive. "The pain is still there, it's not going to go away," he said. "But I can pitch like this."

The Royals scored three runs in the first inning off Tavarez. Ramirez, in the DH role for the first time, got one run back in the second with his 23rd homer and seventh since June 20.

But Doug Howard homered for K.C. in the second, and when Mike Macfarlane homered in the fourth, Tavarez was gone, and the Indians couldn't catch up.

Mesa worked the ninth, allowing a hit but striking out two batters, and pitching coach Mark Wiley said he was encouraged. "Guys were swinging late on him, and he was getting his deception back," said Wiley. "I was very pleased with what I saw."

BELLE HAMMERS 31st HOMER

Hargrove had to be very pleased with what he saw of the Indians the next night, July 16, in their 10-4 victory over the Royals and Chris Haney, one of several left handers who gave them trouble in 1996.

Belle, red hot at the plate again, hammered a two run homer in the first inning, and after the Indians added two runs in the fourth and three in the fifth, it was not much of a contest.

The homer was Belle's 31st of the season, fourth in six games since the All-Star break, and 225th of his career, putting him one behind Earl Averill's club record.

Murray also was a major contributor. He doubled and singled, driving in four runs.

Omar Vizquel, back in the lineup after resting his aching shoulder for two games, also homered and McDowell went seven innings on a yield of six hits and three runs for a second straight victory, raising his record to 8-6.

"We needed that," said Hargrove, aware that the White Sox also had won, their seventh victory in 10 games, keeping them two behind the Tribe.

HERSHISER THE VICTIM OF CARELESSNESS

However, more careless play in the field by the Indians the next night, July 17, cost them - and Hershiser - a 3-2 loss to the Royals.

And there also was great consternation in the clubhouse before the game, when the lineup card was posted and Murray's name was not on it.

"Everybody get ready to write No. 33 on their hats," said Lofton, loud enough for everyone to hear. "He (Murray) is not going to be around much longer."

Ramirez also had something to say. "Eddie Murray has a chance to hit 500 homers ... I'm going into Hargrove's office and talk to him," said Ramirez.

"I'll give you 100 bucks if you do," said Lofton.

Ramirez didn't.

In the game on the field, the Indians were fortunate again in that the White Sox also lost, 4-3, to Minnesota, so the Indians remained two games ahead.

This time an unlikely co-culprit in the sloppy defense was Lofton, the Gold Glove center fielder. Though Lofton was not charged with an error, the Royals appeared to take advantage of him on two occasions, and both were costly.

In the first inning, when K.C. scored twice, Lofton was slow in running down a grounder up the middle by Jose Offerman, who turned it into a double.

After Michael Tucker walked with one out, Offerman scored on Bob Hamelin's single. Then, with two out, Johnny Damon sent another bouncer up the middle. It skipped under Baerga's glove, scoring Tucker, and when Lofton jogged after the ball, then made a lazy throw to Vizquel, Hamelin, no speed merchant, also scored, and easily.

The Indians tied it in the second on Burnitz's single, Baerga's double, Tony Pena's sacrifice fly and another single by Vizquel, but that was it. Tim Belcher slammed the door and reliever Jeff Montgomery kept it closed in the ninth.

Another miscue, this one a chargeable error by Thome, provided the Royals with the go-ahead, and what proved to be the winning run in the third.

Tom Goodwin was credited with a double when he - in a virtual replay of what happened in the first inning - slapped another grounder up the middle.

Baerga waved at it, and when the ball died in the grass in center field, Goodwin sprinted to second, again beating the throw from Lofton.

Hershiser retired the next two batters, but Goodwin scored when Kevin Young grounded to Thome, whose throw to first was in the dirt and got away from Carreon for an error.

It was the Tribe's 12th error on the seven game trip.

"That one hurt," Hargrove said, though he did not criticize Lofton. Instead, he credited Offerman and Damon. "They just turned slow hit balls into doubles," Hargrove said.

INDIANS LEAD STAYS AT TWO

The loss concluded the Indians road trip with a 4-3 record and kept them in first place by two games over the White Sox - who would get no closer the rest of the season.

But that's not to say that the rest of the season was a pleasurable, pressure-less trip to the playoffs.

Far from it.

The Indians returned to Jacobs Field and beat Minnesota three times in a four game series, July 18-21, and the first and last of those dates were most dramatic - and memorable.

Murray, pinch hitting for Burnitz with the score tied and two out in the ninth inning of the opener, smashed a home run, his 12th of the season and No. 491 of his 20 year major league career, giving the Indians a 5-4 victory.

It sent his teammates into near-hysteria and, it seemed, would solidify again his status on the team, ending the speculation that his days with the Indians were numbered.

Though Murray had no public comment, others did.

Speaking of Murray's obvious resentment about his reduced role, Hargrove said, "He's handled it as well as can be expected. I didn't expect him to be a happy camper, and he hasn't been.

"He has been very professional about it, though I'd be disappointed if he just accepted it."

As for sending Murray to the plate to hit for Burnitz in that situation, Hargrove said, "It was a no-brainer. When you have a Hall of Famer sitting there with the power he has ... I think it's pretty automatic.

"In a situation where a home run can win a game, it's an automatic move."

The victory, Danny Graves' first in the major leagues as the second reliever to follow Ogea, the starter, combined with Chicago's 7-1 loss to Kansas City, boosted the Tribe's first place margin to three games.

TRIBE SPLITS WITH TWINS

The Indians split the next two games with Minnesota.

They lost, 3-2, as two bases loaded walks and Thome's error gave the Twins all their runs in the seventh inning on July 19, depriving Nagy of his 12th victory for the sixth consecutive time.

They won, 6-5, the next day, July 20, again in dramatic fashion, as Murray's bases loaded walk forced in the tying run in the ninth, and Espinoza's home run won it in the 11th.

And then it happened.

Murray was traded to Baltimore, the organization with which he began his professional career as a third round pick in the 1973 amateur draft.

Mercker, the pitcher the Indians received in exchange, pitched for Atlanta from 1990-95, faced the Indians in Game 3 of the 1995 World Series, and was 3-6 for the Orioles in 1996 after they'd acquired him for two minor league pitchers in December 1995.

He pitched a no-hitter for the Braves against Los Angeles in 1994.

When the deal was announced, prior to the Indians' 7-5 victory over the Twins on July 21, it evoked more negative comments from several players. Especially outspoken was Martinez.

"It was not right the way they treated (Murray)," said Martinez. "It just wasn't right. I am relieved he is going somewhere where he is going to be happy and he's going to get more playing time."

In his lament on behalf of Murray, Martinez also said, "When you pinch hit for someone like him, it is the worst thing that can be done."

It was a reference to the July 12 game in Minnesota when Hargrove sent Burnitz to the plate as a pinch hitter for Murray.

"You could see the disappointment on (Murray's) face when that happened," continued Martinez.

"But it's best for Eddie to get out of here and go to a team where he is appreciated. (The Indians) brought him back here and cut his salary, then they reduced his role at DH. To me you don't do that. It's not fair, I don't understand it, but I'm just an employee here."

'THEY'RE TRYING TO FIX TOO MUCH'

Martinez also said he thought the Indians were making too many moves - something that would come into even sharper focus a month later.

"They're trying to fix everything at once here," he said. "Julian Tavarez was one of the best setup men in the league last year. They try to make him a starter, he does bad, and they send him down instead of trying to fix him.

"There's a lot of things that are done here that I don't agree with. You never know what's going to happen next. Sometimes I don't feel like I belong here."

Lofton said he was sorry to see Murray leave, but was more cautious in his comments.

"I don't want to put my foot in my mouth, so I better not say too much," he said. "(But) Eddie was good for the game here. He taught me a lot."

Hart said of the trade, "It was a tough decision, but we felt we made a move that was right for the organization. We owe it to our fans to put the best club on the field.

"Eddie has meant a lot to our program, but he was getting limited at-bats here. This gives him a chance to play more, and also will allow Eddie to make a run at 500 homers.

"Eddie was short term for us. It was a stretch for us to pay him the amount that we did."

Murray was paid $3 million in 1995, but was cut to $2 million in 1996.

In 336 at-bats for the Indians in 1996, Murray was hitting .262 with 12 homers and 45 RBI.

He left with 3,159 career hits, 11th on the all-time list; 1,865 RBI, eighth all-time; 541 doubles, 14th all-time; and 491 homers. Of those career totals, Murray had 339 hits and 50 homers for the Tribe.

Murray had nothing to say until he arrived in Baltimore two days later.

But anyone who thought he would rip the Indians was mistaken.

"I enjoyed Cleveland," Murray told the media in Baltimore. "I had a good 2 1/2 years there. I thought I fit in well. The guys accepted me, and we had fun. We were all buddies," he said of his former teammates, "so it was hard on them to see me go.

"But I think, finally, they were glad to see me go and get a chance to hit 500 (homers). I had to leave pretty quickly, though, because it was getting very emotional.

"I didn't think it was possible to come back to Baltimore. I have a lot of fond memories here. I'm really glad Pat Gillick and Mr. (Peter) Angelos fought to make it happen."

Angelos owns the Orioles, and Gillick is their general manager.

MERCKER GOES TO BUFFALO

Murray played for the Orioles from 1977-88, was traded to the Los Angeles Dodgers, for whom he played from 1989-91; then joined the New York Mets as a free agent and played for them in 1992 and 1993.

According to Jim Ingraham of the Lake County *News-Herald* and Lorain *Morning Journal*, the Orioles and Indians originally talked about a deal that included Bonilla for Murray and a prospect, but they couldn't agree on the prospect.

Hart also refused to release Murray when Orioles officials believed he might, so the two teams finally got back together.

As part of the trade, the Orioles agreed to pay the Indians about $500,000, which was the difference in the remaining portion of the two players' salaries. Mercker was making $2.8 million, $800,000 more than Murray.

Four days after the trade Mercker was optioned to Buffalo to begin a program of rebuilding his arm and his confidence. "I don't view it as a demotion," he said. "I view it as spring training."

NAGY STILL SEEKING A 12th VICTORY

Particularly distressing was the loss in the second game on July 19 by Nagy, the Tribe's most dependable pitcher whose 11-3 record and 3.51 ERA had established him as a leading candidate for the A.L. Cy Young Award.

It was his sixth consecutive start in quest of a 12th victory, dating back to June 15 when he beat New York, 10-3. During that period Nagy allowed only 15 earned runs in 44 innings. But he still lost two games, and was not the pitcher of record in four, as the Indians scored a grand total of 21 runs in his behalf.

"All of this is just part of the game," said Nagy. "I don't like it to happen, but it does. All I can do is go out and continue to pitch."

Lofton and Giles belted solo home runs to give Nagy a 2-0 lead through six innings. But with two out in the seventh, Nagy suddenly lost his control. He walked two around a single, then issued another base on balls, forcing in the Twins' first run.

"I don't know what happened," said Nagy. "For some reason I lost my concentration and couldn't get it back. I walk three guys, the bases are loaded, and the next thing I know I'm sitting on the bench kicking myself."

Plunk replaced Nagy and the tying run scored on an error by Thome. Then the go ahead run was forced in as Plunk walked another batter before ending the inning.

In the bottom of the seventh, Murray pinch hit again as the Indians looked for a repeat of the drama he produced two days earlier. The bases were loaded with two out and the same pitcher, Eddie Guardado, was on the mound for the Twins.

But this time Guardado won. Murray grounded out and the Indians didn't threaten again.

MESA IS DOMINANT AGAIN

Espinoza's homer that won the third game of the series against the Twins, 6-5, on July 20, was not the only encouraging aspect of the victory.

Mesa also played a key role as he resembled - for the first time since before the All-Star break - the dominant closer who was successful in 46 of 48 save opportunities in 1995.

Mesa was perfect in striking out two without giving up a hit or a walk in the eighth, ninth and 10th innings.

On the other hand, Tavarez started, was bombed again, this time for eight hits and five runs in 3 1/3 innings. The next day Tavarez was demoted to Buffalo and Greg Swindell was activated from the disabled list.

"The failure of our young pitchers to step up has been the most disappointing thing of our season," said Hart.

BURNITZ MAKES THE DEAL LOOK GOOD

In the finale of the Minnesota series, after the initial shock of the Murray trade had calmed down, Burnitz, stepped forward and - at least for this day - made the deal look great.

The heir to Murray's job as the Tribe's designated hitter against right handed pitchers, Burnitz homered twice, doubled once and drove in three runs, triggering a 7-5 victory on July 21. It kept the Indians four games ahead of the White Sox, a lead that would continue to grow larger.

"I don't think what (Burnitz) did today is unexpected," said Hargrove. "When he hits the ball, it jumps off his bat. Until he hits regularly, it's tough to say how many home runs he's capable of. It's safe to say though, that he's a power hitter."

The Indians wiped out one-run deficits three times, finally taking the lead for keeps in the fifth on Burnitz's first homer. It followed Ramirez's lead-off double and wiped out the Twins' 4-3 lead.

Burnitz homered again in the seventh with the bases bare.

By then McDowell was in the showers, though he lasted long enough - into the top of the seventh, giving up all five of the Twins' runs on 10 hits - to gain his third straight victory and ninth in 15 decisions.

And again it was Shuey, not Mesa, whom Hargrove called upon to close out the game, which he did - but not without a few anxious moments.

Shuey struck out the first batter, then walked the next two before also striking out Dennis Hocking and getting Molitor to ground out. It was Shuey's fourth save.

The game ended the Indians' brief homestand and was witnessed by the 100th consecutive sellout crowd at Jacobs Field, boosting the season atten- dance to 2,007,271.

It was the third time in four years the Tribe went over the two million mark - not bad for a city that almost lost its major league franchise several times in the previous three decades because of poor support.

HERSHISER ON A 6-2 ROLL

The Indians also were well supported in Toronto when they visited the Skydome for a three game series against the Blue Jays, July 22-24.

Many Cleveland fans, unable to buy tickets for the Indians' soldout games at Jacobs Field, journeyed to Toronto to see their favorite team, which was just the opposite from the way it had been several years previously.

Then, with the Blue Jays winning the A.L. pennant in 1992 and 1993, and playing in the brand new Skydome, Toronto fans had to go to Cleveland, where the Indians were playing in front of sparse crowds at the Stadium, to cheer for the Blue Jays.

Belle led the Indians to a 4-2 victory with a three run double in the third inning of the opener, though much of the credit for the big hit belonged to Thome.

With runners on first and third with two out, Thome walked on three balls - not four - loading the bases because everybody else, including umpire Mike Everitt, lost track of the count.

With the count 2-and-2 on Thome, Blue Jays pitcher Erik Hanson's next pitch was wide of the plate. Thome dropped his bat and trotted to first base. Nobody stopped him and the umpire, a minor league substitute, didn't call him back.

"I knew it was only ball three," said Thome. "It was just one of those funky situations."

Belle followed with a drive to deep left center. Joe Carter backed against the wall and had the ball in his glove, but couldn't hold it. Center fielder Otis Nixon, also trying to make the catch, hit Carter, jarring the ball loose. All three base runners scored.

Blue Jays manager Cito Gaston took the blame for the mistake. "Normally you just rely on the umpire, but we all should have had the correct count," said Gaston. "I take full responsibility."

Hanson said, "I thought the count was 2-and-2 (when he made the next pitch), and I was shocked when Thome ran to first base (on ball three). But the umpire didn't say anything, and when nobody else questioned it, I figured I was wrong."

The three runs on Belle's triple were enough for Hershiser, whose record climbed to 10-6 with the victory. In nine starts since June 8, Hershiser was 6-2 with a 0.85 ERA.

"Orel can focus about as good as anyone I've ever seen," said Hargrove. "I'm just glad he's on our side - and I don't mean for just what he does on the field."

Thome and Belle collaborated again for another run in the eighth. Thome doubled with one out and Belle singled for his 90th RBI.

Hershiser left after seven innings and Paul Assenmacher and Mesa finished. Mesa, seemingly back in form, took over with one out in the eighth and retired five batters in order, striking out three of them for his 25th save.

And the Indians' lead climbed to five games over the White Sox, who lost again, 6-5, to Oakland.

OGEA CONTINUES AS FIFTH STARTER

The Indians and Blue Jays split the next two games, Toronto winning, 3-1, on July 23, and the Tribe, with Martinez coming off the disabled list and pitching his first game since May 31, prevailed, 10-0, on July 24.

In the loss, to Pat Hentgen, the Indians stranded six runners in the first three innings, as the Blue Jays jumped ahead on Carter's 350th career homer leading off the second inning against Ogea.

Vizquel solo homered in the third, but that's all Hentgen and two relievers allowed in limiting the Tribe to five hits.

Toronto won it in the fifth on Shawn Green's two run homer.

"Those two pitches, the one that Carter hit and the one to Green, I wish I had back," said Ogea. "They were mistakes."

Despite the loss, Hargrove said Ogea pitched well for the third straight time. "Chad has had some bad outings, but on the whole he has been good and will continue as our fifth starter," Hargrove said.

MARTINEZ GETS 240th CAREER VICTORY

Martinez's performance the next night was even more encouraging as he ended a 25 day stay on the disabled list with a strained flexor tendon in his right elbow.

Martinez only pitched five innings - he called it "a five and fly" - but allowed just three hits and two walks in 71 pitches, and reported no ill effects after the game.

Swindell, Graves and Shuey wrapped up the shutout through the final four innings, providing Martinez with his ninth victory in 14 decisions, and 240th of his career.

(It would, however, be the final game Martinez would win in a Cleveland uniform, as his elbow trouble would flare up again, forcing him back on the disabled list twice in the next six weeks and off the roster.)

To make room for Martinez the Indians designated Scott Leius for assignment, and in preparation for the activation of Julio Franco from the disabled list where he'd been since July 11, Mercker was optioned to Buffalo.

Baerga also provided a measure of encouragement. He homered in the second inning for the first time in 24 games, since June 27, and also singled and doubled, raising his average to .268.

The Tribe scored six runs in the fifth, making it easy for Martinez to "fly," and Vizquel capped the outburst with a three run homer in the sixth.

THE 'BIG DOGS' COME THROUGH

And then the Indians moved on to Baltimore where Belle became the most prolific home run hitter in club history. He hammered two homers, giving him 34 for the season and a career total of 228, two more than Averill hit for the Tribe from 1929-39.

Belle's homers, which also accounted for five RBI for a season total of 96, led the Indians to another big victory, 10-7, over the Orioles on July 25.

Nagy, who had been the victim of poor support, offensively and by the relief corps in his previous six starts, was the recipient of the explosion sparked by Belle's two run homer in the first, and solo shot in the third.

It raised Nagy's record to 12-3, but was his first victory in 40 days. He was excused in the sixth after the Tribe had taken a 7-3 lead.

The victory also raised their lead over Chicago to a season high seven games as the White Sox lost to Texas, 4-3, for a fourth straight time.

The Indians' record since the All-Star break climbed to 10-5, while the White Sox lost 10 of 15 games during that period.

"We can feel a whole lot better than what we did at the start of the second half," said Hargrove, though he cautioned, "but we've still got two months of baseball to play. There's a long way to go."

Which was true.

But the fact is, the "big dogs" - Belle and Mesa - finally were beginning to "hunt" again, as Hart said they had to do, or the Indians would be in trouble.

And because they were, the final two months looked much brighter for the Tribe than they had appeared to be two weeks earlier.

11

GOODBYE TO THE 'HEART AND SOUL' OF THE TRIBE

July 26-August 14

There was great excitement and expectation as the Indians resumed their strong surge in the second half of the season as the "Big Dogs" continued to hunt to John Hart's satisfaction, pounding Baltimore, 14-9, on July 26.

Albert Belle led the 20 hit assault on the Orioles with his 35th home run, a double and two singles, driving in three runs for a league-leading total of 99.

They helped the Tribe overcome Greg Swindell's ineffective starting pitching - he was mercifully removed after three innings - to win for reliever Paul Assenmacher.

It gave the Indians an 11th victory in their last 16 games, and maintained their seven game lead over Chicago.

Then, after splitting the next two games with the Orioles on July 27 and 28 - the latter victory made possible by Kenny Lofton's remarkable catch of what would have been Roberto Alomar's game-winning home run - Hart commandeered the headlines.

He detonated another blockbuster deal that stunned the fans and angered many of the Indians, trading away the man that Hart himself had previously called the "heart and soul" of the team.

Carlos Baerga.

The deal, in which Baerga and Alvaro Espinoza were sent to the New York Mets for infielders Jose Vizcaino and Jeff Kent, also contradicted what Hart had said several weeks earlier.

Then, responding to published speculation that Baerga was on the block, Hart said of the report:

"This is totally and officially unfounded. It's not accurate. There's no point to discuss it any further."

Then he did, saying, "This is a joke ... a joke. It's not happening. Carlos Baerga is going nowhere ... nowhere. The whole thing is bizarre. Just bizarre."

'WE WERE LIMITED AT SECOND BASE'

After the trade with the Mets was made on July 29, an open date in the schedule, interrupting the charity golf tournament hosted annually by Baerga and Belle, Hart said that the Indians were compelled to make a change.

"We felt we were limited at second base, and the big offense we were used to seeing from Carlos wasn't there this season."

Hart also acknowledged he'd been talking to the Mets "for about a week to 10 days" about a trade, although, as New York General Manager Joe McIlvaine said, Baerga's name wasn't mentioned until three days earlier.

"We believe this makes us a better club today than we were yesterday," added Hart.

Mike Hargrove expressed similar sentiments. "I'm sure some of our players are upset," he said, "but if we worry about players' feelings when we're trying to improve the club, we're not doing our job."

The Indians' rationale was that Vizcaino, a switch-hitter, would take over - and strengthen - second base, and also could play shortstop if/when Omar Vizquel's aching shoulder forced him out of the lineup.

And Kent would replace Espinoza as a utility infielder who could play third base against left handed pitchers, giving Jim Thome a day off, and also see service at second and first base.

"It will be an honor for me to play next to Omar (Vizquel)," said Vizcaino, 28, who was hitting .303 for the Mets. Kent, 28, brought a .290 average with nine homers and 39 RBI.

Though Baerga's average had dropped to .267 (with 10 homers and 55 runs batted in) - 38 points below his lifetime .305 mark - it was his lack of range at second base, and 15 errors in 100 games that bothered the Indian chiefs.

"Simply stated, we needed to strengthen our defense," Hargrove echoed Hart.

MORE THAN MEETS THE EYE

There was, however, more to the deal than met the eye, according to sources within, and close to the organization.

Rumors had been rampant for several months that management was concerned about Baerga's off-the-field habits and activities.

"I'd be lying if I said I didn't go out after games," Baerga replied when asked the obvious question. "But I always knew what my responsibilities were. I had my family with me on almost every road trip. I take care of my family.

"So, yeah, I'd get limos on the road. I went out. But I was more careful in the things I was doing this year than I was in the past few years."

It also was said that Baerga was unwilling to do the "extra" things that had helped make him a star since his acquisition as a minor leaguer from San Diego in December 1989.

When the deal was announced, Hargrove responded to a reporter's question by saying that Baerga had a problem with his "priorities."

But, when asked to elaborate, Hargrove said, "There are some factors we don't want to get into."

'WE ARE TAKING ALL THE CHANCES'

Some strange comments also were elicited by the Mets officials.

McIlvaine told the New York media, "We know we're not getting Saint

Carlos ... but we think he can help our team."

And Dallas Green, who was then the Mets' manager (but would be fired a few weeks later), said, "We are taking all the chances."

The Indians' problems with Baerga obviously began in February when he reported for spring training weighing between 220 and 230, some 20 to 30 pounds heavy.

Though he subsequently trimmed away some of the excess avoirdupois in a rigorous training program under the direction of strength coach Fernando Montes, Baerga never really regained the esteem in which he'd previously been held.

The deal also freed the Indians of Baerga's large salary. He was making a reported $4.7 million, and would be paid the same amount in each 1997 and 1998.

Vizcaino's contract called for him to make $2.2 million in 1996, and $2.2 million in 1997. Kent was paid $1.96 million in 1996, and he would become eligible for salary arbitration when the season ended.

The Indians also had to send a reported $75,000 to the Mets as partial payment of Espinoza's $400,000 salary.

"Carlos played as hard as always, but he didn't practice as hard, and that hurt him and us," said one member of the team. "Basically, he never turned it on until 7:05 (game time), and he was always quick to get away (after games) to party."

Baerga was bitterly disappointed..

So were his legion of fans in Cleveland.

"It was like I was born to this team," he said. "I never thought this day would come. I put my heart in this team. I really enjoyed the time here. People loved me, and I think it's unfair for them to bring in another second baseman.

"I am surprised because I didn't think the team needed a trade like this. I think we have to get pitching to get better. Our offense was doing real good."

And then he asked, "How are you going to trade a winning team away? But that's the way they want to do it."

INDIANS WANTED ROBERTO ALOMAR

As for the allegations that he did not take proper care of himself, Baerga said, "If you do the job on the field, they shouldn't tell you to change anything you do off the field."

Baerga claimed he'd been playing with a sore left wrist all season and never complained about it, and that the real reason the Indians were upset with him was because he refused to move to third base.

"The front office knows about (the injury)," he said. "I've had two MRIs on it. They know I was hurt. I keep playing because I don't like to be on the bench. I showed that in the playoffs and World Series last year."

The latter was a reference to the fact that, in the 1995 post season games, Baerga played with a hairline fracture in his left ankle.

Baerga also claimed the Indians told him during the winter that they wanted to try to sign free agent second baseman Roberto Alomar. But they couldn't unless Baerga would agree to change positions.

"I told them no, and that's when all this started," he said. "By them showing interest in Robbie Alomar, it was embarrassing to me.

"Then they started talking about me coming to spring training over-weight. That was embarrassing, too.

"To say I am overweight is (expletive)

Before leaving, Baerga took a parting shot at Hargrove - which, inci-dentally, was returned by the manager.

Baerga said, "When a manager comes to you after a trade like this and all he says is four words, that tells you something.

"All (Hargrove) said to me was ''I'm sorry, good luck.' That was it. We'd been together for five years and that's all he said. That pretty much made me feel worthless."

Hargrove vehemently disputed Baerga's version of their farewell ses-sion. "I'm not going into any detail, but what Carlos was quoted as saying what I said is not true. And the man who wrote it, knows it's not true."

MARTINEZ IS PARTICULARLY CRITICAL

Particularly angry, and outspoken in his criticism of the Baerga-Espinoza trade was Dennis Martinez.

"Around here if you don't do what they ask you to do, they get you out of here," said Martinez, referring also to the deal that sent Eddie Murray to the Orioles (for pitcher Kent Mercker) on July 21.

"I know where I stand," said Martinez, acknowledging that he could be the next player to go. "People don't like to hear the truth. They want the play-ers to say good things about them. But when a player says something they don't agree with, they might do something to hurt that player.

"Everyone (in the clubhouse) is on their tiptoes. They don't know what's going on. They're in limbo. And when you have people like that, it doesn't work. I hope it does. I hope we get to the next level and win a world champion-ship.

"That's what I want. That's what I am going to fight for - if I'm here."

Martinez's remarks did not endear him to management, though neither Hart nor Hargrove had an immediate response.

Though Lofton had nothing to say about the deal, his silence seemed to speak volumes. When asked his opinion, Lofton snapped, "No comment," leav-ing little doubt about his sentiments.

Veteran catcher Tony Pena might have offered the best summary of the trade. "What all this shows to me," he said, "is that John Hart has a lot of (guts). Give him credit.

"It cannot be easy for the front office to trade someone who is recog-nized as the heart and soul of the team, but he did. He has to live with that.

"What he is trying to do is improve the club. And, I think, they are worried about Omar (Vizquel, who has had a sore shoulder all season). I don't have any problem with what (Hart) did."

Another who thought the Indians were wrong in trading Baerga was Mark Clark, the pitcher Hart shipped to the Mets on the final day of spring training - a deal that subsequently proved to be a poor one.

"As soon as somebody struggles in Cleveland, boom! Hart tries to get rid of him," said Clark. "(Hart) is scared because the pressure is on to win it this year."

TRIBE FANS ALSO ARE ANGERED

The strongest comments by a fan were made by Tom Shirer, 28, of Wickliffe, Ohio, who said:

"Carlos Baerga is the epitome of unselfishness. He signed long term before this team was a winner. And now they've taken advantage of him. I will never root for this team again. I can't root for a team that lies to me. They say he is the core of the team, (then) one bad year and they get rid of him."

But Orel Hershiser was equally outspoken in his endorsement of the deal.

"Carlos has made a lot of great contributions to this organization, and I'm sure he'll be missed. But I also believe we're a stronger team because of (the deal). We're stronger defensively, and probably stronger against left handed pitching," said Hershiser.

"We've got a Gold Glover at shortstop, a Gold Glover in center field, and a Gold Glover at catcher. I think maybe fans look at this trade and say, 'Why?' but they don't see the defensive lapses (at second base) that those with experienced baseball eyes have seen.

"I think the fans should support John (Hart). He's continued to address the problems and places where they felt (the Indians) needed to improve."

'LEADERSHIP IS A THREE RUN HOMER'

When asked if Baerga was a team leader, Hershiser chose his words carefully. "In some ways he was, and in others, no," said the pitcher. "What is it that somebody once said? That leadership is a three run homer?

"Leadership comes when you're producing on the field, and when a guy isn't producing on the field, sometimes it's tough to be a leader."

Hershiser also spoke out about those who publicly disapproved of the Murray-Mercker deal.

"I don't think the team reacted badly to Eddie being traded," he said. "The guys were sad to see him leave, but they were glad to see him get more playing time."

Hershiser also cautioned the media about making premature judgments.

"I think it's unfair to make predictions," he said. "You don't know the personalities of the guys coming in. People wondered about the (Mark) Carreon for (Jim) Poole trade and look at what Carreon's doing for us."

The best explanation of the Indians' compulsion to trade Baerga perhaps was stated by Bob August in the Lake County *News-Herald* and Lorain *Morning Journal:*

"Privately, Indians officials reached the conclusion that Baerga enjoyed life off the field too much for him to remain productive on it.

"Baerga's penchant for renting limousines to take him to and from ballparks on the road only underscored his infatuation with the trappings of being a celebrity at the cost of paying the price at the job that got him there in the first place.

"In short, the problem as Indians officials saw it - the reason Carlos Baerga is a New York Met today - is that he became too enamored with the big league life style to realize that his job should come first.

"A couple of weeks from now, when all of the emotions from the trade have died down,' said one member of the Indians staff, 'I think Carlos is going to look back on this time and realize he really blew it".

'VIZCAINO IS LIKE HAVING ANOTHER COACH'

Another who thought Hart made a good deal was John McHale, former president of the Montreal Expos, who remembered Vizcaino from the days they were together in winter ball.

"Whoever said, 'Let's get Jose Vizcaino' is a very good baseball man," said McHale. "Jose comes to play every day. He's ready mentally and physically. He's like having another coach on your team. He'll steal a big base, get a big hit. John Hart got a good player."

On the other hand, the Baerga deal pleased Ron Schueler, the general manager of the White Sox, but for a different reason.

Schueler viewed it as beneficial to the White Sox, who had lost 11 of 17 games since the All-Star break, and still trailed the Indians by seven lengths.

"Now they've traded away two of their leaders, Baerga as well as Murray, and Martinez and McDowell are hurting," the Chicago *Tribune* quoted Schueler.

Schueler and owner Jerry Reinsdorf had been making disparaging remarks about the Tribe most of the season.

"The (A.L. Central) winner is going to be somebody that puts a hot streak together at the right time," said Schueler. "I think our games against Cleveland in September (Sept. 16-18) are going to mean something."

INDIANS SEEK DAVID WELLS

Before leaving Baltimore, and with the July 31 trading deadline only 72 hours away, Hart met with Pat Gillick, his Orioles counterpart, after which both thought they'd laid the groundwork for another major deal.

Hart long had coveted David Wells, the 33 year old left hander who'd pitched for Detroit and Cincinnati in 1995, the Tigers in 1993 and 1994, and Toronto from 1987-92 - and had a history of success against the Tribe..

According to written reports, Gillick agreed to send Wells to the Tribe for outfielder Jeromy Burnitz and pitcher Alan Embree, pending the approval of Orioles owner Peter Angelos.

Gillick favored the deal because, in his opinion, it was time to rebuild the Orioles, who were then 12 games behind New York in the American League East.

But Angelos was unwilling to give up on the season that early and nullified the proposed trade, much to the consternation of Hart, who would be even more chagrined later.

With that rejection, Hart said he did not anticipate anything "major" happening before the deadline.

"We have four quality starting pitchers now, and it would be tough for us to find another one who can improve that mix," said Hart.

"We will not trade away any of our young pitchers unless we can get a guy we see as being a No. 1 starter. I don't see any guys like that out there."

Hargrove said of the Indians' inability to add an established, left handed starting pitcher, "I'm not disappointed. If we could have brought in another starter, that would have helped.

"But at the same time I have a lot of confidence in the starters we have. Our guys, one through five, are solid."

McDOWELL TO THE DISABLED LIST

However, Hart's and Hargrove's confidence in the Indians' pitching staff had to be questioned as, two days before the Baerga deal, they lost the services of Jack McDowell.

When signed as a free agent on Dec. 14, 1995, McDowell was expected to be the missing link, the money pitcher who would take the Tribe to the next level in 1996, a victory in the World Series.

But McDowell lost three consecutive starts after the All-Star break, reducing his won-lost record to 9-6 and raising his ERA to 4.50, and was placed on the disabled list July 26.

McDowell's injury, described as a strained muscle in his right forearm, was "a little more serious than we expected," Hargrove said. It marked the first time in McDowell's major league career that he was disabled.

Utility infielder Casey Candaele was recalled from Class AAA Buffalo to replace McDowell on the roster, and he immediately became a member of the Indians' makeshift lineup that was overwhelmed by the Orioles, 14-2, on July 27.

Candaele played second base in place of Baerga, who was said to be suffering a strained groin, with Espinoza at shortstop because of Vizquel's strained right hamstring, and Brian Giles went to center field and Pena caught as Lofton and Sandy Alomar were given the day off.

The loss was charged to Hershiser, though he didn't blame the substitutes. "Our lineup had no effect on me," he said. "Everyone knows that's not our regular lineup. You have to go out and pitch your game regardless."

Which Hershiser didn't.

He was rocked for 11 hits and 10 runs, seven of them in the sixth inning when Hershiser was kayoed by a grand slam by Rafael Palmeiro, and Wells raised his lifetime record against the Indians to 7-3, and 2-0 in 1996.

"I'll take one bad start out of 10 anytime," said Hershiser, who had allowed only six earned runs over 63 2/3 innings in his previous nine starts.

LOFTON'S REMARKABLE, GAME-SAVING CATCH

It was a different story the next day, July 28, primarily because Lofton was back in center field, although the margin of the 6-3 victory was provided by Thome's 13th inning, three run homer.

Lofton, who'd won three Gold Glove awards in his previous four seasons, stole what would have been a game-winning, two run homer off the bat of Roberto Alomar in the 12th.

Lofton leaped high - and reached over - the center field fence to catch the ball for the second out of the inning, and maintain the 3-3 tie.

Then Lofton provided an encore. He charged in to field a single by

Mike Devereaux, the next batter, and fired a strike to Thome to retire Luis Polonia and end the threat.

An inning later, after Sandy Alomar walked and was sacrifice bunted to second, Lofton beat out an infield single and stole second, setting the stage for Thome's two-out homer.

Candaele, the longtime minor leaguer who'd seen limited service in the National League with Houston, also homered for the first time in the major leagues since Sept. 1, 1993.

So did B.J. Surhoff, off Chad Ogea who started for the Tribe in another effort to nail down the fifth place in the rotation.

Lofton said of the homer he stole from Roberto Alomar, "I'd rather make a catch like that than hit a home run." However, he denied it was the best he'd ever made, "though I'd say it was the best because of the situation."

So would Jose Mesa, who was on the mound at the time and got credit for the victory.

'TRADE HART ... NOT CARLOS'

With their new second base combination - Vizquel at short and Vizcaino at second, although sometimes Vizcaino was the shortstop and Kent the second baseman - the Indians returned on July 30 to the friendly confines of Jacobs Field.

This time, however, there were some angry patrons among the 100th consecutive sellout crowd, and an airplane circled overhead dragging a banner that read: "Trade Hart ... Not Carlos."

It was one of the few times that fans had shown any hostility toward the man who was credited with rebuilding the Indians and bringing a pennant to Cleveland for the first time in 41 years.

But if it bothered Hart, he wouldn't admit it. "That's baseball," was his only comment, as the Indians lost, 3-1, to Toronto and a previously unknown rookie pitcher named Huck Flener.

The Indians public relations department also received "hundreds" of calls protesting the trading of Baerga, according to Vice President Bob DiBiasio. "We expected it," he said. "Carlos was a very popular player."

Though no team meeting was held before the game, Hargrove said, "I talked to just about every player individually ... I wanted to get a read on how they were feeling. There wasn't one who was struggling with (the repercussions of the trade)."

Hargrove also met with Vizcaino and Kent. "I told them they might get booed, but that it wouldn't be directed so much at them as it was a way of showing the fans' support for Baerga," Hargrove said.

The loss was charged to Martinez, who gave up all of Toronto's runs on six hits in five innings. It would turn out to be the last decision in a Cleveland uniform for Martinez, though he would start one more game, without being the pitcher of record, nearly a month later.

TRIBE'S LEAD CUT TO SIX GAMES

The loss to the Blue Jays cut the Tribe's lead to six games over Chicago, which beat Oakland, 2-1.

Vizcaino singled in his first at-bat, and played shortstop with Kent at second base. Both were booed when neither covered second on a double by Ed Sprague in the third inning, but otherwise the newcomers played well.

"Given the circumstances and the uncertainty they faced coming in, and replacing a popular player like Carlos, I thought they did a good job," said Hargrove.

It also was upon the occasion of the Indians' first game back in Cleveland since the trade of Baerga and Espinoza that Belle noted their empty lockers in the clubhouse and let his feelings be known.

Belle turned the nameplate above his locker backward, so that it could not be read, and said, according to one observer, "Next year this locker will be empty, too."

It was an apparent reference to his contractual status with the Indians; he would be eligible to become a free agent at the end of the season.

'LIKE DEJA VU ALL OVER AGAIN'

As Yogi Berra would have said, it was *deja vu* all over again - for several reasons - the next night, July 31, as Belle hammered his sixth career grand slam and 36th homer of the season with two out in the last of the ninth inning to beat the Blue Jays, 4-2.

It also marked the 12th time the Indians came back in their last at-bat to win, after doing so 27 times in 1995.

Belle's grand slam was set up by Burnitz's pinch single leading the ninth, and two walks by Mike Timlin with one out. After Thome fouled out, Belle drove a 1-and-0 pitch from reliever Bill Risley into the left field plaza.

The victory was credited to Assenmacher, the Tribe's fourth pitcher to follow Charles Nagy, who gave up three hits and a run through the first five innings. The game was interrupted by a two-hour, 21-minute rain delay in the third.

The victory hiked the Indians' lead to seven games again as Chicago lost for the 12th time in 20 games since the All-Star break, 5-4, to Oakland.

LOPEZ RECALLED TO REPLACE McDOWELL

But August began for the Indians with a 5-3 setback handed them by the Blue Jays, as an unhappy Albie Lopez was the victim of poor support.

Lopez was recalled earlier in the day from Buffalo, as Embree was placed on the disabled list with bursitis in his left hip.

Lopez was to get two starts in place of McDowell and pitched well enough in the first one to win most games, except that the Indians wasted numerous opportunities on his behalf. They got 12 hits, three each by Giles and Julio Franco, but few at the right time and left eight runners stranded..

"I'm through playing guessing games," grumbled Lopez when asked if he thought he improved his chances of staying with the Indians the rest of the season. Lopez's record with the Bisons was an impressive 10-2 with a 3.87 ERA.

"I'm just trying to get through this season and see what happens. The Indians don't have any more options on me, so they'll either have to keep me in the big leagues, or trade me next spring."

Hargrove wouldn't comment on whatever the future might hold for Lopez, but of the present, he said, "Albie certainly pitched better than he did the last time he was here. We saw him pitch tonight, not just throw the ball. He showed he was confident in his ability to make tough pitches."

Solo home runs by John Olerud in the seventh, and Joe Carter off Mesa in the ninth won it for the Blue Jays after the Indians had battled back from a 3-0 deficit to tie the score in the fourth.

INDIANS LOSE TO WELLS AGAIN

The loss began a two week period in which the Indians split another four game series against Baltimore, and embarked upon a nine game western trip that started promisingly in Seattle, but faltered in Oakland and Anaheim.

The bottom line: the Indians went 7-6 but, fortunately, lost only one game of their lead over the White Sox, who also slumped badly and all but fell out of the race.

The Indians rolled over the Orioles, 11-1 and 14-2, on Aug. 2 and Aug. 4, behind Hershiser and Brian Anderson, but were in turn embarrassed by 9-4 and 13-10 losses on Aug. 3 and Aug. 5 to Jessie Orosco, a former Tribesman, and Wells, their longtime nemesis.

"It is amazing ... I have no idea why we hit their pitching the way we do," Hargrove said of the 11-1 victory over Baltimore. Belle's 37th homer was one of four the Indians included among their 16 hits that made a loser of Scott Erickson.

Instead of celebrating, however, Belle, again for an unknown reason, attacked the Indians' post game spread in the clubhouse with his bat. Not only did he shatter dishes, he also broke up the table and the food that was on it, and knocked the phone off the wall.

MURRAY RETURNS TO JACOBS FIELD

Lofton, Carreon and Burnitz also homered in the game that marked Murray's first return to Jacobs Field in an Orioles uniform. In his first 11 games since he was traded to Baltimore, Murray hit two home runs, giving him 14 for the season and a career total of 493.

In one of the few interviews granted by Murray, he said he was happy to be playing for the Orioles because, "This is a chance for me to be in the lineup every day," which wasn't the case with the Tribe.

"There are a few people in the game - especially the guys (the Indians) in that other locker room - who really wanted to see me hit 500 homers."

While many of his Tribe teammates were angry when Murray was traded, they were even more upset earlier when he was benched against right handed pitchers.

It was a particularly touchy situation on July 12 when, in the ninth inning of a game in Minnesota, Burnitz was sent to the plate as a pinch hitter for the future Hall of Famer.

"Sometimes if you don't have anything good to say, you try not to say anything. But it was tough looking at the guys getting ticked off. When I wasn't in the lineup they kept coming up to me and saying, 'Are you hurt? Why aren't you playing?'" said Murray.

"What I'll remember about Cleveland are the people. What they said in 'Field of Dreams' is true. 'Build it and they will come.' Those people in Cleveland filled Jacobs Field every night."

ORIOLES FINALLY WIN AT JACOBS FIELD

The next day the Indians grounded into two double plays - raising their league lead in that statistic to 118 - both of them killing potential rallies, and suffered a 9-4 loss charged to Ogea. It broke the Orioles' 10 game losing streak at Jacobs Field.

The Indians also left 10 runners stranded, giving them a season total of 862, also the most in the A.L.

Manny Ramirez blasted his 25th homer in the eighth inning, but by then it was too little and too late. He also singled three times, but the Orioles got homers from Brady Anderson, his 34th, and Bobby Bonilla.

Also on the down side for the Tribe was that Franco re-injured his right hamstring, which he hurt the first time on June 22 and landed him on the disabled list originally on July 11. Franco would go back on the disabled list Aug. 6.

There was another incident in which Belle came under criticism again, this one in the ninth inning, with the game all but over, when he hit a long drive to right center that he thought would leave the park for his 38th homer.

Instead, the ball banged off the wall and Belle, jogging to first, never got beyond that base as Thome was thrown out at the plate, trying to score from first base.

It was obvious that Hargrove did not appreciate Belle's lack of hustle, but when asked about it, he said, "I was watching Jimmy (trying to score), not Albert."

MARTINEZ OUT, BRIAN ANDERSON IN

Martinez was scheduled to start the next day, Aug. 4, but never got to the mound as his elbow injury flared up again as he warmed up for the game.

As a precautionary measure the Indians had summoned Brian Anderson from Buffalo in case Martinez was unable to pitch. Thus, Martinez returned to the disabled list and Anderson was officially placed on the major league roster - and started against the Orioles.

"We brought Brian up in case we needed him, and it was a good thing we did," said Hargrove.

The way the game went, it also was a good thing for Anderson, although the 14-2 blow out of the Orioles was not as one-sided as it sounds.

The Indians were clinging to a 3-2 lead when they exploded after two were out for 11 runs in the eighth inning as Thome and Giles bashed homers.

But Lofton was the main topic of conversation afterwards. Not only did he deliver a solo homer in the third, single in the eighth, draw a walk and steal two bases to raise his league-leading total to 53, he also made another remarkable catch that had to be seen to be believed.

"I was stunned," said Sandy Alomar, who was in the Indians' bull pen when Lofton leaped high - and, again, *over* - the fence to steal what would have been a two run homer by Surhoff in the top of the eighth.

It would have put the Orioles ahead, 4-3, but instead, was the third out, enabling the Indians to come to life and send 14 batters to the plate in the bottom of the inning.

"Kenny climbed the fence like Spiderman," said Alomar. "It was the most unbelievable catch I ever saw."

Bull pen coach Luis Isaac was equally awed. "I thought I was dreaming," he said. "(Lofton) must have been four feet over the fence. We just started screaming. We knew that was the game."

GRAVES: 'IT WAS AMAZING'

Danny Graves, who also was seated in the bull pen, said, "It was amazing. I'll never see another catch like that as long as I live. I'll talk about it forever."

Lofton was asked to compare the catch to the one he made against the Orioles on July 28. That one deprived Roberto Alomar of what would have been a game winning homer.

"This one was much better," Lofton said, "The wall (at Jacobs Field) is higher, although the other one (at Camden Yards) was a game saver. If I don't make it, we lose. This time we still had a chance to come back and score some runs.

"I love making catches like that, more than hitting a home run. I like helping the pitcher out when he's made a mistake. Whenever you do that, it can be a game saver."

Of the offensive explosion by the Indians, Hargrove said, "I don't think I've ever seen that many runs scored with two out."

Anderson, the Geneva, Ohio left hander who grew up cheering for the Indians, pitched 5 1/3 innings to earn his first victory since being acquired from California at the start of spring training.

As for Martinez, nobody was writing him off - yet. But there seemed to be little doubt that his sore elbow would continue to plague him (which it did).

"Anytime any one of your pitchers has back-to-back (trips) to the D.L., regardless of age, it's a concern," said Hargrove, "although the doctor (Louis Keppler) thinks Martinez will be OK with rest."

NAGY STILL SEEKING VICTORY No. 13

The Orioles wreaked a share of revenge the next night, beating the Indians, 13-10, and again it was Wells, the same longtime tormentor they tried to acquire in a trade, who was credited with the victory in the slugfest.

Actually, it wasn't as close as the score indicated as the Indians rallied in the ninth for six runs against three relievers before Lofton, who solo homered to start the inning, popped out as the 10th batter to end it.

Nagy started, again seeking a 13th victory, but left in the sixth with the scored tied, 3-3. The Orioles went ahead, 7-3, against Assenmacher and Graves in the seventh, and broke the game open with six more runs in the eighth off Graves.

Though he didn't let it show, there was little doubt that Nagy was consumed with frustration.

After his first 14 starts Nagy's record was 11-1 with a 3.72 ERA and, not only did it appear that he would become the Indians' first 20 game winner since Gaylord Perry in 1974, he also was the leading candidate to win the A.l. Cy Young Award.

In nine starts since then, however, Nagy was 1-2 with six no-decisions.

"The problem is, these days pitchers tend to get a lot of no-decisions because the bull pens are so much better than they were 20 years ago," said pitching coach Mark Wiley.

"Twenty years ago you might leave a pitcher in when the game is tied, and the team might end up winning and the pitcher would get the credit. Today, if it's tied late in the game, the pitcher is frequently taken out."

In another roster move, Anderson, who won his first game for the Indians the previous day, was returned to Buffalo and Julian Tavarez recalled.

And the next day it was Franco's turn to go back on the disabled list for the second time, because of his strained right hamstring. Called up from Buffalo to fill the vacancy on the roster was Mercker, the pitcher obtained from Baltimore in the deal for Murray.

INDIANS CREATE THE QUAKE THIS TIME

The last time the Indians were in Seattle their game on May 2 against the Mariners was interrupted by an earthquake.

This time, in the first stop on a three city western trip, the Indians created their own quake.

They swept the Mariners, 4-3, 5-4 and 2-1.

The opener, on Aug. 6, was a victory by Lopez who took a one hitter and a 4-1 lead into the sixth inning, tired in the seventh and was put in jeopardy because of an error by Vizcaino.

The Mariners scored twice after Eric Plunk replaced Lopez, but Tavarez blanked Seattle in the eighth. Mesa struggled but prevailed with a scoreless ninth to record his 26th save, his first since July 22 - and only his first in a one run game since June 10.

Mesa gave up two hits, putting the tying and winning runs on base, but ended the game by pitching a double play ball to Joey Cora.

Mesa impressed Wiley who said, "Jose was throwing between 97 and 99 (miles per hour) ... he's back to where he was."

Bob Wells, the Mariners' winningest pitcher with 11 victories, was hit for all the Tribe runs in the fifth inning, the big blow being a two run single by Carreon.

Then Randy Johnson, the 1995 A.L. Cy Young award winner, took over in the sixth in his first appearance after nearly three months on the disabled list with a back injury. He pitched two scoreless innings.

LIKE THE GOOD OLD DAYS OF 1995

It was like old times - the good old days of 1995 - the next night, Aug. 7, when the Indians erupted for three runs in the ninth to overcome a 4-2 Mariners' lead and register their 17th victory in 27 games since the All-Star break.

It was the "V-Squad," Vizquel and Vizcaino, that delivered the big blows off Norm Charlton, the left handed reliever (formerly known as one of the "Nasty Boys") who usually dominated the Tribe.

And, ironically, it was Jamie Moyer, another lefty who seldom gave the Indians trouble, who held them in check through the first eight innings.

Vizquel launched the comeback with a two-out, solo homer off Charlton, and Lofton singled, then scored the tying run on Vizcaino's double.

The go ahead run came around on Carreon's infield single and Cora's throwing error, the Mariners' fourth miscue of the game. Mesa earned his 27th save, but not without a major contribution by Ramirez.

Alex Rodriguez singled with one out, but was thrown out trying to stretch it into a double on a strong throw by Ramirez. Then Mesa got the next two batters, ending the game.

The victory was credited to Tavarez, though he was burned in the eighth, his only inning in relief of Hershiser. Dan Wilson greeted Tavarez with a home run, boosting the Mariners' lead to 4-2.

Hershiser was tagged for Rodriguez's 25th homer in the third, but squirmed out of bases loaded situations in the fourth and fifth. The Mariners went ahead, 3-2, in the seventh when Hargrove left himself open to the second guessers.

Cora led off with a double, Rodriguez walked, and they were advanced to second and third on a sacrifice bunt by Ken Griffey Jr.

With first base open, Hargrove disdained an intentional walk to Jay Buhner that would have loaded the bases and set up a double play. Buhner then singled for the tie breaking run before Paul Sorrento bounced into a double play.

"Mike and I talked about (intentionally walking Buhner), and he gave me the option," said Hershiser. "It was my decision, I wanted to pitch to him. I just made a mistake with a slider."

Said Hargrove, "With a pitcher of Hershiser's caliber, you always give him the option."

Winning as they did, again was reminiscent of 1995, though Hargrove said it was time to forget what happened then.

HARGROVE: 'STOP GRABBING AT LAST YEAR'

"We need to stop grabbing at last year," he said. "Every time we win a game like that people say, 'You had 30 of those kind of games last year.' Well, last year is gone. We are in reality. Reality was not last year. Those kind of years don't come along very often."

Hershiser agreed. "It's not like we came to spring training and Grover (Hargrove) called a meeting and said, 'OK, our goal this year is to surpass our ninth inning comeback wins from last year."

Ogea completed the sweep the next night, Aug. 8, and firmly established himself - finally - as the Indians' fifth starter.

He allowed only one hit through eight innings, a tainted single by Rich Amaral in the second, as the Indians prevailed, 2-1, boosting their A.,L. Central lead over Chicago back to seven games.

Kent, acquired in the Baerga trade, played a key role in both Tribe runs. He singled for a 1-0 lead in the fourth, after Vizcaino's single and Belle's walk, and led off the seventh with a double and scored on Thome's single.

Mesa came out of the bull pen to record another save, his 28th and third in the series, but again not without some very anxious moments. He struck out Cora, but after going 0-and-2 on Rodriguez, was hammered for a homer by the Mariners shortstop who would go on to win the A.L. batting championship.

Griffey followed with a single and represented the tying run, before Mesa struck out Buhner and Sorrento to end the suspense.

The tainted hit off Ogea came with two out as Amaral bounced a grounder to the right side of the infield. Carreon broke to his right to get it, but realizing he had no chance, hurried back to first base as Vizcaino fielded the ball.

The throw appeared to beat Amaral, but umpire Tim McClelland ruled otherwise. "It wasn't an error," said McClelland. "The throw didn't pull (Carreon) off the bag. In my judgment, Carreon just didn't get to the bag in time."

Carreon disagreed. "I think (Amaral) was out. I was standing on the bag. Amaral even stepped on my ankle."

Ogea concurred. "I was right there on top of the play. I saw it as well as (McClelland)."

THE UMPIRE WINS AGAIN

The umpire, of course, won the argument.

It didn't matter - at least not at the time - as Amaral stole second, continued to third as Alomar's throw flew into center field when nobody covered the base, but Doug Strange struck out to end the inning.

As it turned out, Strange was the first of 17 consecutive Mariners retired by Ogea.

Ogea said he wasn't upset by Hargrove's decision to take him out after eight innings. "There was some disagreement among the team, some guys on the bench were like, 'What? He's taking him out with a one hitter?' But it didn't bother me.

"Sure, instinctively, I wanted to stay in and pitch all nine innings. But we've got a guy out there (Mesa) who has 70-some saves the last two years. That's his job to pitch the ninth."

Hargrove said he would have allowed Ogea to pitch the ninth if he'd been working on a no-hitter - which television replays of the Amaral "hit" proved that he should have been, McClelland's ruling notwithstanding.

RUDELY BROUGHT BACK TO REALITY

And then, envisioning their best west coast trip in years, the Indians, after beating Oakland, 10-4, on Aug. 9 in the opener of a three game series, were rudely and quickly brought back to reality by the Athletics.

They lost the next two games, 5-1 and 9-3, and once again began looking over their shoulders at the White Sox, who trailed the Indians by only six games the morning of Aug. 12.

McDowell, fresh off the disabled list (with Graves being returned to Buffalo), pitched the first five innings and left with a 4-3 lead that was protected by Paul Shuey, Mercker and Tavarez.

McDowell still wasn't pain-free, but said his sore right forearm was much improved. "It's going to hurt for the rest of the year," he said, "but at least it's not as sore as it was,"

The latter remark did not bode well for the rest of the season.

The victory gave McDowell a 10-6 record - and 4-0 since the All-Star break - establishing him as one of only four major league pitchers to win at least 10 games every season since 1990.

The others were Greg Maddux and Tom Glavine of Atlanta, and Kevin Tapani of Minnesota, Los Angeles and the White Sox.

After McDowell was in the showers, the victory became a laugher as Belle crashed his 38th homer to feature a four run seventh inning, and Thome and Giles each got three of the Tribe's 15 hits.

NAGY AND LOPEZ ARE ROCKED

It wasn't so funny the next two days, however, as the Athletics played long ball to beat Nagy and Lopez, back-to-back.

A couple of guys named Jose Herrera and Willie Adams administered the harshest punishment in Oakland's 5-1 beating of the Tribe in the second game of the series.

All of the Athletics' runs came on homers, two by Herrera and the other by Terry Steinbach, and Adams, making his first major league start, scattered seven hits, including Thome's solo homer, over six innings for the victory.

"What can I say?" asked Hargrove. "They beat us. The one guy (Herrera) hit two good pitches out of the park. We come in here and he's hitting about .230 (actually, .258), but against us he's hitting five thousand. And the other guy (Adams) pitched a good game. That's all."

Pena agreed, with one exception. "Herrera hit two *great* pitches, especially the second (in the third inning). It was about an inch off the ground when he hit it," said the veteran catcher who went 0-for-3, raising his hitless streak to 20 consecutive at-bats.

"I can remember the last time I was on base," Pena said. "It's not like I'm tired. I'm just trying too hard. That's what it is."

As for Herrera's homers, "The guy is a low ball hitter ... sometimes you have to learn the hard way," said Nagy, whose record fell to 12-4. It was his first loss since July 19.

Steinbach's homer, a three run shot in the fourth inning, was his 28th.

"Oakland has a lot of guys who hit home runs, and the ball jumps out of this park, but you can't change the way you pitch. There are a lot of small parks in this league. That includes Jacobs Field," added Nagy.

FROM BAD TO WORSE

It went from bad to worse for the Indians in the finale of the Oakland series, as another rookie pitcher, John Wasdin, beat them, 9-3. Until then Wasdin's record was 0-3 with a bloated 14.21 ERA.

No wonder the Indians were looking over their shoulders at Chicago when they left town after the beating.

Although the Tribe started fast, taking a 2-0 lead after Lofton cracked a home run in the first inning, Lopez frittered it away and didn't last long on the mound.

The Athletics tied the score in the second, and with the score deadlocked at 3-3 in the fifth, they broke the game wide open, sending Lopez to the showers when they exploded for six runs, three of them on Scott Brosius' 19th homer.

Tavarez replaced Lopez but wasn't much better, and suddenly the west coast trip that started so promisingly for the Indians, had become a cause for concern.

Thome, who also homered for the second time in three games, said of the rookie pitchers who shut down the Tribe twice in a row, "I don't think we were at a disadvantage just because we haven't seen those two starters that much.

"They still have to throw the ball across the plate, and we still have to make adjustments. We didn't do that."

Then what was the problem? Hargrove said there was none. "We just got beat."

TRIBE LEAD CUT TO FIVE

Which the Indians did again, twice in their next three games against the Angels in Anaheim, concluding a 5-4 trip that cut their lead over Chicago to five lengths, equaling the shortest it had been since July 22.

Hershiser, pitching well again, was a 5-4 winner over California in the Aug. 12 opener, but Ogea and McDowell couldn't maintain the momentum as the Indians were beaten, 4-2 and 8-7, on Aug. 13 and 14.

Belle and Alomar, both in prolonged batting slumps, seemed to break out of them in support of Hershiser, whose record climbed to 12-7 - and 7-3 in his last 13 starts.

Hershiser's sinker was working so well that Hargrove said, "His ball has such dramatic and late breaking action to it, that people think he's cutting the ball, or even throwing a spitter."

It even took a year for Alomar to be convinced that Hershiser was not cheating. "Sandy was afraid to say anything to me last year," said Hershiser. "He didn't want to know what I was doing to the ball."

Wiley said the sinker is Hershiser's natural gift. "The way his arm and shoulder are constructed, and the way he releases the ball allow him to throw like that."

Whatever it is, Hershiser's sinker worked to near perfection against the Angels. He gave up five hits through seven innings, and left with a 5-1 lead after walking the first two batters in the eighth.

Belle, who was 3-for-22 in the first six games of the trip, gave the Indians a 3-1 lead that they never relinquished with a two run single in the third inning.

Alomar, 1-for-18 on the trip, and 12-for-79 since July 3, went 3-for-4, driving in two runs with a sixth inning double.

Then, in the eighth, Belle stole what would have been a three run homer from Chili Davis with a leaping catch in front of the left field stands. It was so good that Lofton jogged over from his center field position to congratulate Belle.

However, the next batter, Jim Edmonds doubled off Assenmacher for one run, Shuey took over and promptly walked Tim Salmon to load the bases, then uncorked a wild pitch for another run.

California's third run of the inning and fourth of the game scored on a ground out, and Mesa retired the Angels in order, on 15 pitches in the ninth for his 29th save.

BELLE GETS EARLY WAKE-UP CALL

Ogea didn't pitch badly the next night, but neither did he get much offensive help, despite 11 hits by the Indians - or defensive help either. Their only runs came on solo homers by Belle, his 39th in the second, and Lofton in the third inning.

Obviously, Belle was suffering no ill effects from the early wake-up call he received that morning from an intrepid - if insensitive, blockheaded - radio talk show host from San Diego.

David Singer, from station XTRA, knocked on the door of Belle's hotel room at 7:30 a.m. with a cellular phone to request an interview.

Belle answered the knock and, after a brief but controlled exchange - which was carried over the air - slammed the door on Singer, who was then escorted out of the hotel by security officers.

The Indians filed a complaint with the A.L. and Phyllis Merhige, vice president of administration, said the station would not be given credentials for post season games as a penalty for Singer's actions.

The Angels also got two solo homers in the game that night, by Jim Edmonds and J.T. Snow off Ogea in the first and fifth. They broke the 2-2 tie with an unearned run in the sixth on an error by Vizcaino, and made it 4-2 with three singles off Eric Plunk in the eighth.

"Chad pitched well, but again we couldn't get a hit at the right time," Hargrove said of the eight base runners the Indians stranded, including two others who were thrown out at third and at the plate in the seventh.

Ramirez also was unable to score from first on a long, two out double by Carreon in the fourth, and two innings later was picked off first by Shawn Boskie.

McDOWELL FAILS TO HOLD 6-0 LEAD

McDowell was in no mood to be interviewed the next night, after he failed to hold a 6-0 lead and couldn't get past the third inning in the Tribe's 8-7 loss that ended the three city, nine game trip on a sorry note.

"I didn't get a chance to know how my arm felt ... they took me out of the game in the third inning with a lead," snapped McDowell.

Then, this parting shot, "I've never seen anything like that in my life," and stalked away.

To make matters worse for the Indians, their late inning rally was halted by one of their former farmhands, Pep Harris, who was traded to the Angels with Jason Grimsley for Anderson in February.

Grimsley had started against the Tribe, but couldn't do much of anything right in the first two innings. He was scorched for six runs - all of which, plus one, McDowell gave back to the Angels before he was mercifully replaced by Mercker (who wasn't an improvement).

Before Mercker was banished, also in the third, the Angels had all the runs they needed, despite being blanked over the final six innings by Tavarez, Shuey and Assenmacher.

Because his right forearm was still sore, by his own admission, McDowell threw few curve balls, relying almost exclusively on his fast ball and split fingered pitch, and obviously they weren't good enough.

The Angels scored four runs - all after two were out - on five hits in the second, and four more in the third.

When Hargrove went to the mound to replace McDowell with one run in and runners on first and third with one out, the pitcher obviously was angry, neither waiting for Mercker to arrive, nor making eye contact with the manager.

Hargrove wouldn't discuss the incident later, saying only that he was sure that McDowell's breach of major league protocol would not happen again - indicating that the issue was resolved behind closed doors.

HARGROVE'S JOB IN JEOPARDY?

And so, the Indians returned to Cleveland with a five game lead over the White Sox amid new rumors that, because of the problems on the west coast trip, Hargrove's job would be on the line, depending upon the team's performance in the post season.

All of which was predicated on owner Richard Jacobs' pre-season avowal that the organization's "single mission" was "to prepare ourselves so the 1996 World Series will be won by the Cleveland Indians."

*Sandy Alomar watches the ball as it goes into the
stands for a home run against the Brewers*

12

ANOTHER ROLLER COASTER RIDE

August 15-31

Back home with a not-so-comfortable five game lead over the Chicago White Sox on Aug. 15, the Indians were given permission to print post season game tickets - and then climbed back on the roller coaster they'd been riding most of the second half.

Their record since the All-Star break was 20-14, but only 9-8 after being blown out, 14-2, in Baltimore on July 27, and they'd lost four of five games to California and Oakland to wind up a 5-4 west coast trip.

All of which kept General Manager John Hart busy, despite the July 31 expiration of the trading deadline, as he continued to seek the two commodities he felt the Indians needed to get back to the World Series:

•Another starting pitcher because of the ongoing physical problems suffered by Dennis Martinez (who, 11 days earlier, returned to the disabled list for the second time with a strained flexor tendon in his right elbow), and the puzzling inconsistency of Jack McDowell (who also had spent time on the disabled list in late July).

•A right-handed designated hitter to help combat what was becoming a diet of left handed pitchers, against which the Indians' record was 18-17, compared to 54-32 vs. right handers.

Hart's initial effort was to land Denny Neagle, a crafty southpaw whom the Pittsburgh Pirates were making available to the highest bidder because of his salary, reported to be $2.3 million in 1996 and $3.5 million in 1997.

Hart's offer for Neagle was surprisingly generous: he invited the Pirates to pick any three players from the Indians' farm system, without ruling any of them untouchable, not even pitchers Albie Lopez, Bartolo Colon, Jaret Wright, Daron Kirkreit, or Danny Graves; shortstop-second baseman Enrique Wilson, third baseman Russell Branyan, or first basemen Richie Sexson or Sean Casey - all of whom had been advertised by the organization as being "can't miss" prospects.

When the Pirates rejected the Indians' bid and dealt Neagle to Atlanta in late-August for three Braves' farmhands, Hart said, "Quite frankly, I'm stunned!"

Quite frankly, many close observers of the Indians also were stunned that Hart would make such an offer for Neagle, described as a "finesse" pitcher whose control had to be near perfect for him to be successful.

INDIANS LEAD WHITE SOX BY FIVE

Hart's attempts to wheel-and-deal continued through the rest of August, although some of the urgency he'd felt because of the Indians' second half inconsistency was dissipated because the White Sox also were struggling.

After closing to within two games of the Indians at the All-Star break, the White Sox experienced trouble of their own, primarily because Frank Thomas was sidelined for nearly three weeks with a stress fracture of his foot. During Thomas' absence the White Sox went 17-17 through Aug. 15.

Despite the Indians' five game lead it was still a race with 6 1/2 weeks remaining as they opened a nine game homestand with a three game series against their "cousins," the Detroit Tigers.

SPIKE LEE: 'IT'S A FAIR PIECE'

It was during the Tigers' visit that television producer Spike Lee came to Jacobs Field to complete an interview with Albert Belle for an HBO special.

Lee had this to say about the controversial Tribe star:

"I knew there was more to (Belle) than I was reading, especially in the New York papers. I was intrigued by him. He's very articulate, very smart, and this is something people don't point out. He's not the first person in sports that didn't want to talk to the media. Once he got going with us, he talked for 90 minutes non-stop.

"(Belle) doesn't (trust people). That's his personality. In the piece, he talks about some of the things he would've done differently. It's obvious some of the things have hurt him with endorsements. He wants to do them."

Of the documentary, Lee said, "I think it's a fair piece. We hear from (Belle's) detractors and we let Albert respond. To me, what he's saying is, 'I am what I am, and nobody's going to mold me differently.' He has a ritual, a routine, and he doesn't want it to be messed with."

At the time of Lee's visit there also was a rumor that Belle had agreed to sign a new contract calling for as much as $50 million over five years that would keep him in Cleveland through 2001, but it was denied by Tribe officials.

ANOTHER NO-DECISION FOR NAGY

As for the series with the Tigers, it proved to be exactly what the Indians needed as they won all three games, 3-1 in 12 innings, 6-3 and 11-3, while the White Sox were losing two of four in Milwaukee.

Sandy Alomar's two run homer with two out in the 12th enabled the Tribe to capture the opener on Aug. 16, making a winner of Paul Assenmacher.

The only negative aspect was that Charles Nagy again was deprived - despite another fine performance - of his 14th victory. Instead, it was his seventh no-decision in his last 11 starts.

Nagy pitched nine strong innings, allowing one run on five hits, two of them in the sixth when the Tigers tied the score, 1-1.

Actually, Nagy could consider himself fortunate that he didn't lose the game, 1-0, as Detroit's starter, Felipe Lira, was even tougher. Lira gave up only two hits over eight innings, with the Tribe scoring its first run in the second on a walk, stolen base, error and sacrifice fly.

"Charlie was outstanding again," said Mike Hargrove. "It's a shame for him we didn't score any runs, and it's a shame for us."

In his first 14 starts in 1996, Nagy was 11-1, including six straight victories between May 3-30. Then, in 11 subsequent starts Nagy went 1-3, despite pitching well enough in those seven no-decisions to win at least six.

At the time it was expected that Nagy would become the Tribe's first 20 game winner since Gaylord Perry (21-13) in 1974, and he also was the front runner for the A.L. Cy Young Award.

"It's not real frustrating, but you do think about it," Nagy spoke of his inability to win. "You think about your good first half, and that you haven't won in a long time in the second half.

"But the only thing you can do is go out and keep grinding away. I've still got eight starts left. There's still a chance to get on another roll."

HERSHISER AND THOME BEAT DETROIT

The Indians continued their roll against the Tigers the next day, Aug. 17, behind Orel Hershiser's 14th consecutive solid performance, though this victory wasn't settled early, and didn't come easily.

Jim Thome blasted his 25th homer, and his two runs batted in gave him a career high 79. The Indians rallied for four runs in the sixth to break a 2-2 tie, giving Hershiser a 9-3 record and 2.23 ERA since June 8.

"Orel came up big for us, even though he didn't have his best stuff," said Hargrove. "And to win when you don't have your best stuff is the mark of a very good pitcher."

Hershiser endured some anxious moments before it was over as he took a 6-2 lead into the seventh inning, then walked two batters and gave up a bases-loaded single with two out.

Eric Plunk came to the rescue and retired Travis Fryman on a long fly that Belle caught on the warning track to end the threat.

When the Tigers scored their third run with two out in the ninth, Jose Mesa came on to end it with six pitches for his 30th save.

TRIBE GOES TO 9-0 vs. DETROIT

Thome did it again - and even more - the next day, Aug. 18, eliciting an appropriate comment from Hargrove: "With Jimmy, anything he does with a bat should not surprise anyone."

In the 11-3 trouncing of the Tigers which gave the Indians a perfect 9-0 mark against Detroit in 1996 and an 18-1 record in three seasons at Jacobs Field, Thome blasted two more homers. One was his first career grand slam, and he also singled twice, driving in six runs.

It boosted Thome's batting average to .320, which was all the more remarkable considering that he started the season with only one hit in his first 20 at-bats.

"I've never had a game where I've had this kind of production," said Thome, whose first home run was initially called a double by umpire Jim Evans.

After a heated debate with Hargrove, and in consultation with the other three umpires, Evans changed his decision.

And that, of course, brought Buddy Bell, the Detroit manager and former Indians coach, out for another argument.

"I thought Buddy was my friend," quipped Thome, whose slam came in the eighth when the Indians scored five times.

It made it easy for Chad Ogea, now solidly entrenched as the Tribe's fifth starter, though he was resting by then. Julian Tavarez blanked the Tigers in the seventh and eighth, and Paul Shuey did the same in the ninth.

Kenny Lofton, off and running toward his fifth consecutive stolen base championship, got the rout started with a first inning single.

It was his 58th stolen bases in 73 attempt, and gave Lofton a three base lead over his closest competitor, Kansas City's Tom Goodwin.

Bell vented his frustration on his hapless Tigers after the game. "We had a meeting," he said, "and, to be honest with you, I think we disrespected this game in particular, and the game of baseball in general.

"We lost the first two games of this series, and I don't think we gave a (expletive) about playing today. We wanted to go home and didn't give a (explerassing)."

McDOWELL: 'I'M JUST NOT IN A GROOVE'

The victory over the Tigers in the series finale, combined with Chicago's 8-7 loss to Milwaukee, gave the Indians a season-high 7 1/2 game lead.

But whatever relief they might have felt was short-lived as the American League West leading Texas Rangers came to town and, just like that, the Indians were back on their roller coaster.

They lost four of their next six games until - thankfully - they returned to Detroit to start another nine game trip.

But first, in the Aug. 19 series opener against Texas, Hargrove's concerns about McDowell were heightened. The Rangers won, 10-3, as McDowell was battered for seven runs on eight hits in three-plus innings.

McDowell was accompanied by a volley of boos as he marched off the field upon being replaced in the fourth by Greg Swindell, who was no great improvement.

Insisting that his troubles were not physical, McDowell said, "I feel I am taking a lot better stuff to the mound than the results have shown. It's hard to explain. I feel strong, but I'm not in a groove. I just don't know."

Hargrove was more explicit. "(McDowell) had no command of his fast ball or splitter (split finger fast ball) and was up with a lot of his pitches. It is something we'll have to talk about. Other than that, we're puzzled.

"I don't know if he's still hurting, or not. He says he's not. Jack says he's fine and I believe him. I don't know about the strength in his arm, but I don't think he's hurting," said Hargrove.

Juan Gonzalez disagreed. The Texas slugger who drove in four runs with a single and double off McDowell, said, "I don't know ... (McDowell) looked hurt to me."

The Rangers got two runs in each of the first two innings, and added another in the third. They kayoed McDowell in the fourth as Ivan Rodriguez reached on Jose Vizcaino's error, and Rusty Greer and Gonzalez doubled back-to-back.

Swindell was greeted with a three run homer by Dean Palmer, and the Rangers were coasting, 9-0, before the Indians got on the board with Belle's solo homer in the bottom of the fourth. It was his 40th of the season.

RAMIREZ'S THIRD GRAND SLAM

The shoe was on the other foot the next night, Aug. 20, as the Indians blasted three homers, including Manny Ramirez's third grand slam of the season, to beat the Rangers, 10-4.

Hargrove best summarized the action when he said, "When these two teams get together, all you can do is sit down and hold on."

The game actually was closer than the six run differential indicated as the Indians led by only one, 5-4, before Ramirez unloaded the bases with two out in the sixth. The blow was struck off Jeff Russell, though three of the runs were charged to another former Tribe reliever, Dennis Cook.

Thome homered off loser Bobby Witt, and Belle walloped his 41st in the eighth off Mike Stanton.

The offensive splurge won it for Lopez and, though he gave up nine hits and four runs in five innings, was the recipient of praise by a seemingly tolerant Hargrove.

"Give him credit," the manager said of Lopez. "He did a good job. He held a good hitting team to four runs, and survived a long (83 minutes) rain delay."

TRIBE LOSES THREE IN EXTRA INNINGS

But again the momentum turned, this time for three consecutive games, all in overtime.

First, the Tribe lost to the Rangers, 10-8, on Greer's two run homer off Tavarez in the 10th inning on Aug. 21, then to Milwaukee, 6-5, in 11 innings on Aug. 23, and again to the Brewers, 4-3, in 10 innings the next night.

However, despite those three defeats the Indians actually gained a half-game on the White Sox, who lost four in a row between Aug. 20-23, the Tribe's first place margin climbing to another season high of eight games.

While it was Greer's 15th homer that beat the Indians in the first of those three losses, it was their leaky defense that caused most of the damage. It resulted in another no-decision for Nagy, although, this time, he didn't deserve anything better.

"The game turned in the sixth inning ... we should have won it ... we let it get away," Hargrove said after the Indians blew a 6-1 lead when Lofton and Thome committed errors that led to the Rangers' seven run rally in the sixth.

The Indians also stranded 17 base runners, matching their season high.

Palmer hammered a two run homer off Nagy to start the scoring, but most of the damage was inflicted against Shuey, who continued his inconsistent pattern of pitching and was charged with the loss.

"Charlie was not happy about coming out of the game, but from the bench it looked like he was tired," Hargrove responded to those who second guessed his decision to replace Nagy with a 6-3 lead.

How unhappy was Nagy?

Uncharacteristically, he didn't remain long enough after the game to answer that question.

BELLE AND VINA MEET AGAIN

The 6-5 loss to the Brewers on Aug. 23 marked the first meeting of Belle and Milwaukee second baseman Fernando Vina since their collision on May 31 that resulted in a two game suspension and $25,000 fine for Belle.

As expected, Vina was greeted with a torrent of boos by the 42,405 fans who comprised the 113th consecutive sellout crowd.

An airplane cruised overhead towing a banner that read: "Vina should play in a dress."

If it bothered Brewers manager Phil Garner, he didn't let it show. "I like that kind of thing," he said. "It proves that the fans are alive, and that they are literate.

It didn't take long for the two players to stage another meeting - though this one didn't cause any trouble. Belle slid into, and upended Vina in a vain attempt to break up a double play in the fifth inning.

Vina had nothing to say about the double play, and little to add when asked about being booed by the fans.

"It doesn't really matter," he said. "Albert is (the fans') great player and deserves their support. The only thing that bothers me is, why am I the villain?

"But I don't want to keep harping on it. Any route I go with this, I am the bad guy here. I thought (Belle) was wrong, but I am trying to handle it with class," which he did.

A bigger villain, at least in this game, was John Jaha, who whacked a three run homer off Hershiser in the third inning. Jaha also doubled, and his leadoff single in the 11th resulted in the Brewers' winning run off Mesa.

Though he's usually used only in save situations, Mesa replaced Hershiser in the 10th with the score tied.

After Jaha singled to start the 11th, he stole second, took third as Kevin Seitzer grounded out, waited as Jose Valentin was intentionally walked, and scored when Lofton couldn't make a diving catch of Marc Newfield's sinking liner that fell for a single.

"(Hershiser) pitched very well ... he made just one bad pitch and it cost us the game," Hargrove said of the ball Jaha hit for his 27th homer.

The Indians tied it in the eighth on two walks and an error that got one run home, but Ramirez was thrown out at the plate by Newfield on a play that, Garner said surprised even him.

"We didn't know he had that kind of an arm," Garner said of the throw by Newfield after catching Mark Carreon's fly in shallow left field.

"The ball wasn't hit too deep, but it was a good try, a good gamble," Hargrove said of Ramirez's unsuccessful bid to score what would have been a go ahead run.

In his next at-bat, Carreon, who had played well for the Tribe since his acquisition from San Francisco in a trade for Jim Poole on July 9, fouled a ball off his left leg. As it turned out, the injury would sideline him the rest of the season.

The victory was credited to former Tribe relief ace Doug Jones after Mike Fetters earned his 24th save by striking out Belle to end the game.

SEITZER'S HIT BEATS THE TRIBE

There was noticeable concern among the Indians after they lost again, 4-3, to the Brewers the next day, reducing their record in extra inning games to 6-8 (compared to 9-0 in 1995, and 14-3 in 1994).

The concern was based primarily on the Tribe's poor defensive play that helped the Brewers score three runs in the third. Though only one error was charged, to Alomar on a wild throw to second, there were other miscues that cost Ogea a chance to win in regulation time.

"It's frustrating, very frustrating," admitted Hargrove. "We gave them at least one run, and we did the same thing a couple of days ago. We're better than that, or should be."

When asked to elaborate on the mistakes, Hargrove said he would not publicly criticize his players. "Let me just say that we seem to get into situations where we try to make things happen when there's nothing there to make happen."

It was an oblique reference to two ill-advised throws by Lofton, as well as the one charged as an error to Alomar.

Hart also was upset by the Indians' poor execution of fundamentals and met with the coaches after the game, making clear his opinion that it was up to them to correct the problems.

Plunk, who took over in the eighth, suffered the loss as Jeff Cirillo singled to start the 10th. Assenmacher came on to retire one batter, and Shuey took over to get the second out.

But then, after a stolen base by pinch runner David Hulse, Seitzer - yes, *that* Seitzer - lined a single to left center for the go ahead run.

Earlier in the game Seitzer, who was then hitting .317, also doubled.

HARGROVE: 'WE ARM WRESTLED; I WON'

The Indians finally beat the pesky Brewers, 8-5, halting a three game losing streak on Aug. 25, in the wake of a team meeting called by Hargrove. "It was time to do some talking," he said.

So what was the subject matter? "I'll just say that we arm wrestled ... and I won," said Hargrove.

"We've all been trying to do too much," is the way Lofton discussed the situation in the wake of Hargrove's "arm wrestling" meeting.

"Other teams have been battling us hard all year. Everyone is at the top of their game when they play us. We just need to keep a clear head. We're a good team. We know that. We just have to go out and flow with it."

The meeting produced a positive result.

Especially by Belle, who observed his 30th birthday with a sixth inning bases loaded single. It drove in two runs and gave the Indians a 6-5 lead that Kent Mercker, Shuey and Mesa protected. Shuey was the winner, and

Mesa got his 31st save with a perfect ninth inning.

It wasn't all positive, however. McDowell started and continued to struggle, though there was some improvement. "Black Jack" gave up a two run homer to Seitzer in the second inning, but hung on through six, yielding five runs on six hits.

"It's something for Jack to build on," is the way Hargrove assessed McDowell's performance, without suggesting that the troubled right hander was out of the woods.

Hargrove said he replaced McDowell "because of a stiff back, though we don't consider it to be serious."

The game also resulted in some severe second guessing of Garner. He had Thome intentionally walked, loading the bases and setting the stage for Belle's two run single off Jones that wiped out the Tribe's 5-4 deficit. Two more runs came in on Alomar's single and a throwing error by the Brewers.

"I walked Thome for a very good reason," said Garner. "He is swinging very well. I have a lot of respect for Belle, but Thome is real hot. It was sort of pick your poison.

"If we pitch to Thome, we give them two shots at going ahead with two great hitters. We eliminated one great hitter and had one to go.

"I was trying to win the game right there. It ain't a good bet to get a double play on Belle, but that was my choice. They had one shot at doing it, and they succeeded."

WHITE SOX CONTINUE TO STUMBLE

Despite their mediocre play through the 5-4 homestand, the Indians maintained their eight game lead as the White Sox continued to stumble, too. They lost five in a row from Aug. 20-24, before beating Toronto, 10-9.

And, while the Indians' record since the All-Star break was 25-18 (.581), Chicago's was 20-25 (.444).

Instead of challenging the Indians for the A.L. Central Division title, the White Sox were hoping to make it into the post season as a wild card.

TRIBE LEADS WHITE SOX BY NINE

It got even better for the Indians the next three days, for one reason: they went to Detroit to begin their final extended road trip.

With the Indians seeking a season sweep of the Tigers, Thome and Nagy got them started with a 2-1 victory on Aug. 26. Nagy pitched a complete game three hitter, and Thome blasted a solo home run, his 29th, in the ninth inning.

It was Thome's fifth homer in nine games as the Indians increased their lead to nine over the slumping White Sox, who suffered their sixth loss in seven games, 3-2, to Milwaukee.

Thome's home run, giving him the most by a Tribe left handed batter since Graig Nettles hit 28 in 1971, provided Nagy with his 13th victory, but only his first in six starts dating back to July 25.

"You just try to put all that stuff out of your mind," said Nagy. "This is a weird game so you've got to do it. But sometimes some of it gets stuck in there. You've got to go home and kick the wall."

The only run Nagy allowed was a homer by Fryman leading the seventh, after 14 Tigers had been retired in order.

"The thing about Charlie," said Hargrove, "is that he's very confident the way he goes about his business. We haven't scored a lot of runs for him, but he still approaches the game the same way all the time."

Thome's homer was one of only four hits allowed by Lira, and Bell's Tigers lost their 84th game.

MARTINEZ'S FINAL 14 PITCHES

Twenty four hours later Thome was at it again, but despite winning, 12-2, the Indians' elation was tempered considerably by something that happened in the first inning of the game.

Martinez, who came off the disabled list and started for the first time since July 30, left after making just 14 pitches, leading to the belief that he had pitched his last game for the Indians.

He retired the first two batters, but Fryman singled, stole second, Ruben Sierra walked, and Bobby Higginson doubled for two runs.

At that point Martinez walked off the mound, clasping his right elbow. Lopez was rushed into the game and was masterful, allaying some of the urgency Hart and Hargrove had felt about acquiring another pitcher.

"Dennis felt his elbow pop (after a curve ball to Higginson)," said Hargrove. "We were surprised. He pitched a simulated game (five days earlier) and felt fine. And he also felt fine in the bull pen before the game."

Hart was still talking trade with teams, but said, "We're not far along with anyone," including the Pirates who, the next day, would trade Neagle to the Braves.

Hart and Hargrove both expressed confidence in Lopez, who allowed only two hits through the seventh inning in the victory over the Tigers. Tavarez and Mercker blanked Detroit in the eighth and ninth.

"Albie gave us a big lift. When we needed the kid to step up, he came through," said Hargrove.

"I'm like the guy they keep behind the glass. It's like, 'Break glass only in case of emergency.' I guess somebody pulled the fire alarm," said Lopez.

Another negative factor in Martinez's failure to come back from his elbow problem was that, to activate him, the Indians were forced to make a roster move with Swindell.

They designated Swindell for assignment, which meant they would have 10 days to either trade or release him. The only way they could keep Swindell by sending him to Buffalo was with his approval.

"As we looked to the post season, we just felt we didn't need Swindell, with Mercker and (Alan) Embree, who could be brought back (from Buffalo)," said Hart. "It was a difficult decision. Greg worked hard and did a good job for us. This doesn't mean we don't like him.

"(But) the staff likes what they've seen of Mercker. He has experience pitching out of the bull pen, and he also has post season experience (with Atlanta)."

HAPPY BIRTHDAY, JIM THOME

In Lopez's victory over the Tigers, Thome, celebrating his 26th birthday, reached base five straight times with four hits, including his 30th homer, and walked in the eighth.

"I'm just trying to keep things as simple as possible," said Thome. "You know, see the ball, hit the ball."

It was Thome's sixth homer in 10 games, and the four hits raised his average to .356 (55-for-155) since the All-Star break.

The Indians tied the score, 2-2, in the third. They went ahead, 4-2, in the fifth on Thome's homer and back-to-back doubles by Ramirez and Jeff Kent. Four more runs came home on four hits in the seventh, and Belle hit a three run homer, his 42nd, in the eighth.

In the wake of Martinez's inability to rejoin the rotation, Hart intensified his efforts to acquire another starting pitcher after being rejected earlier by the Orioles in his quest for David Wells, and then by the Pirates for Neagle and Cincinnati for John Smiley.

Reportedly, Hart could have made a deal for either Jamie Moyer or Terry Mulholland, but said, "We wanted a No. 1 or No. 2 starter, and we like our minor league pitchers better than anyone else who was available."

INDIANS SWEEP THE TIGERS, 12-0

The Indians concluded their domination of the Tigers with a 9-3 victory on Aug. 28, giving them a 12-0 record against Detroit in 1996.

Only four other teams in baseball history swept opponents in one season: Baltimore (12-0) vs. Kansas City, 1970; Baltimore (11-0) vs. Oakland, 1978; Kansas City (12-0) vs. Baltimore, 1988; and Oakland (12-0) vs. New York, 1990.

"All the pressure was on me," quipped Hershiser, the winning pitcher in the game that gave the Indians a three season, 30-5 record against the Tigers.

"I could have been the only guy to lose to Detroit. Then, after we win the World Series this year and we all come back to Cleveland for Old Timers games, that's all anybody would want to talk about, how I was the only guy to lose to the Tigers in 1996."

Hershiser made sure that wouldn't be a problem as he held the Tigers to three runs on eight hits in seven innings, striking out five and walking one.

It raised Hershiser's record to 10-3 in his last 16 starts, to 14-7 for the season, and 30-13 since joining the Indians as a free agent for 1995.

"I don't think there's a situation in a ball game that Orel hasn't been in during his career," said Hargrove. "He knows what he can do and what he can't do. Outside of the first month of this season (when Hershiser was 2-2), he has been very good for us."

Hershiser was well supported by Belle, who smashed his seventh career grand slam, and second of the season in the sixth, when the Indians broke a 2-2 tie with six runs.

Thome also homered in the first inning, his 31st of the season. Against the Tigers in the season series, Thome went 17-for-38 (.447) with six homers and 13 RBI.

Belle's homer, his 43rd, raised his RBI total to 129, equaling his career high set in 1993. It also was Belle's 16th homer in 46 games since the All-Star break, during which he hit .329 (57-for-173) with 55 RBI,

BELL PRAISES INDIANS; FRYMAN DOESN'T

After the game, Bell, the Tigers manager, was in awe of his former team, which he served as bench coach in 1994 and 1995, though Fryman, Detroit's veteran shortstop, spoke disparagingly of the Indians.

"They're still the best team in the league, and they're every bit as good as last year," said Bell, even though the Indians were not as dominating against other teams as they were in 1995.

"The difference," he said, "is that everybody is really up for the games against Cleveland, which makes it more difficult for the Indians to duplicate last season."

Fryman, on the other hand, blasted the Indians for what he called their "cocky" attitude.

"I don't enjoy losing to anybody, and I especially don't like to lose to Cleveland, and I'm looking forward to the day the shoe is on the other foot," said Fryman.

"They are a good ball team and I relish beating teams that are good. But they're not one of my favorite clubs in terms of their demeanor, and the way they carry themselves. For those reasons a lot of guys enjoy beating Cleveland."

Part of Fryman's problem with the Tribe was based on a confrontation he had with Ramirez in the second game of the series. Ramirez, trying to stretch a hit into a double, slid with his spikes high, apparently trying to kick the ball out of Fryman's glove.

Fryman objected to the slide and, after tagging Ramirez, shoved him.

Then, in Ramirez's next trip to the plate, Tigers pitcher Greg Keagle threw a fast ball behind him, and later admitted it was a "message" to the Indians outfielder.

"That was not a good play," Keagle said, referring to Ramirez's hard slide into Fryman. "Just because he screwed up and was out by five steps isn't a reason to go hard into (Fryman) like he did."

Those three victories over the Tigers boosted the Indians' lead over the White Sox to 10 games and - for the first time in 1996 - the *Plain Dealer* published the Tribe's "magic number."

It was 19 - meaning any combination of Cleveland victories and Chicago losses totaling 19 would clinch a second straight division championship for the Indians.

BACK ON THE ROLLER COASTER

Just as quickly, however, the Indians found themselves back on the roller coaster, in the downhill direction again.

After an aggravating, six hour delay leaving Detroit because their chartered plane had a mechanical problem, the Indians suffered two consecutive losses to the Rangers in Texas on Aug. 30 and 31.

They were beaten, 5-3 and 6-3, while the White Sox were winning twice, cutting their deficit back to eight games and time was running out for Hart to make a deal that would help in the post season.

Ogea was hit hard and was the loser in the first game as Rodriguez and Gonzalez smashed back-to-back homers for a 3-0 lead in the first inning, and Roger Pavlik beat the Indians for the third time in 1996. He was 4-0 lifetime against them.

Thome continued his hot streak, smashing his 32nd homer, and Brian Giles hit his fifth since his July 12 promotion from Buffalo, but both were solo shots, leading the third and fourth innings.

Giles also doubled to start the seventh, and scored, cutting the Indians' deficit to one, but they could get no closer.

Prior to the game the Indians activated Julio Franco and placed Martinez back on the disabled list, effectively ending Martinez's tenure with the Indians and, perhaps, his major league career as well.

In his three seasons in Cleveland, Martinez won 32 games and lost 17. It left him with a career mark of 240-183, three victories shy of Juan Marichal, the winningest Latin American pitcher in baseball history.

Despite his arm problems, Martinez said he plans to pitch in 1997, but not with the Indians. "My career with Cleveland is over, dead," he said. "If I come back next year it will be with a team closer to my family in Miami. I don't want to come back here."

Franco, who injured the hamstring muscle in his right leg more than two months earlier, on June 22, was on the D.L. from July 11-25, and had to go back on it again Aug. 6.

"Right now I'd say I'm about 95 percent," Franco said when asked about his condition. "Now it's more mental than anything. I've just got to get my confidence back. If I try to baby my leg, the ball will find me."

TRIBE IS 6-17 vs. TEXAS AND NEW YORK

The next night it was McDowell who took a step backwards. He was knocked out in the sixth inning, and also gave up consecutive homers, to Palmer and Warren Newson in the second inning when the Rangers took a lead they never relinquished.

It was McDowell's ninth loss in 19 decisions, and left him with a 1-3 record and 7.62 ERA in five starts since returning Aug. 9 from the disabled list, though he continued to insist it was not a physical problem.

The winner was Darren Oliver, who also raised his lifetime record against the Indians to 4-0, and to 3-0 in 1996.

It was a turbulent game for the Indians as Hargrove and Alomar were ejected for arguing strike calls by rookie umpire Ray DiMuro.

The problem started early as Lofton, Vizcaino and Franco all were called out on strikes by DiMuro in the first inning, setting the tone for all that followed.

Alomar was chased in the fifth when he protested that he had checked his swing on a third strike. When Alomar threw his bat in anger, he was invited to take an early shower.

An inning later Lofton disagreed with DiMuro, also on a called third strike. When Hargrove went to the plate to question DiMuro's eyesight, he was kicked out of the game.

It was Hargrove's third ejection of the season, and Alomar's second.

Before leaving the dugout Hargrove admonished his players. "I want them to be aggressive, but it doesn't help to go overboard and get thrown out of a game," he said.

Later Hargrove said, "It bothers me if (the players' constant complaining) affects the way the umpires call the game. The good umpires get beyond that, but some of the others don't."

The back-to-back losses gave the Indians a 3-8 record against the Rangers, who would win the A.L. West.

They also were well below .500, at 3-9, vs. New York, which would prevail in the A.L. East.

Losing twice to the Rangers also cut the Indians' lead to eight games over Chicago, and kept their magic number at 19.

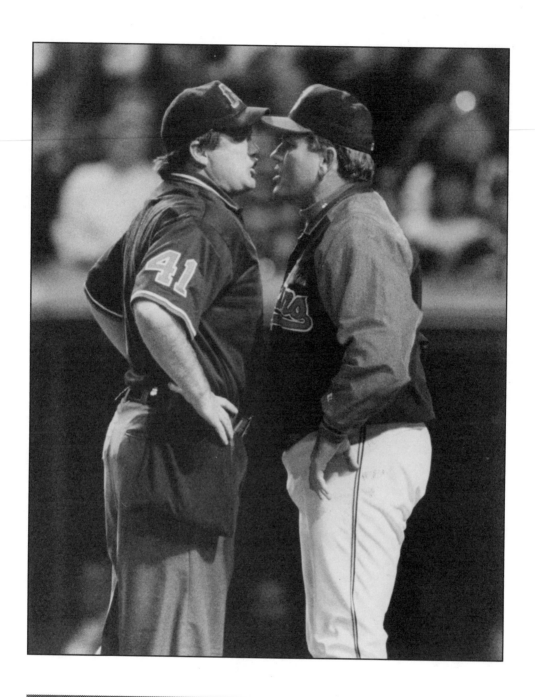

Mike Hargrove goes head to head with umpire Brian O'Nora

13

HELLO KEVIN SEITZER, GOODBYE MARTINEZ

Sept. 1-15

Motivated perhaps by the Indians' futility in consecutive losses to the Texas Rangers, John Hart spent the last couple of innings on the telephone during the game on Aug. 31.

He was feverishly trying to swing a deal for an established pitcher and a "professional" hitter - objectives he'd had for more than a month - and finally was successful for the latter, if not the former.

About 15 minutes before midnight on Aug. 31, the deadline for finalizing post season rosters, Hart closed a deal with Milwaukee for Kevin Seitzer, who'd been a thorn in the side of the Indians in back-to-back losses to the Brewers a week earlier.

To get Seitzer, 34, an 11 year major league veteran with a .296 career batting average, the Indians sent Jeromy Burnitz to Milwaukee.

Burnitz was deemed expendable because of the presence of Brian Giles. Both were young, left handed hitting outfielders with similar abilities. The Brewers were willing to take either one for Seitzer, and the Indians chose to keep Giles.

"We think Giles is more consistent in everything he does, and he's younger (25) than Burnitz (27)," Mike Hargrove explained the choice.

As much as anything, Hart's acquisition of Seitzer was a matter of perseverance.

Seitzer was one of the free agents - Julio Franco, Paul Molitor and Mark Grace were the others - in whom Hart showed interest during the winter.

On the same day, Dec. 7, 1995, that Seitzer re-signed with the Brewers, Franco agreed to terms with the Indians.

A first baseman who started his major league career at third, but now primarily a designated hitter, Seitzer played for Kansas City from 1986-91, Milwaukee in 1992, Oakland and Milwaukee in 1993, and the Brewers in 1994 and 1995.

Seitzer batted .311 for Milwaukee in 1995, and was hitting .316 when he was acquired by the Indians.

Exactly one week earlier, on Aug. 24, it was Seitzer's 10th inning single off Paul Shuey that gave the Brewers a 4-3 victory over the Indians.

That game-winning hit also was a motivating factor in Hart's determination to acquire Seitzer.

"I am ecstatic," Seitzer said of the deal. "Playing in the post season with a shot at winning a World Series ring means everything. It's all I ever wanted in my career."

It would prove to be a significant addition for the Tribe.

SEITZER BREAKS IN WITH FOUR HITS

Seitzer joined the Indians the next day, Sept. 1, meeting them in Texas, and proceded to ignite an offense that had been quieted by the Rangers Roger Pavlik and Darren Oliver.

Batting second as the designated hitter in his debut, Seitzer doubled twice and singled twice in his first four at-bats as the Tribe rebounded for an 8-2 victory over the Rangers.

Franco also played a major role with a grand slam that highlighted the Indians' five run fifth inning in his third game back from the disabled list. The bases-loaded homer was the Tribe's fifth of the season, tying a club record set in 1979.

It also made it easy for Charles Nagy - for a change - to win for only the second time since July 25, despite pitching well in most of his seven starts during that 5 1/2 week period. His record climbed to 14-4, but very easily could have been 18-4.

In his last start against the Rangers on Aug. 21, Nagy took a 6-1 lead into the sixth inning. Four hits later, including a two run homer by Dean Palmer, Nagy was gone and the Rangers went on to win, 10-8.

"Sure, that game was in my mind, especially in the sixth inning," acknowledged Nagy. "We had an almost identical lead and I was facing the same bunch of hitters.

"But this time I got through it."

A big reason he did was because of Albert Belle.

With two out, Mickey Tettleton singled and Kevin Elster hammered a drive to left center field.

"I thought it was gone," said Nagy.

Fortunately, Belle didn't. He raced back to the wall, leaped and caught the ball above the fence for the third out. It was a catch that would have made Kenny Lofton proud.

In fact, as the Indians trotted off the field, Lofton congratulated Belle, who also stole an extra base hit from Rusty Greer an inning earlier.

The victory ended the season series between the two teams with the Rangers on top, 8-4. There was a possibility that the Indians would meet Texas in the Division Series, but only if Seattle won the A.L. West, and the Rangers made the playoffs as the wild card team.

TRIBE'S 'MAGIC NUMBER' SHRINKS TO 18

At the time, Texas had a six game lead over the Mariners, and the Indians - their "magic number" down to 18 - were eight lengths ahead of Chicago with 26 games left to play.

Not only was Seitzer "ecstatic" to be joining the Indians, he said he also was "overjoyed" to be batting second behind Lofton. "I consider myself a table setter," he said.

And that also pleased Jim Thome, who followed Seitzer in the order.

"He's one of the best hitters in baseball," Thome said of Seitzer. "Look at what he did. Flew all night (from Milwaukee), joined us just before the game, and gets four hits. Amazing."

Then Seitzer re-boarded an airplane with his new teammates and paid a return visit to his former teammates in Milwaukee, where the Indians concluded their nine game trip with a three game series against the Brewers.

With the Milwaukee fans taunting Belle the way Clevelanders had booed Fernando Vina when the Brewers played at Jacobs Field, Aug. 23-25, the Indians lost the first two games, 7-6 and 8-2.

Jose Mesa, who seemed to be over his slump, failed in the ninth inning of the opener on Sept. 2, blowing his first save opportunity since July 2, and fifth of the season. The Brewers scored two runs on three hits and Mesa's wild pitch to prevail.

It happened after Jeff Cirillo singled with one out and pinch runner David Hulse stole second with two out. Hulse went to third on John Jaha's single, scored on the wild pitch, and Jose Valentin singled for the winning run.

The loss, the Indians' third in four games, was particularly distressing as they took a 5-1 lead in the third inning that Albie Lopez couldn't protect. He walked three batters after Matt Mieske's leadoff single in the fifth, and the Brewers went on to tie the score after Kent Mercker took over.

And despite the welcome addition of Seitzer, which was expected to alleviate the Indians' problems against southpaws, the disappointing performances of Lopez, as well as Mesa, made clear again that pitching help was needed.

With Dennis Martinez obviously finished for the season, Jack McDowell struggling, and Chad Ogea inconsistent from one start to the next, the Tribe's only reliable starters for the stretch run - and post season - were Nagy and Orel Hershiser.

It was a dilemma that would continue to plague the Indians.

MORE CONTROVERSY INVOLVING BELLE

Belle, who had flattened Vina in a base running collision in a game on May 31, during the Indians' previous trip to Milwaukee, was jeered by the fans, and a large banner in the bleachers said, "Belle Stinks!" But none of it had an effect on his play.

Belle singled to drive in the Tribe's first run in the first inning, and doubled and scored a tie-breaking run in the ninth on Franco's two out single.

It was in the ninth, following his double off former Tribe reliever Doug Jones, that Belle became involved in another on-field mini-controversy.

After cruising into second base, and during a conference on the mound between Jones and Milwaukee manager Phil Garner, Belle took advantage of the time out to jog to the Tribe dugout for a drink.

It infuriated Jones, who said, "I've never seen anything like that," and yelled at Belle, accusing him - and the Indians - of arrogance.

"They need to be humbled a little, brought down to the level with the rest of us," said Jones, though later he laughed and claimed he was only "teasing" Belle by shouting at him on the field.

Omar Vizquel - whose second inning homer, and 9th of the season, was three more than his previous career high - would have had a chance to retire Jaha for the game ending third out, preserving a 6-5 victory for the Tribe, under normal circumstances.

Normal, that is, if Vizquel's shoulder was not aching as it had all season, preventing him from making a strong throw on Jaha's grounder in the hole between shortstop and third base.

"I probably had a play, but I didn't grip the ball, and I was off balance," he said. "I figured it was better to have runners at first and third and go to the next batter, than risk a bad throw."

Three pitches later Mesa threw a fast ball that hit the backstop instead of Tony Pena's glove - "It took off like a jet," the catcher said - allowing Hulse to score the tying run. Then Valentin singled to end it.

Despite the loss, the Indians' lead stayed at eight games and their magic number shrunk to 17 as Chicago also was beaten, 8-6, by Detroit.

ALOMAR: 'THE FIRE ISN'T THERE'

It didn't get any better the next night, raising the specter of the September collapse that knocked California out of the race in 1995, as the Indians - described as being "listless" in the *Plain Dealer* - lost again to the Brewers, 8-2, on Sept. 3.

"An eight game lead is nothing over a month of baseball," cautioned Sandy Alomar. "We're flat, going through the motions and not playing aggressively. We had a great road trip going, but now everybody is flat. The fire isn't there."

Especially not the pitching - not even Hershiser this time.

"It was pretty much a non-athletic night for me. I wasn't executing," he said.

Neither were the Tribe's offense and defense.

Hershiser was tagged for four runs on seven hits and was banished in the fifth, although an error by Manny Ramirez complicated the problem.

Alomar had a perfect game, 3-for-3, with his 10th home run, but it didn't help his disposition. "It doesn't matter if I go 17-for-17. If we lose, it stinks," he said.

And "stink" it did, after the Brewers' Mike Matheny homered in the fourth, and Ramirez failed to catch a long fly by Valentin in the fifth when Milwaukee went ahead, 4-2.

To add to the frustration, Burnitz, playing center field in his second game for the Brewers, made a spectacular, diving catch to end the second inning and rob Vizquel of what would have been a two run single.

The loss enabled the White Sox to cut their deficit to seven games as they beat Detroit, 6-4, holding the Indians magic number at 17.

OGEA'S FOUR-HITTER IS IMPRESSIVE

The mood of the Indians - and especially Hart's and Hargrove's - brightened considerably the next night, Sept. 4, thanks to a four hitter by Ogea in a 7-

0 victory over the Brewers.

Ogea, who had moved ahead of McDowell and the ailing Martinez to become the third starter in the pitching rotation, at least for the time being, hurled his first complete game of the season, and this time the offense cooperated.

Lofton and Thome homered, and Belle drove in two runs with two doubles, giving him a league leading total of 133.

Hargrove commended Ogea - "He really came through for us," said the manager - and also praised Lofton, whose homer and two singles in five at-bats broke a 6-for-34 slump.

"This team goes a lot on how Kenny goes," said Hargrove. "He makes things happen and raises the energy level of everybody. When he doesn't get on base, it makes things that much more difficult."

It ended the nine game trip with a 5-4 record, leaving the Indians seven games ahead of Chicago, needing any combination of 16 victories, and/or White Sox losses to clinch the division championship.

THREE MILLION REQUESTS FOR TICKETS

And, upon their return to Cleveland the Indians' front office was inundated by more than three million postcard requests from fans seeking tickets for the Division Series, American League Championship Series, and the World Series.

Despite their recent mediocrity - the Indians were only 11-11 since Aug. 10 - it was obvious that their fans fully expected another glorious finish and success in the playoffs.

"There's always a danger of looking too far ahead and not paying attention to what it takes to get there," said Hargrove, "(but) this club is not doing that."

Hershiser also expressed confidence. "I think we can use this September to come together as a team," said Hershiser. "Maybe we can do a little male bonding so that everybody is pulling at the same end of the rope when the pressure is on."

All of which led to a heated clubhouse meeting on Sept. 6, the day the Indians were scheduled to open a 10 game homestand, but were rained out game against Seattle after three innings were played.

Actually, Hargrove didn't mind the downpour.

Neither should have McDowell, who did not pitch well again, giving up three runs on four hits before the game was called.

The best that Hargrove could say about McDowell's performance: "He was throwing 91, 92 miles per hour ... when he shut us out here last year with the Yankees, that's what he was throwing."

The problem, Hargrove also said, was that McDowell still wasn't throwing many curve balls since straining a muscle in his forearm. The injury resulted in McDowell going on the disabled list (July 26-Aug. 9) for the first time in his career.

As for the meeting, few spoke specifically about what transpired - "If we wanted you to know what was said, we would have invited you in," Hershiser told one reporter - but, according to another player, "It was the toughest (meeting) of the year."

The rain continued for two days and, when the Indians were finally able to play again, apparently the meeting was all that was needed as they embarked upon a hot streak.

INDIANS EQUAL LONGEST WINNING STREAK

They won seven of eight games against Seattle, California and Oakland, the last six in a row, setting up - appropriately - a division-clinching series against the White Sox in Chicago.

Sept. 6 also was the day that Eddie Murray, traded by the Indians two months earlier, finally hit his coveted 500th career homer in Baltimore off Felipe Lira in a 5-4 loss to Detroit.

It was his 21st homer of the season, and ninth for the Orioles, making Murray only the third player in baseball history with 3,000 hits and 500 homers. The other two are Hank Aaron and Willie Mays.

In addition to Aaron, Mays and Murray, only 12 other players hit 500 homers in their careers, the last to reach that plateau was Mike Schmidt of Philadelphia in 1987.

"Wow! That's quite a neighborhood," the seldom-quoted Murray told the media in Baltimore.

The next day, as the Indians waited in vain for the remnants of "Hurricane Fran" to leave the area, several of them called Murray, offering congratulations. "I wanted him to get it in Cleveland, but now the city of Baltimore has something to celebrate," said Lofton.

"I'm so glad he got it," said Ramirez, whose cap still bore Murray's uniform No. 33 inked on it. "He was trying too hard. I'm glad he got it this year because it's probably going to be his last year."

NAGY: 'I DON'T KNOW HOW I DID THAT'

First, the Tribe split a double header with the Mariners on Sept. 8.

They won the first game, 2-1, as Thome delivered a tie-breaking, eighth inning double, and Nagy pitched a perfect ninth to lock up his third straight victory and fourth complete game.

"Charlie had tremendous stuff, he threw some nasty breaking balls and was as dominating as he's been all season," Hargrove said of Nagy, who scattered six hits and struck out 10.

Nagy was particularly impressive in the sixth, when he struck out Ken Griffey Jr., Edgar Martinez and Jay Buhner on 13 pitches. "I don't know how I did that ... I guess the moon was aligned with Pluto, or something," he said.

In those last three starts, Nagy's ERA was 1.05, and in only 11 of his 29 starts had he allowed more than one earned run.

Nagy had to be sharp to overcome some defensive lapses by his teammates, including one in the first inning. Joey Cora opened the game with a double, took third on an infield out, and scored when Franco misplayed Griffey's routine grounder into a hit.

The Indians tied it in the second on Ramirez's double and Omar Vizquel's two out single.

Then in the eighth, Thome's double scored Vizquel, who had walked, was bunted to second, and took third on an infield grounder. It gave Thome 100 RBI which, he said, "was one of my main goals."

It also established Thome as the second player in Indians history to have 100 runs, 100 RBI and 100 walks in the same season. Al Rosen did it in 1950.

SHUEY AND MESA STRUGGLE AS CLOSERS

It was a different story in the second game of the day-night double header. The Mariners, still fighting to overtake Texas in the A.L. West - they trailed the Rangers by seven lengths at the start of action - beat the Indians, 6-5, as both Shuey and Mesa failed as closers.

Nigel Wilson, who'd hit 30 homers with a .299 average at Class AAA Buffalo and was recalled by the Tribe when rosters were expanded to 40, was a near-hero, before the bull pen faltered.

Sent to the plate as a pinch hitter for Pena with the score tied, 3-3, and a runner aboard in the seventh, Wilson drilled a 3-and-0 pitch from Mike Jackson deep into the second deck of the right field stands.

It was Wilson's first major league hit after 23 at-bats (with 15 strikeouts) for Florida in the National League.

But the victory, which would have been credited to Brian Anderson, was allowed to slip away by, first, Shuey, on a walk and two hits that re-tied the score in the eighth, and then by Mesa - with an assist by Thome - in the ninth.

The Mariners won it on two hits and a walk, and Thome's error on a grounder by Martinez with two out.

The split shrunk the Indians' lead to 6 1/2 games over Chicago, which beat Boston, 7-4. That victory gave the White Sox a one game lead over Baltimore in A.L. wild card race.

With California in town the next four days, the Indians and Mariners were unable to make up the Sept. 6 rainout. However, they would be required to do so on Sept. 30, after the final regular season game, if it had a bearing the playoff status of either team.

BELLE'S SACRIFICE FLY SCORES TWO

Thanks largely to the ineptitude of the Angels, who were last in the A.L. West, the Indians embarked upon a six game winning streak, matching their longest of the season, by sweeping California, 4-3, 7-5, 2-0 and 11-2, Sept. 9-12.

It left little doubt that the Indians' clinching of the A.L. Central was only a matter of time, and that their primary goal was to decide upon their strongest 25 man playoff roster, and to get ready for the post season.

Lofton was the spark that beat the Angels in the opener of the series as the Indians scored three runs in the eighth, two of them - including Lofton with the tie-breaker - scoring on a sacrifice fly by Belle.

Actually, Lofton came home on a throwing error by second baseman Bobby Eenhoorn, though Lofton's speed is what forced the miscue.

Shuey got credit for the victory though he faced only two batters in the top of the eighth, and Mesa, once again throwing 98 mph fast balls in the ninth, got his 32nd save. He struck out three batters after the potential tying run reached on a single.

"We've been playing with intensity the last couple of weeks, and it's paying off," said Hargrove. Without saying so, Hargrove's comment undoubtedly was an oblique reference to the fact that it had been almost two weeks since the acquisition of Seitzer.

Ogea started and coasted before running into trouble in the fourth, when he gave up five singles and the Angels scored all three of their runs.

"Chad lost his concentration, but got it back and that was his only bad inning until he tired (in the seventh)," said Hargrove.

Lofton scored the Tribe's first run in the sixth, after he doubled and stole his 62nd base, though it was only his first in 12 consecutive games, during which he'd fallen behind Kansas City's Tom Goodwin, who had 63.

On the downside, Vizquel, whose shoulder continued to ache, though he wouldn't admit that it had worsened, committed two more throwing errors, giving him 20, a career high.

'THE MOST EXCITING GAME IN TWO YEARS'

Ramirez was the hero the next night, Sept. 10, in a performance that was reminiscent of 1995.

With two out in the last of the ninth and the Tribe trailing, 5-4, against the Angels' ace reliever, Troy Percival, Ramirez blasted a 429 foot, game winning three run homer into the right center field bull pen.

It was the Indians' sixth game-ending homer of the season and was delivered in front of the 119th consecutive sellout crowd at Jacobs Field.

The 42,181 fans in attendance wouldn't leave until Ramirez took two curtain calls, and raised the Indians' season attendance to a franchise record 2,852,882.

"None of our guys wanted to leave either," said Hargrove. "They just wanted to stay in the dugout and savor it.

"This has to be the most exciting game we've had - and that includes last year," added Hargrove.

Lofton, who homered in the first inning, started the rally in the ninth with a walk, and promptly stole second and third, giving him a 64-63 lead over Goodwin in that department.

Thome singled for one run, Belle popped up for the second out, but Franco also singled to set the stage for Ramirez.

It was the second time in 1996 that the Indians beat Percival in the ninth. They did it the first time on May 12 in Anaheim on consecutive homers by Belle, Alomar and Thome for a 4-1 victory.

Home runs also hurt Hershisher; he gave up two of them, solo shots by Jim Edmonds in the first inning and Rex Hudler in the sixth, and left with one on and one out in the top of the ninth. Paul Assenmacher got out of the jam and was the winner, thanks to Ramirez.

HARGROVE: 'THIS IS WHAT WE EXPECTED'

Then - finally - the Indians got that for which they thought they'd contracted nine months earlier, when they signed McDowell on Dec. 14, 1995, to a two year contract worth $9.6 million.

McDowell pitched seven strong innings, blanking the Angels on five hits, and with splendid relief pitching by Eric Plunk in the eighth and Mesa in the ninth, beat California, 2-0. It was his 11th victory - and first in more than a month - in 20 decisions.

"This is what we expected all along was coming from Jack," said Hargrove.

The seven innings by McDowell were the most he'd pitched since July 16, and the only serious threat "Black Jack" faced came in the third, when George Arias tripled with one out, but was left waiting. McDowell retired Hudler on a grounder to Jeff Kent at third base, then struck out Edmonds.

The Indians scored early, in the first inning, then sat back and went meekly to Chuck Finley (one of the left handers in whom Hart had shown interest), and Darrell May.

Lofton, as usual, started it, though this time he reached on an error, and quickly stole his 65th base. He went to third on Jose Vizcaino's infield single, and scored - and so did Vizcaino - on Hudler's throwing error as the Indians attempted a double steal.

"Lofton deked me," lamented Hudler. "I was concerned about him stealing home. I should have taken the out with Vizcaino, but that's what speed does. Lofton intimidates you with (his speed)."

McDowell, who usually was around after an unsuccessful outing to explain what he (or someone else) did wrong, was nowhere to be found after the game. It hiked the Indians' lead over the White Sox back to nine games, and reduced their magic number for Chicago's elimination to eight.

It was during that victory over the Angels on Sept. 11 that Belle, however inadvertently, made news again.

This time because he attacked a thermostat in the clubhouse.

That's right. A thermostat.

Reportedly, because Belle prefers it cool (read: *cold*), he kept visiting the locker room between innings to turn the heat down - and, each time he'd go back to the field, someone would turn it up.

Finally, sometime during the game, Belle took his bat to, not one but, two thermostats in the clubhouse, destroying them and ensuring, he thought, a temperature down around 60 degrees, although it actually was closer to 30 before it was repaired.

And, thereafter, Belle's nickname amongst his teammates (albeit privately) was "Mr. Freeze."

CLUB RECORD TIED BY BELLE, THOME, RAMIREZ

On Sept. 12, after the first of Thome's two, two run homers, the Indians, for the first time since 1950 and seventh in franchise history, had three players with 100 RBI in the same season.

Thome homered in the first and seventh innings, giving him 103 RBI as the Indians bombed the Angels, 11-2. Franco also homered twice and Belle once (No. 45), and Lofton stole his 66th and 67th bases as the Tribe rolled to a fourth straight victory.

The other times the Indians had three players with 100 RBI in the same season were in 1948 (Joe Gordon, Ken Keltner, Lou Boudreau), 1938 (Keltner, Jeff Heath, Hal Trosky), 1935 (Trosky, Joe Vosmik, Odell Hale), 1934 (Trosky, Earl Averill, Hale), 1930 (Eddie Morgan, Johnny Hodapp, Averill), and 1920 (Larry Gardner, Tris Speaker and Elmer Smith).

The victory was credited, appropriately enough, to Anderson, the southpaw who was the Angels' first round (third overall) choice in the 1993 amateur draft. He was 13-13 in 1994 and 1995, and was acquired by the Indians in spring training.

Anderson left after five innings with Mercker, Shuey and Julian Tavarez blanking the Angels in the final four.

It was the Indians' 33rd victory in 56 games since the All-Star break, boosting their best record in the major leagues to 87-58. Afterwards, Thome expressed what many had been thinking.

"I think, in the last three games, we've started to pick up some momentum," he said. "Tonight, we won the same way we won games last season. I don't think we've peaked all year, but now, that end of the season excitement is starting to come. Tonight it was really fun.

"In the beginning of the year I think we were just going through the motions. We just expected to do it. Now we're really starting to get it done."

MARTINEZ CALLS IT QUITS

But, again as often is the case, there was a downside.

Martinez, whom the Indians had hoped could overcome his elbow trouble and be of service in the post season, finally gave up.

And he did so angrily.

In what was to have been a 15 minute workout in the bull pen prior to the game, Martinez gave up after about six minutes. "He had to shut it down, and right now it does not look good," said Hargrove.

Martinez was visibly upset, saying, "I don't know what they had in mind. I was ready to throw for an hour. It (was) a big day for me."

Martinez said that five minutes before the Indians began batting practice, he was told that Hershiser would be worked out in the bull pen.

"I was pumped up to go out and find out for myself just where I am," he said. "Now I am upset."

Hargrove explained why the pre-game workout was postponed. "We had organizational meetings and didn't get out of them until 5:30 (p.m.). There was no lack of communication. It was only a lack of time.

"It was a misunderstanding on Dennis' part. He did not hear it the right way."

Whatever, it was obvious that Martinez's career with the Indians was over.

"Even though they are saying otherwise," Martinez said, "I kind of feel they have given up on me. Which is OK. They have their decisions to make."

The next night Martinez said, "I told (pitching coach) Mark Wiley that

I wasn't going to pitch anymore this season."

Martinez also said he was not going to pitch for the Indians next year - but that he plans to continue his career, probably with the Florida Marlins in the N.L.

Hart called Martinez's complaints "absurd," but admitted, "We do have to look at the reality of the situation. (Martinez) hasn't pitched effectively in seven weeks. Realistically it is hard to tell if he can come back."

NAGY: 'WE'RE STARTING TO COME TOGETHER'

Another rainout, thanks to Hurricane Fran, brought another double header, and the Indians' momentum continued. They beat Oakland, 9-2 and 9-8, on Sept. 14, hiking their lead over the White Sox to 10 games.

Nagy won his 16th and fourth in a row in the opener, and Plunk got credit for the victory in the nightcap in relief of Ogea - and there no longer could be any doubt about the Indians' ability to duplicate their success of 1995.

Especially not in Nagy's mind. "The personalities on this club are starting to come together," he said. "We're really playing aggressively. It's fun to be out there now."

Was he suggesting that it wasn't fun before?

The interview ended without Nagy saying more.

But he spoke eloquently with his pitching - except for a first inning home run he surrendered to Mark McGwire, who hit another in the nightcap, making him the 13th man in baseball history to hit 50 homers in one season.

"Charlie has pitched well enough to be considered for the Cy Young Award," Hargrove endorsed Nagy. "He's been consistent since day one. He's given us a chance to win almost every time out and, in some cases, he's almost won the game by himself."

However, unfortunately for Nagy, three other A.L. pitchers had won more games: the Yankees' Andy Pettitte, 21; Baltimore's Mike Mussina, 19; and Toronto's Pat Hentgen, 17.

Seitzer was the Tribe's hitting star in the opener with a double in the fourth inning that turned a one run lead into a comfortable, 6-2, advantage, which was more than enough for Nagy.

ANOTHER RECORD FOR TRIBE TRIO

Belle bashed his 46th homer in the second game, a three run shot that gave him 140 RBI, the most in the major leagues since Don Mattingly's 145 for the New York Yankees in 1985.

Ramirez also homered in each game, giving him 30 for the season. His homer in the eighth inning of the nightcap provided the winning run.

It established the Indians as the first team in baseball history to have three players to hit 30 homers and drive in 100 runs in the same season. The other two were Belle (46, 140) and Thome (35, 108). Ramirez's homers gave him 101 RBI.

Thome also made it into the Indians' record book by walking three times in the double header. His first base on balls in the opener was his 111th, tying the mark set by Hargrove when he played first base for the Tribe in 1980.

Then Thome broke the record by walking twice in the second game.

"The walks probably mean more to me than all my other stats," said Thome, though he quickly qualified the statement.

"Don't get me wrong. I like driving in 100 runs, but when you have as many walks as I do, it means you're patient. I look, at Frank Thomas as being a great hitter because he draws a lot of walks."

It also was a big day for Lofton, who stole five bases, giving him a career high of 72.

The second game almost got away from the Tribe as Danny Graves, who replaced Ogea in the fifth, walked three after giving up a leadoff single to Scott Bournigal. It cut the Indians' lead to 8-7.

Then, after Graves blanked the Athletics in the sixth, Plunk did the same in the seventh and eighth, and Ramirez's homer gave the Tribe a two run cushion, Mesa also created some anxious moments in the ninth.

"I almost got sick three times," said Hargrove after Oakland scored one run and loaded the bases before Mesa got the final out for his 34th save.

SEASON ATTENDANCE TOPS THREE MILLION

The winning streak ended at six the next day, but - with the exception of shaky performances by Hershiser and Mesa - the 10-9, 10 inning loss to Oakland didn't really matter.

In a way, despite the defeat, it was a day to celebrate as the 124th consecutive sellout crowd of 42,226 that filled Jacobs Field boosted the Indians' season attendance to 3,021,849 in 73 dates. It was the first time in franchise history the three million mark was surpassed.

Amy Root of Plymouth, Ohio was designated as the three millionth fan to enter the park, and was showered with an assortment of gifts.

Hershiser was hit hard through the first six innings, but the Tribe rallied for two runs and a tie in the ninth, only to blow it in the 10th when Mesa gave up two walks and two hits, and Lofton committed a costly throwing error.

A two run double by Scott Spiezio, and a two run homer by Ernie Young were the big hits off Hershiser as the Athletics constructed a 5-0 lead in the fourth inning, and led, 8-4, in the sixth.

Ramirez homered in the fourth and Thome in the sixth, and the Indians pulled even in the ninth on two singles, three walks and a sacrifice fly. But Mesa couldn't shut down the Athletics in the 10th.

Mesa wasn't talking afterwards, but Hershiser did - and accepted full responsibility for the loss.

"All in all, I let us down today," he said. "I'm pretty much the reason we lost. It was not because of Jose Mesa, it was because of me. I pitched very poorly. I had terrible location. I had great velocity, but zero movement. I just had a really, really bad day."

But only one day.

When asked if he was concerned about the future, the thinking man's pitcher replied, "Concern comes from when you feel like you really don't have your health or you feel like you don't know how to pitch, or you have no idea what your mechanics are doing.

"I don't have any of those feelings. I just feel like I've had some bad outings. I had a long, consistent run of good outings. The natural progression of things says you're going to have a couple of rough outings ... but there's more important things ahead."

And, again, Hershiser was correct.

Immediately ahead was a return visit to Chicago, one that the Indians - unlike their last trip to the Windy City, June 27-30 - truly relished.

Three months earlier the Indians were struggling, and their hold on first place was at stake.

Now it was different.

Now the Indians had the best record in the major leagues, a 10 game lead over the White Sox with 13 to play, and their magic number was down to four.

Jim Thome hits a grand slam off Detroit Tigers pitcher Gregg Olson

14

TIME TO START CELEBRATING

September 16-29

The scenario could not have been more fitting had it been scripted by a Hollywood writer.

There were the Indians, in Chicago, poised to clinch their second straight American League Central Division championship against the White Sox.

The same White Sox whose owner, Jerry Reinsdorf, and general manager, Ron Schueler, had been saying most of the season (though not so much lately) that the Indians were "catchable" because their pitching was "questionable."

Reinsdorf was particularly caustic in his remarks about Jack McDowell, whose major league career began with the White Sox, and who'd had ongoing problems with the Chicago owner before being traded to the Yankees in 1995.

"Jack hasn't had a good year since 1993 (when he won the A.L. Cy Young Award)," snorted Reinsdorf in April.

And it was Schueler, a former (but not very successful) pitcher himself, who said in spring training that the Indians' pitching was "suspect" because of the advanced ages of Dennis Martinez, Orel Hershiser and McDowell.

Even as recently as late-July, Schueler predicted that his team's chances of winning the A.L. Central were enhanced because "the Indians traded away two of their leaders, (Carlos) Baerga as well as (Eddie) Murray, and Martinez and McDowell are hurting."

That's also when Schueler said, "I think our games against Cleveland in September (Sept. 16-18) are going to mean something."

Which they did.

But not for the reason Schueler thought.

While the Indians were coasting with the best record in baseball, 89-59, and were on the brink of clinching the division title with any combination of four victories and/or Chicago losses, the White Sox needed to win as many games as possible to capture a wild card berth into the playoffs.

Which they didn't.

McDOWELL HEAPS INSULT UPON INJURY

Heaping insult upon injury, it was McDowell, in his best performance of the season, who beat the White Sox, 4-3, in the first of those three games that Schueler predicted would mean something.

It hiked the Indians' lead to 11 games with 12 to play.

It also hiked Chicago's deficit to three games behind Baltimore in the wild card race.

McDowell, who was called by some, "Mr. October," in anticipation of what was expected of him in the playoffs, said after beating the White Sox, "I couldn't be happier."

But otherwise Black Jack didn't gloat about the victory over his former team.

With a 12-9 record, 3-3 since leaving the disabled list on Aug. 9, and 2-0 in his last two starts, McDowell proclaimed his physical problems were a thing of the past.

"In my first couple of starts I was feeling my way," he said. "It was only a matter of getting into my game and figuring out who I was."

As Mike Hargrove said, "When Jack came off the disabled list in August, I kept telling people that I saw good signs. But they kept looking at me like I was crazier than a bedbug."

The White Sox jumped on McDowell early, scoring a run in the first inning on Tony Phillips' single and Frank Thomas' double. They added two more in the third on back-to-back homers by Thomas and Harold Baines.

But that was all they got.

The Indians retaliated against Wilson Alvarez for two runs in the fifth on a bases loaded walk and Julio Franco's single, and two more in the sixth, driven in with the second of Kevin Seitzer's three hits.

"When we clinch there's going to be a parade and I'm going to be leading it," said Seitzer. "For me to come to a team like this is a miracle. I'm blessed."

INDIANS CLINCH SECOND STRAIGHT TITLE

The only parade the next night was the Indians' romping around the bases in the first two innings. They beat the White Sox, 9-4, to become the first Cleveland team to win consecutive championships.

The Indians of 1921 couldn't do it (they were second by 4 1/2 games), and neither could they in 1949 (third by eight), nor in 1955 (second by three).

"That was as close as I've come to losing control of my emotions," said Hargrove, savoring the victory.

Predictably - and understandably - Seitzer was beside himself with jubilation, saying that winning the division title and getting into the playoffs was "a dream come true" for him.

It also was a dream that he helped make possible, as Hargrove and the his players said as they sprayed each other with champagne and beer during the victory celebration.

Seitzer, with a .322 batting average, blasted a grand slam off Alex Fernandez in the second inning, and the Tribe coasted behind Brian Anderson and Eric Plunk the rest of the way.

The only problem - though the champagne-drenched Seitzer said it as a joke - "I can't play tomorrow ... I'm water-logged."

Then, "I've watched this on television before, but that's the closest

I've ever come. It is awesome to be a part of it," he said.

"The addition of Seitzer was a key (to winning the division championship)," which was much more difficult than in 1995, said Hargrove.

"We had to do things we didn't have to do last year. That made this season tougher. We had to make tough decisions and we hit a lot more bumps along the road. But that also made this one that much sweeter."

Those "tough decisions" and "bumps along the road" were obvious - though unspecified - references to the trades that sent Baerga and Murray away, and the distractions that were created by the controversies involving Albert Belle.

"It took us a while to get over the Baerga trade because he was a young athlete and a franchise-type player," said Sandy Alomar. "But what (the Baerga deal) tells me is that the organization is willing to do anything to win. We respect the decisions by John Hart."

ALOMAR: 'THIS YEAR WE EARNED IT'

Alomar said it also was tougher for the Indians in 1996 because, "Teams geared up to play us ... everybody wanted to beat us, which made things difficult.

"This year we earned it. This year, every time we went into a city, teams said, 'These are the A.L. champs, let's kick their butts.'"

Charles Nagy said it this way: "Last year we did some unbelievable things that probably won't be matched for a long time. We pounded people to death, and we were the sentimental favorites because we hadn't won in 40-some years.

"But now, we're the bad boys everyone wants to beat. But that's OK. It comes with the turf.

"This year we realized the importance of doing the little things you need to do to win."

SEITZER WAS THE 'MISSING LINK'

Franco called Seitzer the "missing link" in the Indians' drive to repeat after struggling at mid-season when they went 18-21, allowing the White Sox to advance to within two games of first place.

"(Seitzer) has brought more to this ball club than we expected. Every time he goes to the plate everybody expects him to get a hit," said Franco.

Winning the division title also was special for Anderson, the native of Geneva, Ohio and a lifelong fan of the Indians.

"I always wanted to be a part of the first Cleveland team to be a champion.

"And to have the opportunity to take the ball in the game where we clinch it is just unbelievable," said Anderson.

Plunk pitched the last three innings for a save, which was a nice gesture on the part of Hargrove.

"I felt like Eric deserved to finish that game because of all he's done for this ball club and organization," said the manager. "He's No. 1 among the unsung heroes. Without the job he's done, we would not be in the position we are now. I don't think a lot of people realize that."

It was appreciated by Plunk, who would be eligible for free agency at the end of the season. "I've never been on the mound for something like this ... it was nice," he said.

Kenny Lofton, whose second inning bunt single gave him 200 hits, the most by an Indians left handed batter since Dale Mitchell's 203 in 1949, used the occasion to put down those who didn't believe the Tribe would repeat.

"We've had our critics who said we're not doing this or that," he said. "Everyone tried to shoot us down, but we've still got the best record in baseball."

ALOMAR: 'WE WANTED TO ATTACK'

It was as though the Indians couldn't wait to beat the White Sox in the clincher. Jim Thome singled with two out in the first inning, and things snowballed after that.

Belle, Franco and Manny Ramirez followed with consecutive singles, and to add to Fernandez's embarrassment, Franco stole home and the Indians led, 3-0, before the White Sox went to the plate.

Thomas solo homered in the bottom of the first, but the Indians came right back and more than made up for it in the second inning.

Alomar and Lofton singled around a walk to Omar Vizquel, and Seitzer unleashed his grand slam before Fernandez retired a batter.

After Thome grounded out, Belle, Franco and Ramirez singled again for another run and the rout was on, assuring the Indians of their most satisfying victory of the season.

"We were really pumped up," acknowledged Alomar. "We wanted to attack, to finish it right away. It is unbelievable what this team can do when it wants to accomplish something."

They were words to remember.

So were Nagy's, when he said, "This is the first step to where we want to go."

CASEY CANDAELE: 'LET'S GO HERD'

Then, adding more insult to injury the next night, Sept. 18, the Indians beat the White Sox, 4-3, with a lineup composed primarily of players recalled from the Class AAA Buffalo Bisons, a.k.a. the "Thundering Herd."

It was Cleveland's 11th victory in 13 games.

The loss, the seventh in the White Sox's last nine games, further damaged their wild card chances. They fell 3 1/2 lengths behind Baltimore, and also trailed Seattle by a half game in the consolation race.

Six of the Tribe's starters spent some or all of the season with the Bisons. So did Albie Lopez, who started on the mound, as did two of the three pitchers who worked in relief, Kent Mercker and Julian Tavarez.

The only regulars who were with the Indians since April 1 were Tony Pena and Ramirez. Jeff Kent, played for the New York Mets until he came to Cleveland in the Baerga trade on July 29.

"When I saw the lineup card before the game," said Candaele, "I said,

'This might be the second best team in the American League - the Buffalo Bisons.'"

It had Candaele at second base, Geronimo Pena, 3b; Brian Giles, rf; Ramirez, dh; Nigel Wilson, lf; Kent, 1b; Ryan Thompson, cf; Tony Pena, c; and Damian Jackson, ss.

"Someone asked me if I should have fielded a more representative lineup with the White Sox still in the wild card chase," said Hargrove. "I just thought our regulars deserved a day off."

Candaele opened the game with a double and immediately scored on Geronimo Pena's homer. The White Sox scored in their half of the first on two singles around two passed balls by Tony Pena, but it was the only run Lopez allowed through five innings.

Hits by Giles and Wilson in the sixth raised the Indians' lead to 3-1, and they made it 4-1 in the ninth on Kent's single and a two out double by Jackson.

Then Jose Mesa came out of the bull pen to provide what was the only disquieting aspect of the game. Though Mesa got his 35th save in 40 opportunities, it was not without a struggle.

The first two batters reached on a walk and a double, one run came in on an infield out, and another scored on a two out single by Domingo Cedeno, before Mesa finally put a stop to the rally.

COASTING THE REST OF THE WAY

Everything that followed for the Indians was a comfortable ride to the end of the regular season that would help, they thought, prepare them for the playoffs.

They returned to Jacobs Field and beat Kansas City three out of four, Sept. 19-22, winning the opener behind Chad Ogea. He gave up only three hits, one of them a solo homer by Craig Paquette, to win, 9-1, and strengthen his hold on the third spot in the pitching rotation, ahead of McDowell.

"I feel I deserve it, I feel I can pitch as well in the playoffs as anyone," he said. "I'll be disappointed if I am not the third starter. The only thing the others have that I don't is experience." The victory raised his record to 9-5.

Hargrove was non-committal regarding the pitching rotation, but said, "The personality of this club has changed in the last month or so."

It was an obvious reference to the addition of Seitzer, who was acquired on Aug. 31.

"The chemistry is as good as I've ever seen it here. There seems to be a feeling of closeness that had been missing in the past."

ROOKIE OUT-PITCHES NAGY

The Tribe's four game winning streak ended the next night, 6-4, Sept. 20, as Nagy was out-pitched by the Royals' Brian Bevil, making his first major league start. It was Nagy's worst outing in a month.

"Charlie really struggled," said Hargrove. "His split-finger (fast ball) wasn't working, and he had no location ... no consistency. It was just one of those nights. What more can I tell you?"

Nagy threw 114 pitches in five innings, and the loss was his third in 25 starts at Jacobs Field where his career record had been 40-21.

Still, he might have avoided the loss if reliever Danny Graves had not given up two runs in the sixth.

HERSHISER'S RECORD CLIMBS TO 15-8

Hershiser, with the help of home runs by Thome and Thompson, waltzed to his 15th victory in 23 decisions the next day, Sept. 21, beating the Royals, 13-4.

It became a laugher that was decided for all practical purposes in the fourth, when the Tribe went ahead, 5-2, on Thome's three run homer. It was his 37th of the season, second most by a left handed hitter in franchise history since Hal Trosky's 42 in 1936.

Thompson, who came to the Indians (with pitcher Reid Cornelius) in the trade for Mark Clark, homered in the eighth.

McDOWELL WINS HIS THIRD STRAIGHT

Then it was McDowell, on Sept. 22, who made clear his desire to be the Tribe's No. 3 starter in the playoffs. Black Jack won his third straight game, 6-5, over Kansas City with eighth inning relief help from Paul Assenmacher and Paul Shuey, and Mesa in the ninth.

If it influenced Hargrove, he didn't admit as much. "It was a good outing for Jack," said the manager. "We saw some good things, but we also saw some things we didn't necessarily like."

Among the latter were the three runs the Royals scored in the fifth, taking a 4-1 lead on three hits and a walk. The Indians got two of them back in their half of the fifth, and won the game with three runs - aided by two K.C. errors - in the seventh.

Mesa, who'd had a couple of ragged outings earlier in the month, retired the Royals in order in the ninth, but was booed when he went 2-and-0 against the first batter he faced, Mike Macfarlane.

"It shocked me that fans would boo Mesa after just two pitches," said Hargrove.

If it bothered Mesa, he didn't hang around the clubhouse long enough to say.

ANOTHER MINI-CONTROVERSY

The game, which resulted in the Indians' 15th victory in 20 games since the acquisition of Seitzer, also produced a mini-controversy between him and Belle.

Belle, going for the RBI championship - he led the A.L. with 142 at the time - singled in the seventh inning and apparently was upset because Seitzer did not score from second on the hit.

While jogging to first base, Belle waved at Seitzer to indicate that he should not have stopped at third.

When the inning ended, after the Indians had scored twice to take a one run lead, Belle returned to the dugout and refused to acknowledge the high fives of his teammates, including Seitzer.

"No one could have scored on that hit," Hargrove answered the obvious question. "If Albert wanted (Seitzer) to score, he should have hit (the ball) over the outfielder's head."

Seitzer talked with Hargrove after the game, but the manager said he did not meet with Belle.

INDIANS WIN 11th IN FINAL AT-BAT

Three victories against Minnesota followed, 7-6, 7-5 and 6-3, in the final regular season homestand, Sept. 23-25 - though the possibility of a make-up game on Sept. 30 against Seattle still existed. It would be played if it would have a bearing on the Mariners' playoff chances.

Ramirez's solo homer with two out in the eighth won it on behalf of Graves, who hardly deserved the victory. He was the second of three relievers to follow Lopez, with Mesa blanking the Twins with a one-two-three ninth for his 37th save.

It was the Indians' 31st come from behind victory, and the 11th in their final at-bat (compared to 17 losses). The seven runs, capped by Ramirez's homer, gave the Tribe 927 for the season, bettering the club record of 925 set in 1921.

Though Lopez was staked to a 4-0 lead, he couldn't stand the prosperity. The Twins scored twice in the fifth, and knocked Lopez out of the game in the sixth, when Graves also was hit hard and the Indians fell behind, 6-4.

Franco came through with a two run single that tied the score in the bottom of the sixth, and Ramirez, hitting Jose Parra's 3-and-0 pitch out of the park, won it.

But not before the Indians were jolted by what appeared to be a serious injury suffered by Lofton.

Lofton, who was leading the A.L. with 75 stolen bases (in 92 attempts), was third with 205 hits, and fourth with 130 runs, fouled a pitch off his left foot, had to be helped off the field and wound up in the hospital.

Fortunately, x-rays of the injury were negative, and Lofton missed only the next two games.

BELLE MOVES AHEAD OF AVERILL

Ogea won the next night, Sept. 24, thanks to Belle, who homered, singled and doubled in a 7-5 victory over the Twins. He drove in three more runs, giving him 146, moving him into second place among the Indians' all-time leaders, ahead of Earl Averill, who had 143 in 1931.

With only four games left, Trosky's 1936 club record of 162 RBI was obviously out of Belle's reach.

"I think Albert is trying to put a capper on a very, very good season," Hargrove said of the left fielder who was battling Seattle's Alex Rodriguez, Baltimore's Brady Anderson, Texas' Juan Gonzalez, and Chicago's Thomas for the A.L.'s Most Valuable Player award.

Belle, eligible to become a free agent at the end of the season, should have won the award in 1995. He lost out to Boston's Mo Vaughn because, in the opinion of many, Vaughn was more popular among the writers who do the voting.

Belle's homer was struck in the third inning when Alomar was ejected by umpire Brian O'Nora for disputing a called third strike. Moments later Hargrove also was ordered to leave when he argued because Alomar was booted.

"I thought (Alomar) was thrown out too quick," said Hargrove. "Sandy had a gripe and he vented it, and you've got to do what you think is right. It was a competitive situation."

Alomar was steaming after the game. "Who cares," he said. "There is no justice here."

It was Hargrove's fourth ejection of the season, and Alomar's third.

Belle's homer, a three run shot, put the Indians ahead, 4-3. The Twins tied it in the fourth on a solo homer by Marty Cordova, but the Indians got three more in the fifth on Franco's two run double and Tony Pena's single.

Tavarez and Plunk blanked Minnesota in the seventh and eighth, setting up Mesa, who was erratic again. He walked the first batter, wild pitched him to second with one out, hit Chuck Knoblauch with a pitch with two out, and served a run scoring double to Rich Becker.

Finally, with the tying and go ahead runs in scoring position, Mesa induced Paul Molitor to ground out to rack up his 38th save.

NAGY BEATS TWINS FOR 17TH VICTORY

Martinez, who had pitched so well for the Indians - and provided the credibility they needed to become a contender when he joined them as a free agent in 1994 - was honored prior to the last regular season home game on Sept. 25.

It was the finale because the make-up game with Seattle, which had been rained out on Sept. 7, didn't have to be played. Baltimore clinched the wild card berth, eliminating the Mariners on the second last day.

After their salute to Martinez, the Indians beat the Twins, 6-3, as Nagy pitched and won his final regular season start in front of 42,469 fans.

It was an easy victory for Nagy, whose record peaked at 17-5, and the 98th for the Indians, leaving them with three opportunities to win two more games to reach the century mark for the second straight season.

It also gave them an 18-5 mark in September - ever since Seitzer joined the club.

"Mr. Nagy dominated the game," was the succinct analysis of Tom Kelly, manager of the Twins.

Nagy went all the way, scattering five hits, and was coasting with a 6-1 cushion until the ninth. It gave him a two year, 33-11 record in 61 starts.

His 17 victories tied a career high and, if not for his 10 no-decision starts, there was little doubt Nagy would have been the prime candidate for the A.L. Cy Young award.

"If you look at what Charlie has done this season," said Hargrove, "and compared it to what other people have done, I don't know how anyone could be more consistent.

"Other pitchers have won more games, but I don't think anyone has been more consistent."

Then Hargrove put in a plug for Nagy and Belle, as well as Lofton, for post season honors.

"I believe we have two legitimate MVP candidates in Belle and Lofton, and a Cy Young candidate in Nagy."

Martinez, in his three seasons in Cleveland, won 32 games - plus another on Oct. 17, 1995, in Game 6 of the A.L. Championship Series when he beat the Mariners in the Seattle Kingdome. It gave the Indians their first pennant since 1954.

"El Presidente," as the Indians called Martinez, was given a crystal vase, 32 personalized baseballs for each of his victories, and a $5,000 check to donate to the Fabretto Children's Fund in Nicaragua.

After receiving a standing ovation, Martinez took the microphone and saluted the fans, calling them "the greatest in baseball."

THREE K.C. ROOKIES BEAT THE TRIBE

With three regular season games in Kansas City remaining, the major concern of Hart and Hargrove - as well as six or seven "fringe" players - was the composition of the 25-man eligibility roster for the post season.

On the "bubble," so to speak, to fill five spots on the list, were infielders Jackson, Candaele, and Mark Carreon (who also could play the outfield), outfielder Wilson, and pitchers Mercker, Anderson, Alan Embree, Tavarez, Graves and Lopez.

But first was the unfinished business against the Royals.

The Indians lost the first game, 11-6, on Sept. 27, making it necessary to win the next two if they were to reach the century mark in victories again.

Kansas City jumped on Hershiser early, continued to pound on two of four relievers late, and three rookie pitchers - Jose Rosado, Bevil and Jamie Bluma - held the Indians in check.

"We were flat tonight," said Hargrove. "You could come up with 100 reasons and all of them might be right.

"But, for whatever reason, Kansas City handed our heads to us."

Lofton returned to the lineup after a two game absence and singled in five trips, giving him 208 hits, becoming the 18th player in franchise history to get that many in one season.

Ramirez homered (No. 33) in the fourth inning when the Indians went ahead, 3-2, but Hershiser couldn't hold it. The Royals went on top, 5-3, in the fifth, raised their lead to 7-3 against Embree in the sixth, and to 11-4 with four runs off Assenmacher in the eighth, after Thome solo homered (No. 38) in the top of the eighth.

INDIANS WIN No. 99 FOR MERCKER

Victory No. 99 was registered on Sept. 28 when McDowell pitched five so-so innings, but Mercker was the winner. Alomar solo homered in the seventh to break a tie as the Indians beat the Royals, 5-4.

Belle also blasted his 48th homer, a two run shot in the sixth, giving him a league-leading RBI total of 148, the most in the major leagues since George Foster of Cincinnati drove in 149 runs in 1977.

McDowell, who allowed four runs on eight hits in five innings, hadn't lost a start in the final month of the season since Sept. 18, 1993. Though Hargrove wasn't yet ready to make it official, it appeared that Black Jack would be the choice over Ogea as the third starter in the playoffs.

For Mercker, it was his first victory for the Indians since his acquisition from Baltimore for Murray two months earlier.

It also was on Sept. 28 that the Indians learned their opponent in the Division Series would be Baltimore. The Orioles won the wild card race by beating Toronto, 3-2, on a 10th inning home run by Sandy Alomar's brother, Roberto, Baltimore's second baseman.

Ogea was the loser - which cost him the third spot in the starting rotation in the playoffs - as the Indians were beaten in their regular season finale, 4-1, by Kansas City, Sept. 29.

Trying to shrug off the disappointment, Ogea said, "I figured they'd go with somebody who had post season experience, although, I would have preferred that they (Hart and Hargrove) told me instead of you guys.

"But whatever capacity they need me to pitch in, I'll be ready. I realize McDowell is more of an investment than me ... but that's all I'm going to say now."

The Indians averted a shutout at the hands of Tim Belcher when Belle doubled to lead the ninth, went to third on Kent's single and scored on a sacrifice fly by Giles.

Thome, who finished with a .311 average, 38 homers and 116 RBI, said personal goals might have caused the Tribe's attention to wander from the fundamental ball they played so well through most of September.

"I think a lot of guys got caught up in that," he said. "Albert (Belle) wanted to get 50 homers (he finished with 48), and I wanted to get 40. I told Albert, I'm going to set you up so you can get the RBI title," which Belle won for a third time.

LOFTON WINS FIFTH STOLEN BASE TITLE

Lofton went hitless in the finale, but batted .317 with 210 hits, third most in the A.L. (behind Molitor's 225, and Knoblauch's 140), the most by a Tribesman in 60 years, and the 16th highest total in club history.

Lofton's 132 runs scored also were third in the A.L. (behind Alex Rodriguez's 141, and Knoblauch's 140), and ranked fifth in the Tribe all-time records, behind Averill's 140 in 1931, Tris Speaker's 137 in 1920, Averill's 136 in 1936, and Speaker's 133 in 1923.

Lofton also easily won his fifth consecutive A.L. stolen base championship with a career high 75 (in 92 attempts), nine more than K.C.'s Tom Goodwin.

In addition to Belle winning the RBI title, his 48 homers were fourth behind Mark McGwire's 52, Brady Anderson's 50, and Ken Griffey Jr.'s 49; and his 124 runs were sixth behind Alex Rodriguez, Knoblauch, Lofton, Robbie Alomar (132) and Griffey (125).

Thome's 122 runs were seventh best in the A.L.

Other Indians among the league leaders were Ramirez, sixth, with 45 doubles; Vizquel, fifth, with 35 stolen bases; and Mesa's 39 saves were second to John Wetteland of New York, who had 43.

HARGROVE: 'WE'VE GOT TO START OVER AGAIN'

And so the Indians ended the regular season with a 99-62 record, a 14 1/2 game lead over Chicago, and played before 3,318,174 fans at Jacobs Field, most in franchise history, with an ongoing mark of 131 consecutive capacity crowds.

They won 10 of their last 13 games, and had a 19-7 record since Sept. 1, when Seitzer joined the team.

"It would have been nice to win 100 games, but our record still was the best in the major leagues ... I'm satisfied with that," said Hargrove.

"Now we've got to start it all over again and get to where we didn't go last year."

Final 1996 Standings

AMERICAN LEAGUE

NATIONAL LEAGUE

CENTRAL	W	L	PCT.	GB	CENTRAL	W	L	PCT.	GB
Cleveland	99	62	.615	----	St. Louis	88	74	.543	----
Chicago	85	77	.525	14.5	Houston	82	80	.506	6.0
Minnesota	80	82	.494	19.5	Cincinnati	81	81	.500	7.0
Milwaukee	78	84	.481	19.5	Chicago	76	86	.469	12.0
Kansas City	75	86	.466	24.0	Pittsburg	73	89	.451	15.0

EAST	W	L	PCT.	GB	EAST	W	L	PCT.	GB
New York	92	70	.568	----	Atlanta	96	66	.593	----
Baltimore	88	74	.543	4.0	Montreal	88	74	.543	8.0
Boston	85	77	.525	7.0	Florida	80	82	.494	16.0
Toronto	74	88	.457	18.0	New York	71	91	.438	25.0
Detroit	53	109	.327	39.0	Philadelphia	67	95	.414	29.0

WEST	W	L	PCT.	GB	WEST	W	L	PCT.	GB
Texas	90	72	.556	----	San Diego	91	71	.562	----
Seattle	85	76	.528	4.5	Los Angeles	90	72	.556	1.0
Oakland	78	84	.481	12.0	Colorado	83	79	.512	8.0
California	70	91	.435	19.5	San Francisco	68	94	.420	23.0

Indians pitcher Charles Nagy hoists the Central Division championship flag on September 19, 1996 at Jacobs field.

Jim Thome slides into second base in a game against the Califonia Angels.

*Albert Belle watches the ball go into the right field stands
for a home run aginst the Seattle Mariners.*

*Orel Hershiser waits in the dugout during a rain
delayed game against the Boston Red Sox*

15

A DREAM SEASON
ENDS TO SOON

September 30-October 5

It was to be the first step to where the Indians planned - really, *expected* - to go, the goal they didn't reach in 1995, losing as they did in six games to the Atlanta Braves.

To the peak, the pinnacle, the World Championship.

Sure, the Indians had their troubles and travail, ups and downs in 1996, a season that was more a roller coaster ride than a swift and direct journey to redemption.

They didn't take charge in the American League Central Division until the second half was well underway, almost blowing the lead at the All-Star break, and traded away two of the players who had been among the best in baseball.

But, finally, they won going away, clinching a second straight division championship with 11 games to play by beating in a direct confrontation the team, the Chicago White Sox, whose management had maligned the Indians most of the season,

And, perhaps best of all - or so everybody thought - the first step toward the rematch with the Braves in the World Series would be against the Baltimore Orioles, who didn't qualify for the post season tournament as the A.L.'s wild card team until the day before the regular season ended.

The Indians beat them seven times in their 12 meetings, and the Orioles were a team whose overall record (88-74) was 11 1/2 games worse.

ORIOLES EMBROILED IN CONTROVERSY

The Orioles came into the playoffs embroiled in a nasty controversy involving one of their best players, second baseman Roberto Alomar, that many thought would be a major distraction.

Three days before the season ended, during a game in Toronto, Alomar spat in the face of umpire John Hirschbeck.

Alomar was suspended for five games by A.L. President Gene Budig, but immediately appealed, effectively forestalling the implementation of the penalty until the start of the 1997 season.

It shocked baseball purists and infuriated the Major League Umpires Association, which initially refused to work any games in which Alomar played.

The umpires' strike finally was averted in a 12th hour negotiating session, but there's no doubt the anger remained.

The Indians, whose catcher, Sandy Alomar Jr., is Roberto Alomar's older brother, made no great show of indignation, accepting - ostensibly, at least - the situation as something over which they had no control.

Besides, though nobody publicly admitted as much, it seemed evident that the Orioles, with or without Alomar, could be brushed aside, enabling the Tribe to get on with its stated objective - to win the pennant and avenge their 1995 loss to the Braves.

The truth be told, there was greater concern about the Indians' presumed next opponent, the New York Yankees or Texas Rangers, at the next level of the playoffs for the A.L. Championship Series.

So it was that the Indians, with a high level of confidence, took on the Orioles in the best-of-five Division Series that began in Baltimore, Oct. 1, and would continue at Oriole Park at Camden Yards for Game 2 on Oct. 2.

And then, because the Indians were supposed to have the home field advantage, Game 3 - as well as Games 4 and 5, if necessary - would be played at Jacobs Field.

HART QUESTIONS PLAYOFF FORMAT

It was a playoff format that Tribe General Manager John Hart questioned at the onset, even before the first pitch was made.

To Hart's way of thinking, he said more than once, the Indians didn't really get an advantage, despite compiling the best record in the A.L., and playing the team that reached the Division Series with the worst mark.

"First," he said, "the five game playoff really levels the field. I think everybody in baseball wants to go to a best-of-seven in the first round. That's a much fairer test."

Hart was even more resolute in his contention that the Indians weren't really getting a home field advantage.

"I'm for giving (the wild card team) the first game at home," he said, "and then packing up and going to the other park for the next two games, and/ or fourth, and/or fifth, if necessary.

"That would be a true home field advantage for the team that deserved it on the basis of having the best record."

Hart's point subsequently was proved to have been well taken, although, unfortunately for the Indians, by then it was too late.

ORIOLES WIN DIVISION SERIES OPENER, 10-4

Just as Jack McDowell's nearly-tragic automobile accident on the eve of spring training might have been a portent of trouble ahead, perhaps Charles Nagy missing the team bus to Camden Yards for Game 1 on Oct. 1, also was a negative omen.

Nagy walked to the ball park and arrived in plenty of time, so missing the bus wasn't the cause of the Indians' problem.

Home runs were. The Orioles hit four of them, by Brady Anderson and B.J. Surhoff off Nagy, and by Surhoff and Bobby Bonilla (a grand slam) off Paul Shuey.

David Wells also was part of the problem.

Yes, *that* David Wells. The left handed pitcher the Indians tried so hard to acquire - and thought they did a few hours before the July 31 trading deadline.

The same David Wells who won only one of his last six starts, but whose 11-14 season record (and 5.14 ERA) included two victories in two games against the Tribe.

The Orioles attacked early, Anderson hitting a first inning, leadoff homer. Manny Ramirez got it back with a solo homer in the second, but everything that followed was downhill for the Tribe.

Surhoff homered to make it 2-1 in the Baltimore half of the second, and the Orioles added two more runs in the third on Todd Zeile's single, Rafael Palmeiro's one out double, and Cal Ripken's two out single.

The Indians cut their deficit to 4-3 in the fourth on hits by Ramirez, Jeff Kent and Sandy Alomar, and Omar Vizquel's sacrifice fly, but it never got any better.

Nagy was kayoed in the sixth when he walked two around a single by Anderson, and the Orioles exploded against Alan Embree and Shuey for five runs, breaking the game wide open.

Each team scored a run in the seventh, the Indians on Vizquel's double, stolen base and Kenny Lofton's single, and the Orioles on Surhoff's second homer.

The turning point, in the opinion of Sandy Alomar, was in the sixth when Nagy walked Zeile on a 3-and-2 pitch with one out and runners on first and second.

NAGY: 'I THOUGHT IT WAS A STRIKE'

Nagy fired a curve that broke down and away - on the outside corner, Alomar said - to the right handed Zeile.

Umpire Drew Coble called it ball four.

"I thought it was a strike, (Coble) thought it was a ball," said Nagy.

"In a game like that, when you've been battling your butt off, you've got a right to be upset, and I was," he said, but to no avail, of course.

"(Nagy) threw the same pitch two pitches before and I called it a ball. How could I call that one a strike?" asked Coble.

Whatever, "That was the turning point .. the whole game turned after that," said Sandy Alomar.

Embree replaced the very irate Nagy and got Roberto Alomar to loft a routine fly to Ramirez in short right field. Chris Hoiles, no speed merchant, tagged up at third base and broke for the plate. He should have been thrown out by Ramirez, who led the league in outfield assists.

However, Ramirez made a basket catch and, instead of throwing home, tossed the ball to second base.

"I wanted to go home, but the (fly) ball died on me," said Ramirez. "I couldn't throw to the plate after that."

Mike Hargrove didn't question Ramirez's decision. At least not publicly. "I have to assume the ball didn't carry the way (Ramirez) thought it would," said the manager. "From the way he played it, I thought he made the right throw."

A hit batsman followed, loading the bases, and Shuey came in to replace Embree. He was greeted with the grand slam off the bat of Bonilla, who hit a low fast ball on a 3-and-2 count.

"I know Shuey throws extremely hard ... I was trying to get a ball below my hands, not chase anything high," said Bonilla. He also was the subject of trade talks at mid-season before Orioles owner Peter Angelos stepped in and nullified any proposed deal for him.

.The four runs produced by Bonilla's homer were more than enough for the Orioles to win, even before Surhoff's homer leading the seventh.

HARGROVE IS SECOND GUESSED

Hargrove left himself open to the second guessers by sticking with Nagy as long as he did, and when he finally made a change by bringing in Embree instead of the more experienced Paul Assenmacher.

"I considered taking Charlie out in the third, the fourth and the fifth inning," said Hargrove. "But with good pitchers, if you give them time to settle in, frequently they will."

As for his choice of Embree, there would not have been a reason to question the strategy if Ramirez had thrown out Hoiles at the plate after catching the short fly by Roberto Alomar.

The Indians seemed stunned by the loss. "Their lineup reminds me of us last year," said Jim Thome, who - though it wasn't disclosed until later - suffered a fractured hamate bone in his right hand while batting against reliever Randy Myers in the ninth inning.

Though he had trouble gripping the bat, Thome insisted upon playing, and did, though he was far below par the rest of the series.

"It's not good that we got beat, but maybe in some ways it will prove to be a good thing," Thome rationalized the loss . "Now we know what we're up against, and what we've got to go out and do.

"We've got to win (Game 2), and go home where we're comfortable in Jacobs Field."

ORIOLES TAKE 2-0 LEAD IN DIVISION SERIES

Orel Hershiser, who said of Camden Yards, "They could take this park and move it to Japan and it would do quite well," couldn't even the score for the Indians in the second game, Oct. 2.

The Orioles won, 7-4, and suddenly the Indians' expectation for revenge - to reach the World Series and beat the Braves - was in serious jeopardy.

Baltimore jumped off to another early lead when Kevin Seitzer booted a grounder with two out and two runners aboard via walks in the first inning. It scored Roberto Alomar.

Seitzer was playing first base in place of Julio Franco because, as Hargrove explained, the grounds were wet after rain delayed the start by 37 minutes, and he did not want to take a chance of Franco re-injuring his right hamstring.

The Orioles added three runs to their margin in the fifth as Anderson led off with another homer. Then, with two out, Palmeiro singled, Bonilla walked and Ripken doubled for another run.

The third run of the inning scored on a double by Murray, though further trouble was averted when Ripken was thrown out at the plate on Vizquel's relay from Albert Belle.

Scott Erickson, who was 13-12 during the regular season, but only 1-2 vs. the Indians, held them scoreless until the sixth when they retaliated with three runs.

Lofton singled with one out, stole second and third, and scored on Seitzer's infield grounder. Thome, his broken hand notwithstanding, lashed a single to center, and Belle homered into the left field stands.

The Tribe tied it, 4-4, in the eighth on hits by Seitzer and Thome, Belle's walk, and Franco's sacrifice fly. But reliever Armando Benitez struck out Ramirez, and retired Sandy Alomar on a pop fly to his brother Roberto.

"At that point the momentum switched back to us," said Ripken

A PLAY THAT LONG WILL BE REMEMBERED

The Orioles won it with another three run outburst in the eighth against Eric Plunk, Assenmacher and Julian Tavarez.

Bonilla walked and went to third as Ripken doubled with one out. After Murray was intentionally walked, loading the bases, Assenmacher replaced Plunk, and it was then that this game turned, once and for all.

It happened on a play that was hotly disputed by the Indians, and undoubtedly will be remembered for a long time.

Surhoff bounced back to Assenmacher and it seemed that a perfect double play - home to first - would result, getting the Indians out of the inning without damage.

Assenmacher's toss to the plate forced pinch runner Mike Devereaux, but Sandy Alomar's relay bounced past Kent, who had taken over at first base for defensive purposes.

The Indians argued that Alomar's throw was wild because he was afraid of hitting Surhoff, who had not run outside the base line as required by the rules. Television replays confirmed their contention.

But neither plate umpire Greg Kosc, nor Tim Tschida, who worked at first base, or Coble, the crew chief, agreed. Not only was Surhoff safe, he reached second on the throw that got past Kent, with Ripken scoring the tie breaking run, and Murray taking third.

After pinch hitter Hoiles was intentionally walked, re-loading the bases, the situation went from bad to worse as Anderson's sacrifice got another run home.

Tavarez replaced Assenmacher and walked Zeile, then gave up a run scoring single by Roberto Alomar for a 7-4 lead before the uprising mercifully ended.

The Indians went down in order in the ninth and, behind in games, 0-2, were staring elimination in the face as they returned to Jacobs Field for what had been - mistakenly - called a "home field advantage."

As Hargrove said to the media afterwards, "You guys asked me how deep a hole we were in yesterday, and I told you it was deep, but not too deep.

It's much deeper today.

"It's a real, tired old cliché to say we've got to take it one game at a time, but we really do. We need to win (Game 3). Then we'll worry about winning (Game 4). Then (Game 6)."

TSCHIDA: 'IT WAS SIMPLY AN ERRANT THROW'

Of the controversial play that opened the door to the Orioles' three run eighth, Hargrove said, "Obviously, Sandy (Alomar) did not make a good throw. (But) our contention was that he had to alter his throw because Surhoff was running inside the line.

"That's an umpire's judgment (call), and they said it (Surhoff running inside the line) didn't have anything to do with how the play turned out."

Tschida said, "The fact that a base runner is inside the line doesn't in and of itself constitute interference. His being inside the line has to prevent whoever is covering the bag from catching the ball (for it to be interference).

"In our opinion, it was simply an errant throw."

Alomar argued, "I tried to aim the ball because I couldn't see Kent. Surhoff was in the way. I knew Surhoff would be out if I hit him, but that's hard to do in a big game. You miss and the ball might end up in the right field corner."

Kent was irate. "Surhoff caused us to botch the play. He got his big butt in the way. It was a good play on his part. He got away with one," said Kent.

When asked why Seitzer started at first base instead of Franco, a better fielder, Hargrove replied, "Whenever the field is wet, we prefer to let Seitzer play first because Julio's hamstring can give him problems on fields that are wet."

Hargrove held an impromptu meeting with his players in the dugout during the fourth inning and, at least for the time being, it helped. They went on to score three runs in the seventh, cutting their deficit to 4-3, and tied it in the eighth.

"It just seemed like a good time to get them together, to talk," said Hargrove. "I thought we were tight, trying to do too much in every at-bat. I'd never seen this club that way.

"I told them, 'Be who you are. We got to where we are by you being that way. Take it one swing at a time, one hit at a time.' Everyone was trying to hit the ball out of the park on every swing."

Only four other teams in baseball history came back from 0-2 deficits, as the Indians were facing: Los Angeles over Houston in 1981, Milwaukee over California in 1982, San Diego over Chicago Cubs in 1984, and Seattle over New York Yankees in 1995.

But Lofton, for one, did not want to discuss the Indians' chances. "Life is tough," he said. "You deal with it. We all have to deal with it. I don't know (if the team is pressing), all I know is we've got three games to play."

McDOWELL HOLDS TRIBE HOPES IN GAME 3

McDowell, who was signed to a two year, $9.6 million contract for this very purpose - to pitch "money" games for the Indians - took the mound for Game 3, Oct. 4.

Despite being staked to 1-0 and 3-1 leads, he was shaky from the on-set.

And it was Lofton, the triggerman again, who took matters into his own hands in the first inning.

He led off for the Tribe by reaching second on a two base error by Bonilla, stole third and scored on Seitzer's ground out, pumping up the 44,250 fans in Jacobs Field. It was the first time the Indians had scored first.

But the Orioles were not intimidated and quickly nullified the run.

Bonilla and Murray singled around one out in the second inning and, after Surhoff fanned for the second out, Murray stole second and Hoiles walked. Then McDowell hit Anderson with a pitch, forcing in a tying run, but managed to strike out Zeile to end the rally.

Ramirez started the bottom of the second with a homer off Mike Mussina, and the "V" squad, Vizquel and Jose Vizcaino, produced another run, with help from Zeile.

Vizquel beat out a bunt single, took second on Zeile's throwing error, and came home on Vizcaino's double.

But again, McDowell couldn't stand the prosperity.

Ripken and Murray singled to open the fourth, and Surhoff smashed his third homer of the Series, giving the Orioles a 4-3 lead.

The Indians re-tied it in the bottom of the third, but as they'd done so often, wasted an opportunity to score more after Vizquel singled again with one out, and came home as Vizcaino doubled again.

But Vizcaino was thrown out at third on a grounder by Lofton and, after Seitzer singled, Thome struck out.

Three innings later the Indians finally exploded, taking advantage of Jesse Orosco, the veteran left hander who pitched for Cleveland from 1989-91.

CANDAELE WANTS TO BUNT, BUT CAN'T

Orosco had replaced Mussina and walked Lofton and Seitzer, the first two batters in the seventh. Casey Candaele was sent to the plate as a pinch hitter for Thome with orders to bunt the runners to second and third.

Candaele tried and if he'd been successful the Orioles would have intentionally walked Belle, the next batter.

But Orosco couldn't throw a strike that Candaele could bunt, and he also walked.

Thus, the bases were loaded for Belle to deliver one of the biggest hits in the history of the Cleveland franchise against Benitez, who had replaced Orosco.

Down in the count, 1-and-2, Belle crushed a fast ball for a grand slam into the left field bleachers, giving the Indians an 8-4 lead - and new life.

They scored another run on two singles and a stolen base in the eighth, and Jose Mesa, the sixth Indians pitcher, gave up a hit but blanked the Orioles in the ninth, preserving the victory that was credited to Assenmacher.

Belle wasn't talking, but Benitez didn't hide from inquiring reporters. "The first two pitches were fast balls," he said.

Both were in the 97-98 miles per hour range, according to the Indians' radar gun. The third pitch was a 72 mph change-up that Belle fouled off, and the fourth, another fast ball missed the strike zone.

"Then I threw him another fast ball, but I didn't get behind it," said Benitez.

Belle did. It was the second grand slam in a post season game by an Indians player. Elmer Smith got the first one in the fifth game of the 1920 World Series.

Hargrove said of Belle, "Albert has legitimized our lineup since he's been here. This game was another piece of evidence of just how focused a competitor he is.

"In the eighth inning, when he struck out with runners on second and third, he was really upset. And that's after hitting a grand slam in his previous at-bat."

HART: 'WE LIVE TO DIE ANOTHER DAY'

While Belle rightfully deserved most of the credit for keeping the Indians alive, Lofton came in for praise.

As coach Dave Nelson said, "As long as Kenny gets on base, we're in good shape ... we're a different team."

Nobody could argue with Nelson's logic. Though Lofton went hitless in the victory that renewed the waning hopes of the Indians and their fans, he reached on an error, a fielder's choice, stole three bases and scored twice.

And, as Hart said, "We live to die another day."

Nagy went back to the mound in Game 4, Oct. 5, with only three days rest for the first time in his career, trying to keep the Indians' flickering hopes alive.

He almost did it.

Except for back-to-back homers by Palmeiro and Bonilla leading the second inning, Nagy was masterful for as long as he lasted, six innings.

Then, after making 110 pitches and striking out 12 batters, he sat down, hoping that Embree and the rest of the Tribe bull pen could protect a 3-2 lead and force a fifth and final game.

They couldn't - but almost did.

Of the strikeouts, Nagy said, "That's something I can't explain. I was making my pitches and they were swinging and missing. I was getting tired (in the sixth inning) and turned it over to the bull pen. They did a good job."

With Wells also working for the Orioles with three days rest since his series opening, 10-4, victory, the Tribe tied the score in the fourth. Sandy Alomar singled with two out to drive in Franco, who'd singled, and Ramirez, who was aboard with a double.

The Indians went ahead with a run in the fifth as Vizcaino singled, was bunted to second and scored on Vizquel's single.

It stayed that way, with the Indians clinging to a 3-2 lead through the eighth, as they couldn't score again against four Baltimore relievers, including Benitez, the victim of Belle's game winning grand slam in Game 3.

And then, in the ninth, the Orioles scored a tying run, and won it in the 12th.

ROBERTO ALOMAR, THE HERO

The hero - the Oriole whose hit sent the game into overtime, and then whose homer ended the Indians season - was Roberto Alomar, the guy who should not have been allowed to play, in the opinion of the umpires and most baseball fans.

Booed in his every plate appearance at Jacobs Field, Alomar singled to left in the ninth off Mesa with two on and two out. It brought pinch runner Manny Alexander home with the run that tied the score.

Mesa, the Tribe's fifth reliever, had entered the game in the ninth and promptly struck out Pete Incaviglia.

But he couldn't retire the next two batters, Surhoff and Anderson, both of whom looped soft singles to center, the second of which appeared catchable.

Apparently fooled by Anderson's big swing, Lofton broke back when the ball was hit, then couldn't recover quickly enough. He made a last second dive for the ball, but it bounced off his wrist for a second single.

Zeile fouled to Franco for the second out, but Alomar refused to let Mesa end the game and prolong the series.

With the count 1-and-2 against Alomar, Mesa fired a slider down and in to the switch-hitting second baseman. "I hardly saw it," Alomar said later.

But he saw enough of the ball to send another soft single to center that also barely eluded Lofton's desperate dive.

Palmeiro flied out to end the rally, but the damage was done, though the Indians mounted one last threat in their half of the ninth against Terry Mathews, who had replaced Wells an inning earlier.

Ramirez coaxed a walk to start it, and was bunted to second. When Palmeiro muffed Sandy Alomar's pop fly for an error, Tribe hopes soared.

Orosco, a goat in Game 3, was rushed to the mound in relief of Mathews, and this time - to the great dismay of the Indians - did what he was supposed to do.

Orosco retired Vizcaino on a grounder and, with Ramirez representing the winning run at third base, Lofton was caught looking at a called third strike. It ended the inning and, as it turned out, the Indians, too.

TRIBE HITLESS THROUGH LAST FIVE

They were held hitless through the final five innings, from the time Vizquel singled off Wells with two out in the seventh (and was caught stealing).

Mesa, pitching in his longest relief stint in two seasons because the Tribe bull pen was spent, held the Orioles at bay through the next two innings, though not without some anxious moments in the 10th.

After Ripken and Murray singled back-to-back with one out, the Indians caught a break. When Ripken rounded second too far on Murray's single to right, he was cut down on a strong throw from Ramirez. Then Pete Incaviglia struck out.

It stayed, 3-3, until Alomar, leading the 12th, drilled his game winning homer into the right center field stands.

"I just swung the bat hard and (Mesa) threw the ball where I was looking for it," said Alomar.

Mesa retired the next two batters, but when the Orioles threatened to pad their lead on a double by Ripken, Chad Ogea took over as the Tribe's seventh pitcher. He intentionally walked Murray, and Devereaux flied out to end the rally.

Then, with the scoreboard at Jacobs Field flashing the message it had displayed the entire game - "Not in our House! Not in our House!" - the Orioles did indeed do it in the
Indians' house.

With Myers on the mound in relief of Orosco, the Indians finally were stopped, once and for all in 1996, as their last three batters went peacefully.

Vizcaino bunted and was thrown out by Zeile. Lofton flied to Devereaux. And Vizquel was called out on strikes.

And with that third strike from Myers, the Indians' hopes - *expectation*, really - of reaching and winning the World Series were finally, cruelly ended.

A dream season had slipped away, and the cheers of the fans turned to tears.

'HE WAS STRUCK OUT' - VIZQUEL

"It was like somebody stabbed a knife in your heart," is the way Vizquel lamented the loss.

He also lamented the third pitch Mesa made to Roberto Alomar in the fateful ninth inning. Not the one Alomar hit for the game tying single, the pitch before that, when the count was 0-and-2.

"We had two strikes on him, and two outs," said Vizquel. "Then Jose threw strike three. It was right down the middle. But the umpire (Larry Young) called it a ball. I couldn't believe it. You'd think that the umpires were mad at us instead of (Alomar).

"He was struck out," or should have been, in Vizquel's opinion. "It was like it was just not meant to be for us."

The third strike that Young called a ball also was a subject that Hart addressed in the Indians somber clubhouse.

"The key is that we didn't get the last strike on Alomar," he said, without making a major issue of it.

"The guy (Alomar) is a professional hitter. He was looking to protect the plate and just make contact. That's what a good hitter does. The bottom line is, we didn't get the job done in the ninth."

Vizquel also talked about the jubilation the Indians felt when Sandy Alomar singled for two runs, tying the score, 2-2, in the fourth.

"When Sandy got that hit, we all went crazy," said Vizquel. "It was just a matter of time, we thought, until we'd win.

"We probably had too much confidence, but we had a right to be confident. We had the best record in baseball. We were the best team, they (the Orioles) just played better. They did the little things better, and they pitched better than we did.

"It probably was to their advantage that they were in a pennant race until the (second) last day of the season," added the disconsolate Gold Glove shortstop.

HARGROVE: 'NO SECOND THOUGHTS'

As for Mesa still being in the game in the 12th - his fourth inning - when Alomar homered, Hargrove defended the strategy.

"I have no second thoughts (about leaving Mesa in the game)," said Hargrove. "He's been good for us all year, he was very strong the inning before. We went to him and asked if he could still pitch and he said yes, that he still felt fine."

Others, including pitching coach Mark Wiley and Ogea, who took over in the 12th after Alomar's homer, also endorsed the decision to stick with Mesa.

"You have to leave (Mesa) in. You don't know that the game won't go 20 innings. I hate to say it, but I'm the last resort because I can pitch a lot of innings," said Ogea.

And, as Wiley said, "We wanted our horse (Mesa) in there. Sometimes you just have to give the hitter credit ... and Robbie Alomar is a heck of a hitter.

"Jose and the rest of our pitchers left everything they had out there. If someone wants to second guess anything we did, including leaving Mesa in the game, tell them to come and see me.

"We had the game set up perfectly. The pitch Robbie hit (to tie the game in the ninth) was a good one. It was a slider down and in and Robbie just hit it. That's as good a pitching performance as I've ever seen from our club considering the kind of pressure involved."

Of the record 23 strikeouts by the Indians, Wiley exclaimed, "I kept saying to myself, 'You can't strike out that many guys and lose.' But we did."

In addition to the 12 batters Nagy fanned in his six innings, Embree got one in one-third of an inning, Assenmacher two in two-thirds, Plunk two in one, and Mesa six in 3 2/3.

Orioles pitchers struck out 10 Indians for a game total of 33, also a post season record.

"It comes down to how many runs you score, not how many you strike out," said Hargrove.

HART: 'WE HAD OUR CHANCES'

The Indians got only seven hits, all off Wells in seven innings, and 35 in the four games.

"What hurt us in the entire series," said Hart, "was our inability to get the key hits and drive in the big runs. We had our chances to open up games, but couldn't."

Mesa, who stopped talking to reporters after his slump in late-June, remained in character. When reporters requested an interview, Mesa waved them away. "I don't say nothing," he said.

On the other side of Jacobs Field, in the jubilant Orioles clubhouse, Dave Johnson praised his team - and especially Alomar, who went 5-for-17 (.294) in the four games against the Indians.

"After he got the hit to tie the game, you almost knew the script was already written, that when he had the chance to win it, he was going to win it," said the Orioles manager.

Referring to the vocal abuse Alomar received from the fans, Johnson said, "Robbie is a great player, and to be a great player you have to concentrate at a higher level."

Alomar was subdued in the wake of the victory he provided the Orioles, and contrite as he spoke of the incident that will mar his reputation, probably forever.

"I talked to my family. I thank my family and I thank God," he said. "I pray a lot. God knows what's going on. I regret what I did. I didn't mean it to be that way. Sometimes in the heat of battle you do things that you can't recall what's going on.

"I know what kind of person I am, and people who know me know what kind of person I am. You can't judge one person by one mistake."

And, as Ripken said, "Some of the life and joy was pulled out of Alomar this week (because of the spitting controversy), but it seemed like the longer the game went on, he got it back.

"Then, when he got his (game tying) hit, it blew life back into the team."

And out of the Indians.

GAME 1 BOX SCORE

HITTING

CLEVELAND	AB	R	H	RBI	BALTIMORE	AB	R	H	RBI
Lofton cf	5	0	1	1	Anderson cf	5	2	2	1
Seitzer dh	5	0	1	0	Zeile 3b	4	2	2	0
Thome 3b	4	0	1	0	R. Alomar 2b	4	0	1	1
Belle lf	4	0	0	0	Palmiero 1b	4	2	1	1
Franco 1b	4	0	1	0	Bonilla rf	3	1	1	4
Ramierez rf	4	2	3	1	Devereaux pr-ph	0	0	0	0
Kent 2b	4	1	1	0	C. Ripkin ss	5	0	3	1
S. Alomar c	3	0	1	1	Murray dh	4	0	0	0
Giles ph	1	0	0	0	Surhoff lf	4	2	2	2
Pena c	0	0	0	0	Hoiles c	2	1	0	0
Vizquel ss	2	1	1	1	Parent c	0	0	0	0
TOTAL	36	4	10	4	TOTAL	35	10	12	10

Cleveland ....010 200 100 -- 4
Baltimore ....112 005 10x -- 7

E-Zeile. LOB - Cleveland 8, Baltimore 8. 2B - Palmeiro, Kent, C. Ripken, Vizquel.
HR - Anderson (1), Ramierez (1), Surhoff 2 (2), Bonilla (1). SB - Vizquel (1). SF -Vizquel,
R. Alomar

PITCHING

CLEVELAND	IP	H	R	ER	W	SO	BALTIMORE	IP	H	R	ER	W	SO
Nagy L, 0-1	5 1/3	9	7	7	3	1	Wells W, 1-0	6 2/3	8	4	4	1	3
Embree	1/3	0	1	1	0	0	Orosco	0	0	0	0	0	0
Shuey	1 1/3	3	2	2	0	2	Mathews	2/3	2	0	0	0	0
Tavarez	1	0	0	0	1	1	Rhodes	2/3	0	0	0	0	1
							Myers S, 2	1	0	0	0	0	2

HBP - by Nagy (Hoiles), by Embree (Palmiero), by Orosco (Thome). WP - Mathews.
Time - 3:25. Attendance - 47,644
Umpires - HP, Coble; 1B, Kosk; 2B, Tschida; 3B, Welkeck; LF Shulock; RF, Hendry

GAME 2 BOX SCORE

HITTING

CLEVELAND	AB	R	H	RBI		BALTIMORE	AB	R	H	RBI
Lofton cf	5	1	2	0		Anderson cf	4	1	2	2
Seitzer dh	4	0	2	1		Zeile 3b	4	0	0	0
Kent pr - 1b	0	1	0	0		R. Alomar 2b	4	1	1	1
Thome 3b	4	1	2	0		Palmiero 1b	3	1	1	0
Belle lf	3	1	1	2		Bonilla rf	2	1	0	0
Franco dh	3	0	0	1		Devereaux pr-ph	0	0	0	0
Ramirez rf	4	0	0	0		C. Ripken ss	3	1	2	1
S. Alomar c	4	0	0	0		Murray dh	3	0	2	1
Vizquel ss	3	0	0	0		Alexander pr - dh	0	1	0	0
Vizcaino 2b	3	0	1	0		Surhoff lf	4	0	0	0
						Incaviglia pr - lf	0	1	0	0
						Parent c	3	0	1	0
						Hoiles ph - c	0	0	0	0
TOTAL	33	4	8	4		TOTAL	30	7	9	5

Cleveland ....0 0 0 0 0 3 0 1 0 -- 4
Baltimore ....1 0 0 0 3 0 0 3 x -- 7

E-Seitzer, S. Alomar. DP-Cleveland 1, Baltimore 1. LOB-Cleveland 6, Baltimore 8.
2B-Seitzer, Murray, C. Ripken. HR-Anderson (2), Belle (1). SB-Lofton 2 (2), Vizquel 2.
SF- Franco, Anderson.

PITCHING

CLEVELAND	IP	H	R	ER	W	SO		BALTIMORE	IP	H	R	ER	W	SO
Hershiser	5	7	4	3	3	3		Erickson	6 2/3	6	3	3	2	6
Plunk L, 0-1	2	1	2	2	2	2		Orosco	1/3	2	1	1	0	1
Assenmacher	2/3	0	1	1	1	0		Benitez W, 1-0	1	0	0	0	1	1
Tavarez	1/3	1	0	0	1	0		Myers S, 1	1	0	0	0	0	0

Orosco pitched to 2 batters in the 8th, Plunk pitched to 3 batters in the 8th.
HBP - by Hershiser (C Ripken). Time - 3:27, Attendance - 48,970.
Umpires - HP, Kosc; 1B, Tschida: 2B, Welke; 3B, Shulock; LF, Hendry; RF, Coble

GAME 3 BOX SCORE
HITTING

CLEVELAND	AB	R	H	RBI	BALTIMORE	AB	R	H	RBI
Lofton cf	3	2	0	2	Anderson cf	3	0	0	1
Seitzer dh	4	1	2	1	Zeile 3b	5	0	1	0
Thome 3b	2	0	0	1	R. Alomar 2b	3	0	0	0
Candaele ph	0	1	0	1	R. Palmeiro 1b	4	0	0	0
Kent 3b	1	0	0	0	Bonilla rf	4	1	1	0
Belle lf	4	1	2	1	C. Ripkin ss	4	1	1	0
Franco 1b	4	0	0	0	Murray dh	4	1	2	0
Ramierez rf	4	1	1	0	Surhoff lf	4	1	2	3
S. Alomar c	4	0	0	0	Devereaux pr	0	0	0	0
Vizquel ss	4	3	3	0	Hoiles c	2	0	1	0
Vizcaino 2b	4	0	2	0	Alexander pr	0	0	0	0
					Parent c	1	0	0	0
TOTAL	34	9	10	9	TOTAL	34	4	8	4

Baltimore ....0 1 0   3 0 0   0 0 0 -- 4
Cleveland ....1 2 0   1 0 0   4 1 x -- 9

E- Zeile (2). DP-Cleveland 1, Baltimore 1. LOB-Cleveland 7, Baltimore 7. 2B-Vizcaino 2 (2), HR-Belle (2), Ramierez (2), Surhoff (3). SB-Lofton 3 (5), Vizquel (3), Belle (1). Murray (1).

PITCHING

CLEVELAND	IP	H	R	ER	W	SO	BALTIMORE	IP	H	R	ER	W	SO
J McDowell	5 2/3	6	4	4	1	5	Musina	6	7	4	3	2	6
Embree	1/3	0	0	0	0	0	Orosco L, 0-1	0	0	3	3	3	0
Shuey	2/3	1	0	0	2	0	Benitez	1	1	1	1	0	1
Assenmacher W	1/3	0	0	0	0	0	A. Rhodes	1/3	1	1	1	1	1
Plunk	1	0	0	0	0	2	T. Mathews	2/3	1	0	0	0	0
Mesa	1	1	0	0	0	1							

Orosco pitched to 3 batters in the 7th.
HBP - by J McDowell (B. Anderson). Time - 3:44, Attendance - 44,250
Umpires - HP, Merrill; 1B, Young: 2B, Clark; 3B, Johnson; LF, Evans; RF, Kaiser

GAME 4 BOX SCORE

HITTING

CLEVELAND	AB	R	H	RBI	BALTIMORE	AB	R	H	RBI
Lofton cf	5	0	0	0	Anderson cf	5	0	1	0
Vizquel ss	5	0	2	1	Zeile 3b	6	0	2	0
Seitzer dh	4	0	0	0	R. Alomar 2b	6	1	3	2
Candaele pr - dh	0	0	0	0	R. Palmeiro 1b	6	1	1	1
Belle lf	4	0	0	0	Bonilla rf	6	1	1	1
Franco 1b	4	1	1	0	C. Ripkin ss	6	0	2	0
Ramirez rf	4	1	2	0	Murray dh	4	0	2	0
Kent 3b	3	0	0	0	Incaviglia lf	5	0	1	0
Wilson ph	1	0	0	0	Devereaux lf	1	0	0	0
Thome 3b	0	0	0	0	Hoiles c	3	0	0	0
S. Alomar c	5	0	1	2	Surhoff lf	1	0	1	0
Vizcaino 2b	5	1	1	0	Alexander pr	0	1	0	0
					Parent c	1	0	0	0
TOTAL	40	3	7	3	TOTAL	50	4	14	4

```
Baltimore ...................0 2 0  0 0 0  0 0 1  0 0 1  -- 4
Cleveland ...................0 0 0  2 1 0  0 0 0  0 0 0  -- 3
```

E- Palmeiro. LOB-Cleveland 8, Baltimore 13. 2B-Zeile, C.Ripken (3), Ramirez 2.
HR-R. Alomar, Palmeiro. SB-Vizquel (4), Seitzer. CS- Anderson, Vizquel (2), S. Alomar.
S-Lofton, Kent .

PITCHING

CLEVELAND	IP	H	R	ER	W	SO	BALTIMORE	IP	H	R	ER	W	SO
Nagy	6	6	2	2	2	12	Wells	7	7	3	3	3	3
Embree	1/3	0	0	0	0	1	Mathews	1 1/3	0	0	0	1	1
Shuey	0	1	0	0	0	0	Orosco	2/3	0	0	0	0	1
Assenmacher	2/3	0	0	0	0	2	Benitez W 2-0	2	0	0	0	1	4
Plunk	1	0	0	0	0	2	Myers S 2	1	0	0	0	0	1
Mesa L0-1	3 2/3	7	2	2	0	6							
Ogea	1/3	0	0	0	1	0							

BB - Belle off D.Wells, Murray off Ogea Time - 4:41, Attendance - 44,280
Umpires - HP, Young; 1B, Clark: 2B, Johnson; 3B, Evans; LF, Kaiser; RF, Merrill

DIVISION SERIES COMPOSITE BOX

BATTING SUMMARY

CLEVELAND	G	AB	R	H	2B	3B	HR	RBI	BB	SO	AVG
Vizquel ss	4	14	4	6	1	0	0	2	3	4	.429
M Ramirez rf	4	16	4	6	2	0	2	2	1	4	.375
Vizcaino 2b	3	12	1	4	2	0	0	1	1	1	.333
Thome 3b	4	10	1	3	0	0	0	0	1	5	.300
Seitzer dh - 1b	4	17	1	5	1	0	0	4	2	4	.294
Belle lf	4	15	2	3	0	0	2	6	3	2	.200
Lofton cf	4	18	3	3	0	0	0	1	2	3	.167
Franco 1b - dh	4	15	1	2	0	0	0	1	1	6	.133
S Alomar c	4	16	0	2	0	0	0	3	0	2	.125
Kent 2b-1b-3b	4	8	2	1	1	0	0	0	0	0	.125
Giles ph	1	1	0	0	0	0	0	0	0	1	.000
Wilson ph	1	1	0	0	0	0	0	0	0	0	.000
Candaele ph-dh	2	0	1	0	0	0	0	0	1	0	-----
Pena c	1	0	0	0	0	0	0	0	0	0	-----
Totals	**4**	**143**	**20**	**35**	**7**	**0**	**4**	**20**	**15**	**32**	**.245**

BALTIMORE	G	AB	R	H	2B	3B	HR	RBI	BB	SO	AVG
C. Ripken ss	4	18	2	8	3	0	0	2	0	3	.444
Murray dh	4	15	1	6	1	0	0	1	3	4	.400
Surhoff lf	4	13	3	5	0	0	3	5	0	1	.385
B.Anderson cf	4	17	3	5	0	0	2	4	2	3	.294
R. Alomar 2b	4	17	2	5	0	0	1	4	2	3	.294
Zeile 3b	4	19	2	5	1	0	0	0	2	5	.263
Bonilla rf	4	15	4	3	0	0	2	5	4	6	.200
Parent c	4	5	0	1	0	0	0	0	0	2	.200
Incaviglia pr - lf	2	5	1	1	0	0	0	0	0	4	.200
Palmeiro 1b	4	17	4	3	1	0	1	2	1	6	.176
Hoiles c	4	8	1	1	0	0	0	0	3	3	.143
Devereaux pr-rf-lf	4	1	0	0	0	0	0	0	0	0	.000
Alexander pr-dh	3	0	2	0	0	0	0	0	0	0	-----
Totals	**4**	**150**	**25**	**43**	**6**	**0**	**9**	**23**	**17**	**40**	**.289**

PITCHING SUMMARY

CLEVELAND	G	CG	IP	H	R	ER	BB	SO	HB	WP	W	L	SV	ERA
Assenmacher	3	0	1 2/3	0	0	0	1	2	0	0	1	0	0	0.00
Tavarez	2	0	1 1/3	1	0	0	2	1	0	0	0	0	0	0.00
Ogea	1	0	1/3	0	0	0	1	0	0	0	0	0	0	0.00
Mesa	3	0	4 2/3	8	2	2	0	7	0	0	0	1	0	3.86
Hershiser	1	0	5	7	4	3	3	3	1	0	0	0	0	5.40
J McDowell	1	0	5 2/3	6	4	4	1	5	1	0	0	0	0	6.35
Plunk	3	0	4	1	3	3	2	6	0	0	0	0	0	6.75
Nagy	2	0	11 1/3	15	9	9	5	13	1	0	0	1	0	7.15
Embree	3	0	1	0	1	1	0	1	1	0	0	0	0	9.00
Shuey	3	0	2	5	2	2	2	2	0	0	0	0	0	9.00
Totals	**4**	**0**	**37**	**43**	**25**	**24**	**17**	**40**	**4**	**0**	**1**	**3**	**0**	**5.84**

BALTIMORE	G	CG	IP	H	R	ER	BB	SO	HB	WP	W	L	SV	ERA
R. Myers	3	0	3	0	0	0	0	3	0	0	0	0	2	0.00
T. Mathews	3	0	2 2/3	3	0	0	1	2	0	1	0	0	0	0.00
Benitez	3	0	4	1	1	1	2	6	0	0	2	0	0	2.25
Erickson	1	0	6 2/3	6	3	3	2	6	0	0	0	0	0	4.05
Mussina	1	0	6	7	4	3	2	6	0	0	0	0	0	4.50
D Wells	2	0	13 2/3	15	7	7	4	6	0	0	1	0	0	4.61
A. Rhodes	2	0	1	1	1	1	1	1	0	0	0	0	0	9.00
Orosco	4	0	1	2	4	4	3	2	1	0	0	1	0	36.00
Totals	**4**	**0**	**38**	**35**	**20**	**19**	**15**	**32**	**1**	**0**	**3**	**1**	**2**	**4.50**

Albert Belle is greeted by Manny Ramirez after hitting a Grand slam in game 3, October 4, 1996.

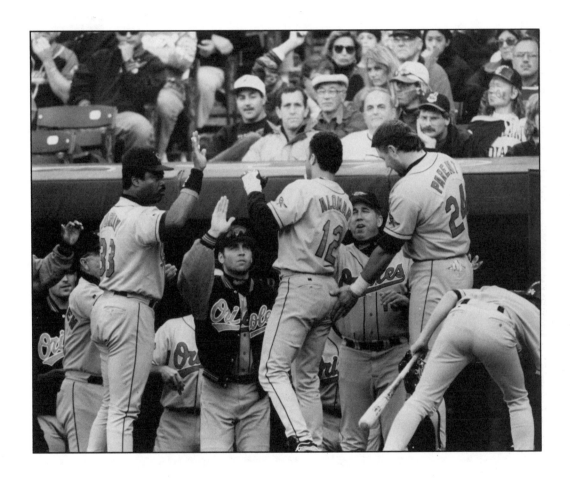

Orioles Roberto Alomar is congratulated by teammates after hitting a home run in the 12th inning of Game 4 .

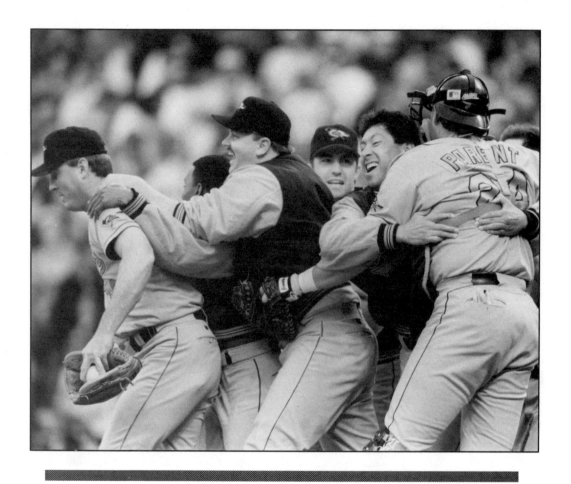

*Orioles celebrate after defeating the Indians, 4-3, in 12 innings
to win the series on October 5, 1996.*

A dejected Indians relief pitcher Jose Mesa and catcher Sandy Alomar watch the Orioles celebrate - Mesa gave up a home run to Roberto Alomar that won Game 4 of the playoffs.

EPILOGUE

So, where did it go wrong for the Indians in 1996?

Well, first, it didn't *all* go wrong.

There was plenty to cheer about, beginning with the best record, 99-62, in the major leagues; and winning a second straight Central Division championship, this one by 14 1/2 games, after leading, or being tied for the lead for all but the first eight games of the season.

What's more, both their hitters and pitchers cumulatively were best in the American League, offensively with a .293 average (five points better than second place New York), and on the mound with a 4.34 earned run average (compared to Chicago's 4.52).

Five players - outfielders Albert Belle and Kenny Lofton, pitchers Charles Nagy and Jose Mesa, and catcher Sandy Alomar Jr. - made the American League all-star team which was managed by Mike Hargrove, and Lofton and shortstop Omar Vizquel won Gold Glove awards.

And the Indians played before a franchise record 3,318,174 fans, including an American League record 131 consecutive (over two seasons) sellout crowds.

Granted, they lost in the first round of the playoffs, to Baltimore, a team that was ninth in the American League in pitching, and tenth in hitting;

But, as a dejected Vizquel said in the somber Indians' clubhouse after their elimination by Baltimore, they didn't lose to a better team, they simply lost to a team that was, at that time, *playing* better.

Obviously, not everything went as planned, as *expected* by General Manager John Hart and Hargrove - along with most of the rest of us - when the Indians embarked April 1 upon the six month marathon that would be the 1996 season.

Dennis Martinez broke down and started only one game after July 30, and none after making just 14 pitches against Detroit on Aug. 27.

Jack McDowell, who was expected to be a kingpin of the pitching staff when he was signed to a multimillion dollar contract as a free agent, was a major disappointment, partly because he also suffered physical problems that caused him to be disabled for the only time in his career.

Mesa, the almost-invincible closer in 1995 when he converted 46 of

48 save opportunities, slumped at mid-season and lost his confidence in a five week period from late-June into early-July.

And the team "chemistry" suffered, too, which, in the opinion of Hart and Hargrove, required trading two popular players, Eddie Murray and Carlos Baerga, deals that were lamented by teammates and fans, but in the end proved beneficial.

Murray, who played well in 1995 when he became a member of baseball's exclusive 3,000 hit club, was angry at management from the onset of the season after being handed a take-it-or-leave-it cut in pay from $3 million to $2 million, and never lost his resentment.

Baerga, who felt he was being demeaned when the Indians suggested they might try to sign Roberto Alomar to play second base, reported to spring training almost 30 pounds over weight and, for whatever reason, seldom resembled the player he'd been in his five previous seasons, especially on defense.

As written by Jim Ingraham in the Lake County *News Herald* and Lorain *Morning Journal*, "What hurt the Indians was not that they traded Eddie Murray and Carlos Baerga, but that they *had* to trade them ... because neither Murray nor Baerga was producing the way they produced the year before. Not even close."

Counter productive, too, were the numerous controversies involving Belle, including reported confrontations with Murray and other teammates, clubhouse tantrums, and his anti-media demeanor.

Something else that didn't help were the constant complaints, the players' whining and whimpering about calls by the umpires, which resulted in eight of them being ejected from games, several times causing severe personnel problems.

It reached the point where Hargrove felt it was necessary to hold a couple of team meetings, including one in the dugout during a game in full view of the press box, to admonish the players for their protests, which created ill-will among the umpires and did more harm than good.

It was not easy for Hargrove. He also had to cope with many inflated egos, and the expectation fostered by the fans and media, as well as the front office - and believed by most of the players - that 1996 would be a duplication of the magic carpet the Indians rode to the pennant in 1995.

It was a matter of complacency, though some preferred to call it arrogance.

In mid-June, when the Indians were struggling to maintain a then-slim lead over the White Sox, Hargrove reportedly was under pressure because, it was charged, too many players had their own agendas, that the team was close to being out of control.

All of which, in the wake of their elimination from the playoffs by the Orioles, begged the question: Was an overhaul necessary?

Definitely not, as Hart made clear when the frustration and disappointment of losing subsided.

But, as he also made clear, some changes were necessary.

Among the most important: Martinez had to be replaced, and perhaps McDowell, too, although there was hope that "Black Jack" would regain the ability (or health) in 1997 that made him one of baseball's best pitchers from 1990-95.

There were other, less weighty decisions.

But an overhaul of the team that won the most games - 199 - in the major leagues in 1995 and 1996?

Again, definitely no.

As Nagy said after the final game, the distressing loss to the Orioles on October 5: "We've got nothing to hang our heads about. We left our heart and soul on the field today."

Indeed they did.

There was no pep rally on Public Square in 1996, as there was in 1995.

And, neither were the politicians proclaiming the greatness of the Indians, nor calling Cleveland the "greatest baseball town in the world" - which it might be anyway - as Gov. George V. Voinovich declared a year ago.

Nor did Indians owner Richard E. Jacobs pledge, as he did in 1995, that the Indians would have a "single mission" when they return to Winter Haven, Florida for spring training "to prepare to win the World Series next year," though that's not to say they won't.

The fact is, even before Hart went shopping for 1997, the Indians still had the best talent in the A.L.

And, just as the cheers of the fans turned to tears, and a dream became a nightmare in 1996, hopefully the cheers will return louder than ever, a new dream will become reality, and there'll be another glorious Indian Summer in Cleveland in 1997.

Mike Hargrove: *Manager*

When the Indians reported for spring training as the defending American League champions, it was presumed by many that Mike Hargrove's toughest tasks would be to decide upon a fifth starting pitcher, two utility infielders and two extra outfielders.

Otherwise, the team that won 100 games in 1995 was set to repeat - and to go one step further - in 1996. Or so almost everybody thought.

But it wasn't that simple, which soon became evident.

Hargrove was faced with the awesome job of guarding against complacency, and having to deal with an assortment of diverse egos and temperaments.

Through it all Hargrove kept his composure and handled the difficult situations well, from the point at mid-season when the Indians almost were overtaken by the Chicago White Sox, during the discord that resulted among some in the clubhouse when Eddie Murray was benched and then traded, and also when Carlos Baerga was dealt to the New York Mets, and finally at the end when the Indians failed in the post season playoffs and were beaten by the Baltimore Orioles.

As Hargrove said in the aftermath of the Division Series, "We didn't win ... but I take away a lot of satisfaction, and a lot of pride from this season."

As well he should.

It hasn't been easy for Hargrove since mid-1991 when he took over the Indians, a team that was in disarray, one that would lose a franchise record 105 games and finish last by 34 lengths.

And the losing continued until 1994, when the Indians' "Blueprint for Success" paid dividends and they became a bonafide pennant contender - in fact, they might have made it to the World Series if the Players Association had not gone on strike in August of that year.

Through those lean years, 1991-93, Hargrove had to concern himself primarily with the nurturing and development of promising but inexperienced talent, a job for which, there can be no doubt, he was well suited.

Hargrove came to be recognized as a "player's manager," and again, with good reason.

He was a major league first baseman for 12 seasons, with the Texas Rangers from 1974 (when he won the American League "Rookie of the Year" award) through 1978, with San Diego in 1979 (until he was traded to Cleveland on June 14 (for Paul Dade in one of the Indians' best-ever deals), and with the Tribe through 1985.

Hargrove was elected the Indians' "Man of the Year" in 1980 when he batted .304, and again in 1981, when his average climbed to .317, and also won the "Good Guy" award in 1985.

The following season Hargrove started his coaching/managerial career at the lowest rung in professional baseball, as the hitting instructor at Batavia (New York) of the short season Class A New York-Penn League.

He managed Kinston (North Carolina) of the Class A Carolina League in 1987, Williamsport (Pennsylvania) of the Class AA Eastern League in 1988, and Colorado Springs of the Class AAA Pacific Coast League in 1989, returning to the Indians as a coach in 1990 under John McNamara.

When McNamara was dismissed on July 6, 1991, Hargrove replaced him as manager.

With the Indians' 99 victories in 1996, Hargrove became the fifth winningest manager in franchise history with a 449-378 (.543) record, and his 5 1/2 years at the helm places him fourth in longevity, behind only Lou Boudreau (1942-50), Tris Speaker (1919-26) and Roger Peckinpaugh (1928-33, 1941).

Mike Hargrove get the "heave - ho" from umpire Rich Garcia.

Richard E. Jacobs: *Owner*

"We bought the team because we wanted to have a little fun, as well as a sense of civic responsibility, and we thought there was a good chance for success."

That's the way Richard E. Jacobs and his brother, David H. Jacobs, justified purchasing the Indians in July 1986 (though it wasn't approved by the American League until five months later).

Baseball fans in Northern Ohio breathed a sigh of relief when Jacobs took over the team because, at the time, speculation was rife that the franchise would be moved out of town.

It had been a loser - on the field and at the turnstiles - for several years and, when the Jacobs brothers came into the picture, the franchise was owned by the estate of the late F.J. (Steve) O'Neill.

O'Neill's nephew, Patrick O'Neill, was in charge of selling the club and had hired Peter Bavasi to run it.

And just as speculation was rife that the Indians would be moved, so were there rumors that Bavasi had the Tampa Bay area targeted as the franchise's new home.

Bavasi had previously worked for St. Petersburg, Florida interests seeking a team for what was then known as the "Suncoast Domed Stadium."

But Jacobs immediately put an end to the rumors that the Indians might be re-located, by re-structuring the front office with veteran baseball executive Henry J. (Hank) Peters in charge.

The rest of the story is history. The Indians went through a couple more difficult seasons until 1994 when they became a bonafide pennant contender.

They won the American League championship in 1995, and posted the best won-lost record in the major leagues in 1996 before losing in the Division Series to Baltimore.

A native of Akron, Ohio and a 1949 graduate of Indiana University, Jacobs is chairman and chief executive officer of the Richard E. Jacobs, Group, whose primary business includes the development, ownership and management of office towers, hotels and regional enclosed malls.

John Hart: *Executive Vice President/ General Manager*

It wasn't easy for the Indians to win a second consecutive Central Division championship in the American League in 1996 - and it certainly wasn't easy for John Hart, executive vice president and general manager of the club.

When cracks appeared in the foundation of the Indians at mid-season and it became obvious they weren't going to ride a magic carpet to the pennant as they did in 1995, Hart made some bold moves that shocked many of the players and most of the fans.

He traded an unhappy and often sullen Eddie Murray to the Baltimore Orioles for pitcher Kent Mercker on July 21. It was what the late Branch Rickey would have termed "addition by subtraction."

Then, undaunted by the negative reaction of some of Murray's former teammates, Hart made an even bigger deal eight days later. He sent Carlos Baerga and Alvaro Espinoza to the New York Mets for Jose Vizcaino and Jeff Kent.

The same Carlos Baerga that Hart himself had once called "the heart and soul of the Indians."

It was a trade that Hart decreed had to be made, primarily to improve the Indians' up-the-middle defense.

"Trading Eddie and Carlos were both very difficult," Hart said.

"With Eddie, we realized he cast a big shadow in our clubhouse, but he wasn't happy here, he couldn't play first base, and we needed a guy who was more versatile.

"With Carlos, we talked for weeks about that one. We kept seeing balls going through the infield, and we have a pitching staff that needed those ground balls picked up."

All of which proved what Hart's predecessor and mentor, Hank Peters, had known all along: that the former minor league catcher, manager and major league coach never lacked courage in his convictions.

It was Peters who brought Hart to the Indians in 1989.

"I'd known John for a long time and respected his values, work ethic and ability to evaluate players," said Peters. "When I was hired by (Indians owner) Dick Jacobs, John Hart was one of the men I wanted to join me, to help me do what needed to be done."

Hart, initially a special assignment scout and Peters' assistant, was promoted to director of baseball operations in 1990. He was named general manager on September 18, 1991, when Peters retired, and in 1993 became executive vice president and general manager.

Under Hart's direction, and the implementation of what has been called the Indians' "Blueprint for Success," the team became a contender in 1994 for the first time in 35 years, won the pennant in 1995, and posted the best record in the major leagues in 1996.

It was through that plan that the Indians identified and signed their best players at an early stage of their development, ensuring they would remain with the organization, as opposed to opting for free agency.

Because of its success, the Tribe's "Blueprint" has been adopted by other clubs.

Honored as "Major League Executive of the Year" by *The Sporting News* in 1994 and 1995, Hart, 48, was a baseball, football and basketball star at Winter Park (Florida) High School, went to Seminole (Florida) Junior College on a baseball scholarship, and earned Junior College All-America honors in 1969 as a catcher.

He was drafted by Montreal and played in the Expos' and Orioles' farm systems for seven years, and was a minor league manager in the Baltimore organization for six years at the Class A, AA and AAA levels, twice winning Manager of the Year honors

Hart was third base coach of the Orioles in 1988, prior to joining Peters in Cleveland, and managed the Indians on an interim basis the final 19 games of that season during with the team's record was 8-11.

Dan O'Dowd:
Director of Baseball Operations/ Assistant General Manager

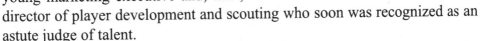

When Hank Peters came to Cleveland at the behest of then new-owner of the Indians, Richard E. Jacobs, there were two young men he wanted to bring with him from the Baltimore Orioles.

One was John Hart, then a coach for the Orioles, now the executive vice president and general manager of the Indians.

The other was Dan O'Dowd, then a bright young marketing executive and, later, assistant director of player development and scouting who soon was recognized as an astute judge of talent.

O'Dowd rejoined Peters in Cleveland in 1989 and has since established himself as one of the Tribe's key decision-makers while serving as Hart's right hand man in the implementation of the "Blueprint for Success."

The "Blueprint" is the Tribe's plan for identifying, signing and developing their best players at an early stage, ensuring that they would remain with the organization, as opposed to opting for free agency.

Much of the Indians' minor league success - five of their six farm clubs had winning records in 1996 - is attributable to the efforts of O'Dowd, Mark Shapiro, director of minor league operations, and Jay Robertson, director of scouting.

Since re-locating with the Indians, O'Dowd, 36, has had opportunities to move on to more prestigious jobs with other clubs and, probably, will do so as the next step up in his professional career.

But for now the Indians are fortunate to have him at Hart's elbow, helping to make the decisions, and steering the Indians in the direction mandated by Peters - and, to be sure, by Jacobs - when he and his brother, the late David, purchased the franchise in July 1986.

At the time there was concern that the Indians would be sold to out-of-town interests and moved elsewhere, fears that were immediately put to rest by the Jacobs brothers, Peters and, most certainly, Hart and O'Dowd.

A graduate of Rollins College in Winter Park, Florida where he played four years of varsity baseball, O'Dowd joined the Orioles in 1984 after a stint as an executive trainee in the office of the Baseball Commissioner.

1996 Batting Statistics

PLAYER	G	AB	R	H	2B	3B	HR	RBI	BB	SO	AVG
S. Alomar	127	418	53	110	23	0	11	50	19	42	.263
A. Belle	158	602	124	187	38	3	48	148	99	87	.311
C. Candele	24	44	8	11	2	0	1	4	1	9	.250
RIGHT		19		4	1	0	0	0	1	5	.211
LEFT		25		7	1	0	1	4	0	4	.280
M. Carreon	38	142	16	46	12	0	2	14	11	9	.324
E. Diaz	4	1	0	0	0	0	0	0	0	0	.000
J. Franco	112	432	72	139	20	1	14	76	61	82	.322
B. Giles	51	121	26	43	14	1	5	27	19	13	.355
D. Jackson	5	10	2	3	2	0	0	1	1	4	.300
J. Kent	39	102	16	27	7	0	3	16	10	22	.265
K. Lofton	154	662	132	210	35	4	14	67	61	82	.317
G. Pena	5	9	1	1	0	0	1	2	1	4	.111
RIGHT		4		0	0	0	0	0	0	2	.000
LEFT		5		1	0	0	1	2	1	2	.200
T. Pena	67	174	14	34	4	0	1	27	15	25	.195
H. Perry	7	12	1	1	1	0	0	0	1	2	.083
M. Ramirez	152	550	94	170	45	3	33	112	85	104	.309
* K. Seitzer	154	573	85	187	35	3	13	78	87	79	.326
CLEV	22	83	11	32	10	0	1	16	14	11	.386
J. Thome	151	505	122	157	28	5	38	116	123	141	.311
R. Thompson	8	22	2	7	0	0	1	5	1	6	.318
J. Vizcaino	48	179	23	51	5	2	0	13	7	24	.285
RIGHT		67		19	2	0	0	4	3	11	.284
LEFT		112		32	3	2	0	9	4	13	.286
O. Vizquel	151	542	98	161	36	1	9	64	56	42	.297
RIGHT		168		46	12	0	4	22	16	12	.274
LEFT		374		115	24	1	5	42	40	30	.307
N. Wilson	10	12	2	3	0	0	2	5	1	6	.250

* Milwaukee statistics

1996 Pitching Statistics

PITCHER	W	L	ERA	G	GS	CG	IP	H	BB	SO
B. Anderson	3	1	4.91	10	9	0	51.1	58	14	21
P. Assenmacher	4	2	3.09	63	0	0	46.2	46	14	44
A. Embree	1	1	6.39	24	0	0	31.0	30	21	33
D. Graves	2	0	4.55	15	0	0	29.2	29	10	22
O. Hershiser	15	9	4.24	33	33	1	206.0	238	58	125
A. Lopez	5	4	6.39	13	10	0	62.0	80	22	45
D. Martinez	9	6	4.50	20	20	1	112.0	122	37	48
J. McDowell	13	9	5.11	30	30	5	192.0	214	67	141
* K. Merker	4	6	6.98	24	12	0	69.2	83	38	29
CLE.	1	0	3.09	10	0	0	11.2	10	3	7
J. Mesa	2	7	3.73	69	0	0	72.1	69	28	64
C. Nagy	17	5	3.41	32	32	5	222.0	217	61	167
C. Ogea	10	6	4.79	29	21	1	146.2	151	42	101
E. Plunk	3	2	2.43	56	0	0	77.2	56	34	85
J. Roa	0	0	10.80	1	0	0	1.2	4	3	0
P. Shuey	5	2	2.85	42	0	0	53.2	45	26	44
J. Tavarez	4	7	5.36	51	4	0	80.2	101	22	46
CLEVELAND	**99**	**62**	**4.34**	**161**	**161**	**13**	**1452.1**	**1530**	**484**	**1033**
OPPONENTS	**62**	**99**	**5.41**	**161**	**161**	**6**	**1436.2**	**1665**	**671**	**844**

*Baltimore Statistics

Day by Day

Game	Date	Opponent	Score	Winning Pitcher	Losing Pitcher	Team Record	Pos.	G.B.
1	4/2	N.Y.	1-7	Cone (1-0)	Martinez (0-1)	0-1	T 3rd	-1.0
2	4/3	N.Y.	1-5	Pettitte (1-0)	McDowell (0-1)	0-2	T 4th	-1.5
3	4/5	TOR	1-7	Guzman (1-0)	Hershiser (0-1)	0-3	5th	-2.0
4	4/6	TOR	5-3	Nagy (1-0)	Hanson (1-1)	1-3	5th	-1.5
5	4/7	TOR	(10)8-3	Martinez (1-1)	Quantrill (0-1)	2-3	T 2nd	-0.5
6	4/10	at BAL	2-3	Oslo 1-0)	r Tavarez (0-1)	2-4	3rd	-1.0
7	4/11	at BAL	4-14	Erickson (1-0)	Hershiser (0-2)	2-5	4th	-1.5
8	4/12	at BOS	3-1	Nagy (2-0)	Sele (0-1)	3-5	T 2nd	-0.5
9	4/13	at BOS	14-2	Martinez (2-1)	Moyer (1-1)	4-5	1st	+0.5
10	4/14	at BOS	(11)7-6	r Tavarez (1-1)	r Stanton (0-1)	5-5	1st	+0.5
11	4/15	at BOS	8-0	McDowell (1-1)	Wakefield (0-2)	6-5	1st	+1.0
12	4/16	at MINN	7-2	Hershiser (1-2)	Radke (3-1)	7-5	1st	+1.5
13	4/17	at MINN	8-9	r Hansell (1-0)	r Shuey (0-1)	7-6	1st	+0.5
14	4/19	BOS	9-4	Martinez (3-1)	Gordon (1-2)	8-6	T 1st	------
15	4/20	BOS	2-1	McDowell (2-1)	Wakefield (0-3)	9-6	T 1st	------
16	4/21	BOS	11-7	r Ogea (1-0)	r Pennington (0-2)	10-6	T 1st	------
17	4/22	BAL	6-3	Nagy (3-0)	Erickson (1-1)	11-6	1st	+1.0
18	4/23	BAL	9-8	r Ogea (2-10)	Mussina (3-2)	12-6	1st	+2.0
19	4/24	at N.Y.	8-10	Kamieniecki (1-0)	Martinez (3-2)	12-7	1st	+1.5
20	4/25	at N.Y.	4-3	r Poole (1-0)	Pettitte (3-2)	13-7	1st	+1.5
21	4/26	at TOR	6-3	Hershiser (2-2)	Hanson (2-4)	14-7	1st	+2.0
22	4/27	at TOR	6-11	r Castillo (2-0)	Nagy (3-1)	14-8	1st	+1.0
23	4/28	at TOR	17-3	Lopez (1-0)	Viola (0-1)	15-8	1st	+1.0
24	4/30	CHI	5-3	Martinez (4-2)	Tapani (2-1)	16-8	1st	+1.5
25	5/1	CHI	9-5	McDowell 30-1)	McCaskill (0-2)	17-8	1st	+2.5
26	5/2-3	at SEA	6-4	Hershiser (3-2)	Wolcott (1-4)	18-8	1st	+3.0
27	5/3	at SEA	5-2	Nagy (4-1)	Hitchcock (3-1)	19-8	1st	+4.5

Day by Day

Game	Date	Opponent	Score	Winning Pitcher	Losing Pitcher	Team Record	Pos.	G.B.
28	5/4	at SEA	1-5	Menhart (1-2)	Lopez (1-1)	19-9	1st	+3.5
29	5/5	at SEA	2-0	Martinez (5-2)	Bosio (3-2)	20-9	1st	+4.5
30	5/6	at OAK	3-5	r Taylor (1-0)	Assenmacher (0-1)	20-10	1st	+4.0
31	5/7	at OAK	4-8	Johns (3-3)	Hershiser (3-3)	20-11	1st	+3.0
32	5/8	at OAK	7-3	Nagy (5-1)	Reyes (3-5)	21-11	1st	+3.0
33	5/10	at CAL	8-13	r Boskie (4-0)	r Lopez (1-2)	21-12	1st	+2.5
34	5/11	at CAL	6-5	McDowell (4-1)	Sanderson (0-2)	22-12	1st	+2.5
35	5/12	at CAL	4-1	r Poole (2-0)	r Percival (0-1)	23-12	1st	+3.5
36	5/14	DET	5-1	Nagy (6-1)	Gohr (2-5)	24-12	1st	+4.5
37	5/15	DET	5-2	Martinez (6-2)	Lima (0-4)	25-12	1st	+4.5
38	5/16	DET	8-3	McDowell (5-1)	Williams (0-2)	26-12	1st	+5.5
39	5/17	TEX	12-10	r Embree (1-0)	r Heredia (1-3)	27-12	1st	+5.5
40	5/18	TEX	3-6	Oliver (3-1)	Anderson (0-1)	27-13	1st	+4.5
41	5/19	TEX	8-5	Nagy (7-1)	Witt (4-3)	28-13	1st	+4.5
42	5/21	MIL	6-5	r Tavarez (2-1)	r Boze (0-2)	29-13	1st	+4.5
43	5/22	MIL	8-10	Karl (4-2)	McDowell (5-2)	29-14	1st	+3.5
44	5/23	MIL	5-1	Hershiser (4-3)	Miranda (3-3)	30-14	1st	+4.0
45	5/24	at DET	6-3	r Plunk (1-0)	Veres (0-3)	31-14	1st	+4.0
46	5/25	at DET	7-6	Nagy (8-1)	r Lewis (1-4)	32-14	1st	+4.0
47	5/26	at DET	5-0	Martinez (7-2)	Williams (0-4)	33-14	1st	+4.0
48	5/27	at TEX	2-3	Pavlik (7-1)	McDowell (5-3)	33-15	1st	+4.0
49	5/28	at TEX	3-11	Oliver (4-2)	Hershiser (4-4)	33-16	1st	+3.0
50	5/29	at TEX	4-5	r Cook (3-0)	r Tavarez (2-2)	33-17	1st	+3.0
51	5/30	at MIL	2-0	Nagy (9-1)	Bones (3-8)	34-17	1st	+3.0
52	5/31	at MIL	10-4	Martinez (8-2)	McDonald (4-3)	35-17	1st	+3.0
53	6/1	at MIL	1-2	r Garcia (1-1)	McDowell (5-4)	35-18	1st	+2.5
54	6/2	at MIL	11-6	r Poole (3-0)	Karl (5-3)	36-18	1st	+2.0

Day by Day

Game	Date	Opponent	Score	Winning Pitcher	Losing Pitcher	Team Record	Pos.	G.B.
55	6/4	SEA	7-10	r Carmona (2-1)	r Mesa (0-1)	36-19	1st.	+1.0
56	6/5	SEA	13-5	r Plunk (2-0)	r Milacki (1-3)	37-19	1st.	+1.0
57	6/6	SEA	2-5	Wells (5-1)	Martinez (8-3)	37-20	1st.	+1.0
58	6/7	CAL	4-3	McDowell (6-4)	Boskie (7-2)	38-20	1st.	+1.0
59	6/8	CAL	5-0	Hershiser (5-4)	Finley (7-4)	39-20	1st.	+1.0
60	6/9	CAL	(13)6-8	r Hancock (1-0)	r Tavarez (2-3)	39-21	T 1st.	-------
61	610	OAK	5-4	Nagy (10-1)	Johns (4-8)	40-21	T 1st.	-------
62	6/11	OAK	(13)6-5	r Ogea (3-0)	r Reyes (4-9)	41-21	1st.	+1.0
63	6/12	OAK	6-9	r M'ntgomry. (1-0)	McDowell (6-5)	41-22	1st.	+1.0
64	6/13	at N.Y.	6-2	Hershiser (6-4)	Rogers (4-3)	42-22	1st.	+1.5
65	6/14	at N.Y.	3-4	Gooden (6-4)	Ogea (3-1)	42-23	1st.	+0.5
66	6/15	at N.Y,	10-3	Nagy (11-1)	Boehringer (0-1)	43-23	1st.	+1.5
67	6/16	at N.Y.	4-5	Pettitte (11-3)	Martinez (8-4)	43-24	1st.	+1.5
68	6/18	BOS	9-7	r Swindell (1-0)	Sele (2-5)	44-24	1st.	+3.0
69	6/19	BOS	11-4	Hershiser (7-4)	Gordon (5-3)	45-24	1st.	+4.0
70	6/20	BOS	5-4	r Shuey (1-1)	r Stanton (3-2)	46-24	1st.	+5.0
71	6/21	at N.Y.	(10)7-8	r Nelson (2-2)	r Mesa (0-2)	46-25	1st.	+5.0
72	6/21	at N.Y.	3-9	Mendoza (2-3)	Tavarez (2-4)	46-26	1st.	+4.5
73	6/22	at N.Y,	9-11	r Brewer (1-0)	Martinz (8-3)	46-27	1st.	+4.5
74	6/23	at N.Y.	5-6	Gooden (7-4)	McDowell (6-6)	46-28	1st.	+3.5
75	6/25	at BOS	4-0	Hershiser (8-4)	Gordon (5-4)	47-28	1st.	+3.5
76	6/26	at BOS	(15)4-6	r Garces (2-2)	r Embree (1-1)	47-29	1st.	+3.0
77	6/27	at CHI	10-15	Fernandez (7-4)	Swindell (1-1)	47-30	1st.	+2.0
78	6/28	at CHI	2-4	Baldwin (7-1)	r Tavaez (2-5)	47-31	1st.	+1.0
79	6/29	at CHI	(10)3-2	r Shuey (2-1)	r Karchner (5-2)	48-31	1st.	+2.0
80	6/30	at CHI	4-2	Hershiser (9-4)	Tapani (8-5)	49-31	1st.	+3.0
81	7/1	KC	2-4	Haney (6-6)	Nagy (11-2)	49-32	1st.	+3.0

Day by Day

Game	Date	Opponent	Score	Winning Pitcher	Losing Pitcher	Team Record	Pos.	G.B.
82	7/2	KC	3-2	r Poole (4-0)	Belcher (6-4)	50-32	1st.	+3.0
83	7/3	KC	6-4	Tavarez (3-5)	r Magnante (1-2)	51-32	1st.	+4.0
84	7/4	CHI	(10)5-6	r Karchner (6-2)	r Mesa (0-3)	51-33	1st.	+3.0
85	7/5	CHI	0-7	Alvarez (10-4)	Hershiser (9-5)	51-34	1st.	+2.0
86	7/6	CHI	2-3	r Karchner (7-2)	r Shuey (2-2)	51-35	1st.	+1.0
87	7/7	CHI	6-1	Ogea (4-1)	Fernandez (8-5)	52-35	1st.	+2.0
88	7/11	at MINN	11-7	McDowell (7-6)	Radke (5-11)	53-35	1st.	+3.0
89	7/12	at MINN	7-5	r Mesa (1-3)	r Stevens (1-1)	54-35	1st.	+3.0
90	7/13	at MINN	19-11	Ogea (5-1)	Aguilera (2-4)	55-35	1st.	+3.0
91	7/14	at MINN	4-5	r Guardado (5-2)	r Plunk (2-1)	55-36	1st.	+2.0
92	7/15	at KC	3-6	r Magnante (2-2)	Tavarez (3-6)	55-37	1st.	+2.0
93	7/16	at KC	10-4	McDowell (8-6)	Haney (8-7)	56-37	1st.	+2.0
94	7/17	at KC	2-3	Belcher (8-5)	Hershiser (9-6)	56-38	1st.	+2.0
95	7/18	MINN	5-4	r Graves (1-0)	r Guardado (5-4)	57-38	1st.	+3.0
96	7/19	MINN	2-3	Rodrigez (9-7)	Nagy (11-3)	57-39	1st.	+3.0
97	7/20	MINN	6-5	r Shuey (3-2)	r Stevens (1-2)	58-39	1st.	+4.0
98	7/21	MINN	7-5	McDowell (9-6)	Radke (5-13)	59-39	1st.	+4.0
99	7/22	at TOR	4-2	Hershiser (10-6)	Hanson (8-12)	60-39	1st.	+5.0
100	7/23	at TOR	1-3	Hentgen (11-6)	Ogea (5-2)	60-40	1st.	+5.0
101	7/24	at TOR	10-0	Martinez (9-5)	Janzen (4-6)	61-40	1st.	+6.0
102	7/25	at BAL	10-7	Nagy (12-3)	Coppinger (5-2)	62-40	1st.	+7.0
103	7/26	at BAL	14-9	rAssenmacher 1-1	Mussina (11-8)	63-40	1st.	+7.0
104	7/27	at BAL	2-14	Wells (7-10)	Hershiser (10-7)	63-41	1st.	+7.0
105	7/28	at BAL	(13)6-3	r Mesa (2-3)	r Stevenson (0-1)	64-41	1st.	+7.0
106	7/30	TOR	1-3	Flener (1-0)	Martinez (9-6)	64-42	1st.	+6.0
107	7/31	TOR	4-2	rAssenmacher 2-1	r Timlin (0-4)	65-42	1st.	+7.0
108	8/1	TOR	3-5	Hanson (10-12)	Lopez (1-3)	65-43	1st.	+6.0

Day by Day

Game	Date	Opponent	Score	Winning Pitcher	Losing Pitcher	Team Record	Pos.	G.B.
109	8/2	BAL	11-1	Hershiser (11-7)	Erickson (5-10)	66-43	1st.	+6.0
110	8/3	BAL	4-9	r Orosco (3-1)	Ogea (5-3)	66-44	1st.	+5.0
111	8/4	BAL	14-2	Anderson (1-1)	Coppinger (6-3)	67-44	1st.	+6.0
112	· 8/5	BAL	10-13	Wells 9-10)	rAssenmacher(2-2)	67-45	1st.	+5.0
113	8/6	at SEA	4-3	Lopez (2-3)	Wells (11-4)	68-45	1st.	+6.0
114	8/7	at SEA	5-4	r Tavarez (4-6)	r Charlton (2-6)	69-45	1st.	+6.0
115	8/8	at SEA	2-1	Ogea (6-3)	Mulholland (0-1)	70-45	1st.	+7.0
116	8/9	at OAK	10-4	McDowell (10-6)	Telgheder (1-3)	71-45	1st.	+7.0
117	8/10	at OAK	1-5	Adams (1-1)	Nagy (12-4)	71-46	1st.	+7.0
118	8/11	at OAK	3-9	Wasdin (7-5)	Lopez (2-4)	71-47	1st.	+6.0
119	8/12	at CAL	5-4	Hershiser (12-7)	Finley (11-11)	72-47	1st.	+6.0
120	8/13	at CAL	2-4	Boskie (11-6)	Ogea (6-4)	72-48	1st.	+5.0
121	8/14	at CAL	7-8	r Gohr (5-8)	McDowell (10-7)	72-49	1st.	+5.0
122	8/16	DET	(12)3-1	r Assenmacher 3-2	r Lewis (3-6)	73-49	1st.	+6.5
123	8/17	DET	6-3	Hershiser (13-7)	Thompson (0-2)	74-49	1st.	+6.5
124	8/18	DET	11-3	Ogea (7-4)	B Williams (3-10)	75-49	1st.	+7.5
125	8/19	TEX	3-10	Pavlik (14-6)	McDowell (10-8)	75-50	1st.	+6.5
126	8/20	TEX	10-4	Lopez (3-4)	Witt (12-9)	76-50	1st.	+7.5
127	8/21	TEX	(10)8-10	Vosberg (1-0)	Tavarez (4-7)	76-51	1st.	+7.5
128	8/23	MIL	(11) 5-6	r Jones (2-0)	r Mesa (2-4)	76-52	1st.	+8.0
129	8/24	MIL	(10) 3-4	r Wickman (5-1)	r Plunk (2-2)	76-53	1st.	+8.0
130	8/25	MIL	8-5	r Shuey (4-2)	r Miranda (7-6)	77-53	1st.	+8.0
131	8/26	at DET	2-1	Nagy (13-4)	Lira (6-11)	78-53	1st.	+9.0
132	8/27	at DET	12-2	Lopez (4-4)	Thompson (1-3)	79-53	1st.	+10.0
133	8/28	at DET	9-3	Hershiser (14-7)	Sager (3-3)	80-53	1st.	+10.0
134	8/30	at TEX	3-5	Pavlik (15-7)	Ogea (7-5)	80-54	1st.	+9.0
135	8/31	at TEX	3-6	Oliver (11-6)	McDowell (10-9)	80-55	1st.	+8.0

Day by Day

Game	Date	Opponent	Score	Winning Pitcher	Losing Pitcher	Team Record	Pos.	G.B.
136	9/1	at TEX	8-2	Nagy (13-4)	Burkett (2-1)	81-55	1st.	+8.0
137	9/2	at MIL	6-7	Jones (4-0)	Mesa (2-5)	81-56	1st.	+8.0
138	9/3	at MIL	2-8	Karl (11-7)	Hershiser (14-8)	81-57	1st.	+7.0
139	9/4	at MIL	7-0	Ogea (8-5)	D'Amico (4-6)	82-57	1st.	+7.0
140	9/8	SEA	2-1	Nagy (15-4)	Mulholland (3-2)	83-57	1st.	+7.0
141	9/8	SEA	5-6	r Charlton (4-6)	r Mesa (2-6)	83-58	1st.	+6.5
142	9/9	CAL	4-3	r Shuey (5-2)	r Holtz (3-3)	84-58	1st.	+7.0
143	9/10	CAL	7-5	rAssenmacher(4-2)	r Percival (0-2)	85-58	1st.	+8.0
144	9/11	CAL	2-0	McDowell (11-9)	Finley (13-15)	86-58	1st.	+9.0
145	9/12	CAL	11-2	Anderson (2-1)	Boskie (12-10)	87-58	1st.	+9.5
146	9/14	OAK	9-2	Nagy (16-4)	Wengert (7-10)	88-58	1st.	+10.0
147	9/14	OAK	9-8	r Plunk (3-2)	Small (0-2)	89-58	1st.	+10.0
148	9/15	OAK	9-10	r Reyes (7-10)	r Mesa (2-7)	89-59	1st.	+10.0
149	9/16	at CHI	4-3	McDowell(12-9)	Alvarez (15-9)	90-59	1st.	+11.0
150	9/17	at CHI	9-4	Anderson (3-1)	Fernandez (14-10)	91-59	1st.	+12.0
151	9/18	at CHI	4-3	Lopez (5-4)	Baldwin (11-6)	92-59	1st.	+13.0
152	9/19	KC	9-1	Ogea (9-5)	Appier (13-10)	93-59	1st.	+13.0
153	9/20	KC	4-6	Bevil (1-0)	Nagy (16-5)	93-60	1st.	+12.0
154	9/21	KC	13-4	Hershiser (15-8)	Rosado (7-6)	94-60	1st.	+13.0
155	9/22	KC	6-5	McDowell (13-9)	r Jacome (0-4)	95-60	1st.	+13.0
156	9/23	MINN	7-6	r Graves (2-0)	Parra (5-5)	96-60	1st.	+13.5
157	9/24	MINN	7-5	Ogea (10-5)	Rodriguez (13-14)	97-60	1st.	+13.5
158	9/25	MINN	6-3	Nagy (17-5)	Robertson (7-17)	98-60	1st.	+14.5
159	9/27	at KC	6-11	Rosado (8-6)	Hershiser (15-9)	98-61	1st.	+13.5
160	9/28	at KC	5-4	Mercker (4-6)	Scanlon (0-1)	99-61	1st.	+14.5
161	9/29	at KC	1-4	Belcher (15-11)	Ogea (10-6)	99-62	1st.	+14.5

How the Indians Were Built ...

Non -Drafted Free Agents	Free Agent Draft (Beginning 1965)	Purchases/ Trades / and Waiver Claims
1987	Albert Belle, of (2)	
1988	Charles Nagy, rhp (1)	
1989	Alan Embree, lhp (5) Jim Thome, inf (3) Brian Giles, of (17)	Sandy Alomar, c from San Diego
1990 Julian Tavarez, rhp		
1991	Manny Ramirez, of (1) Chad Ogea, rhp (3) Albie Lopez, rhp (20)	Kenny Lofton, of from Houston
1992 Eric Plunk, rhp	Paul Shuey, rhp (1)	Jose Mesa, rhp from Baltimore
1993 Jeff Sexton, rhp Dennis Martines, rhp	Daron Kirkreit. rhp (1)	Omar Vizquel, inf from Seattle
1994 Tony Pena, c		
1995 Orel Hershiser, rhp Paul Assenmacher, lhp Casey Candaele, inf Julio Franco, inf Jack McDowell, rhp		

How the Indians Were Built ...

Non -Drafted Free Agents	Free Agent Draft (Beginning 1965)	Purchases/ Trades / and Waiver Claims
1996		Nigel Wilson, of from Cincinnati Mark Carreon, of from SanFrancisco Kent Mercher, lhp from New York Mets Jose Vizcaino, inf from New York Mets Kevin Seitzer, inf from Milwaukee

Transactions

March 31   Traded right handed pitcher Mark Clark to the New York Mets for outfielder Ryan Thompson and right handed pitcher Reid Cornelius; purchased the contracts of infielders Scott Leius and Alvaro Espinoza, and catcher Tony Pena from Class AA Canton-Akron; optioned right handed pitchers Pal Shuey, Joe Roa, and Albie Lopez, left handed pitcher Brian Anderson, outfielder Brian Giles, and infielder Herbert Perry to Class AAA Buffalo; designated for assignment catcher Jesse Levis and outfielder Nigel Wilson; recalled right handed pitcher Daron Kirkreit from Canton-Akron and placed him on the 60 day disabled list (right shoulder surgery).

April 4   Outrighted outfielder Nigel Wilson, and optioned outfielder Ryan Thompson to Buffalo; acquired left handed pitcher Scott Nate and a player to be named later from Milwaukee for catcher Jesse Levis.

April 12   Optioned left handed pitcher Alan Embree to Buffalo; recalled right handed pitcher Paul Shuey from Buffalo.

April 21   Optioned right handed pitcher Paul Shuey to Buffalo; recalled right handed pitcher Albie Lopez from Buffalo.

April 28   Placed right handed pitcher Chad Ogea on the 15 day disabled list (tendinitis in right shoulder); recalled left handed pitcher Alan Embree from Buffalo.

May 14   Optioned right handed pitcher Albie Lopez to Buffalo; recalled right handed pitcher Joe Roa from Buffalo.

May 15   Placed right handed pitcher Chad Ogea on rehabilitation option at Buffalo.

May 17   Optioned right handed pitcher Joe Roa to Buffalo; recalled left handed pitcher Brian Anderson from Buffalo.

May 27   Recalled right handed pitcher Chad Ogea from the rehabilitation option, reinstated him on the active roster, and optioned him to Buffalo

Transactions

June 3   American league announced suspensions for outfielder Albert Belle and right handed pitcher Julian Tavarez.

June 7   Placed infielder Scott Leius on the 15 day disabled list (strained lower back); recalled infielder Herbert Perry from Buffalo.

June 8   Recalled right handed pitcher Chad Ogea from Buffalo; optioned left handed pitcher Alan Embree to Buffalo.

June 10   Recalled right handed pitcher Paul Shuey from Buffalo; optioned left handed pitcher Brian Anderson to Buffalo.

June 15   Signed left handed pitcher Greg Swindell; designated outfielder Wayne Kirby for assignment.

June 22   Recalled left handed pitcher Alan Embree from Buffalo; optioned infielder Herbert Perry to Buffalo.

June 24   Outfielder Wayne Kirby claimed off waivers by the Los Angeles Dodgers.

June 27   Placed infielder Scott Leius on the active roster; optioned left handed pitcher Alan Embree to Buffalo

June 29   Placed right handed pitcher Dennis Martinez on the 15 day disabled list (strained flexor tendon in right elbow); purchased the contract of right handed pitcher Danny Graves from Buffalo; placed right handed pitcher Jeff Sexton on the 60 day emergency disabled list (sprained ligament in right elbow).

July 9   Traded left handed pitcher Jim Poole to the San Francisco Giants for first baseman-outfielder Mark Carreon.

July 11   Placed first baseman Julio Franco on the 15 day disabled list (strained right hamstring); recalled left handed pitcher Alan Embree from Buffalo.

Transactions

July 12   Placed left handed pitcher Greg Swindell on the 15 day disabled list (bicep tendinits in left shoulder); recalled outfielder Brian Giles from Buffalo.

July 21   Traded first baseman-designated hitter Eddie Murray to Baltimore for left handed pitcher Kent Mercker; placed left handed pitcher Greg Swindell on the active roster; optioned right handed pitcher Julian Tavarez to Buffalo.

July 24   Placed right handed pitcher Dennis Martinez on the active roster; designated infielder Scott Leius for assignment.

July 25   Placed first baseman Julio Franco on the active roster; optioned left handed pitcher Kent Mercker to Buffalo.

July 26   Placed right handed pitcher Jack McDowell on the 15 day disabled list (strained muscle in right forearm) retroactive to July 22; purchased the contract of infielder Casey Candaele from Buffalo.

July 29   Traded infielders Carlos Baerga and Alvaro Espinoza to the New York Mets for infielders Jose Vizcaino and Jeff Kent.

August 1   Recalled right handed pitcher Albie Lopez from Buffalo; placed left handed pitcher Alan Embree on the 15 day disabled list (bursitis in left hip); outrighted Scott Leius to Buffalo.

August 4   Placed right handed pitcher Dennis Martinez on the 15 day disabled list (strained flexor tendon in right elbow); recalled left handed pitcher Brian Anderson from Buffalo.

August 5   Recalled right handed pitcher Julian Tavarez from Buffalo; optioned left handed pitcher Brian Anderson to Buffalo.

August 6   Placed first baseman Julio Franco on the 15 day disabled list (strained right hamstring); recalled left handed pitcher Kent Mercker from Buffalo.

Transactions

August 9   Placed right handed pitcher Jack McDowell on the active roster; optioned right handed pitcher Danny Graves to Buffalo.

August 27   Placed right handed pitcher Dennis Martinez on the active roster; designated left handed pitcher Greg Swindell for assignment.

August 30   Placed first baseman Julio Franco on the active roster; placed right handed pitcher Dennis Martinez on the 15 day disabled list (strained flexor tendon in right elbow).

August 31   Traded outfielder Jeromy Burnitz to Milwaukee for infielder-designated hitter Kevin Seitzer; purchased the contract of outfielder Nigel Wilson from Buffalo; placed first baseman-outfielder Mark Carreon on the 15 day disabled list (contusion of the right tibia).

September 1 Recalled catcher Einar Diaz from Canton-Akron.

September 6 Recalled left handed pitcher Alan Embree from the rehabilitation option and placed him on the active roster; outrighted left handed pitcher Greg Swindell to Buffalo.

September 8 Recalled left handed pitcher Brian Anderson from Buffalo.

September 11 Recalled right handed pitcher Danny Graves, outfielder Ryan Thompson, and shortstop Damian Jackson from Buffalo; purchased the contract of infielder Geronimo Pena from Buffalo; placed infielder Herbert Perry on the 60 day disabled list (knee surgery).

September 12 Recalled right handed pitcher Joe Roa from Buffalo.

Indians pitcher Charles Nagy in action against the Orioles in Game 4, October 5, 1996.

*Albert Belle gets ready to slap coach Toby Harrah
as he rounds 3rd base in game with Tigers.*

*Jim Thome watches the ball go into the right field
stands for a grand slam against the Tigers.*

Carlos Baerga in action against the Detroit Tigers.

*Indians shortstop Omar Vizquel fires the ball to first base in time to com-
plete a double play against the White Sox.*

Indians relief pitcher Jose Mesa takes a toss from catcher Sandy Alomar to tag Jose Offerman of Kansas City attempting to score on a wild pitch.

*Omar Vizquel and Jose Vizcaino both go for a pop up
during Game 3 against the Orioles.*

Other Tribe Books by Russell Schneider

Collections of Memories....

Tribe Memories I
Bob Feller...Andre Thornton...Herb Score...Rocky Colavito...Bill Veeck...Sam McDowell...Al Rosen...Al Lopez...and many more from the 1990 - 1991 Schedule/Engagement Book.

Tribe Memories II
Luke Easter...Satchel Paige...Ray Fosse...Ken Harrelson...Jim Piersall...Tito Francona...Hall Trosky...Joe Azcue...Tris Speaker...and many more from the 1991 - 1992 Schedule/Engagement Book.

Tribe Memories III
George Burns...Rich Rollins...Ken Aspromonte...Mudcat Grant...Charlie Spikes...Sonny siebert...Napoleon Lajoie...and many more from the 1992 - 1993 Schedule/Engagement Book.

These books are now offered at close-out prices of $3.00 each or all three for $8.00 (Ohio Sales Tax included). Please include $3.00 per order for 2-3 day delivery and handling.

The Glorious Indian Summer of 1995... When a Season of Dreams Became Reality in Cleveland. Last year's best seller detailing the magical season of 1995. If you missed this book last year, a limited quantity is now available for $10.00 (Ohio Sales Tax included). Please include $3.00 per order for 2-3 day delivery and handling.

TO ORDER BOOKS,
COMPLETE (OR COPY) THE FOLLOWING AND MAIL TO:
TRIBE MEMORIES
P.O.Box 347156
Cleveland, Ohio 44134

Name_____

Address_____

City/ State/ Zip_____

Please circle choices: *Tribe I*   *Tribe II*   *Tribe III*

Indian Summer of 1995